COLLA 2016

The Sixth International Conference on Advanced Collaborative Networks, Systems and Applications

November 13 - 17, 2016

Barcelona, Spain

COLLA 2016 Editors

Thomas Schuster, University of Applied Sciences Pforzheim, Germany

Lasse Berntzen, University College of Southeast, Norway

Printed from e-media with permission by:

Curran Associates, Inc.
57 Morehouse Lane
Red Hook, NY 12571

Some format issues inherent in the e-media version may also appear in this print version.

Printed by Curran Associates, Inc. (2016)

International Academy, Research, and Industry Association (IARIA)
412 Derby Way
Wilmington, DE 19810

Phone: (408) 893-6407
Fax: (408) 527-6351

petre@iaria.org

Additional copies of this publication are available from:

Curran Associates, Inc.
57 Morehouse Lane
Red Hook, NY 12571 USA
Phone: 845-758-0400
Fax: 845-758-2633
Email: curran@proceedings.com
Web: www.proceedings.com

Table of Contents

COLLA 2016

Foreword

The Sixth International Conference on Advanced Collaborative Networks, Systems and Applications (COLLA 2016), held between November 13-17, 2016 - Barcelona, Spain, continued a series of events dedicated to advanced collaborative networks, systems and applications, focusing on new mechanisms, infrastructures, services, tools and benchmarks.

Collaborative systems became a norm due to the globalization of services and infrastructures and to multinational corporation branches. While organizations and individuals relied on collaboration for decades, the advent of new technologies (Web services, Cloud computing, Service-oriented architecture, Semantics and Ontology, etc.) for inter- and intra-organization collaboration created an enabling environment for advanced collaboration.

As a consequence, new developments are expected from current networking and interacting technologies (protocols, interfaces, services, tools) to support the design and deployment of a scalable collaborative environments. Innovative systems and applications design, including collaborative robots, autonomous systems, and consideration for dynamic user behavior is the trend.

We take here the opportunity to warmly thank all the members of the COLLA 2016 Technical Program Committee, as well as the numerous reviewers. The creation of such a high quality conference program would not have been possible without their involvement. We also kindly thank all the authors who dedicated much of their time and efforts to contribute to COLLA 2016. We truly believe that, thanks to all these efforts, the final conference program consisted of top quality contributions.

Also, this event could not have been a reality without the support of many individuals, organizations, and sponsors. We are grateful to the members of the COLLA 2016 organizing committee for their help in handling the logistics and for their work to make this professional meeting a success.

We hope that COLLA 2016 was a successful international forum for the exchange of ideas and results between academia and industry and for the promotion of progress in the field of collaborative networks, systems and applications.

We are convinced that the participants found the event useful and communications very open. We also hope the attendees enjoyed the charm of Barcelona, Spain.

COLLA 2016 Chairs:

COLLA General Chair

Samer Hassan, Universidad Complutense de Madrid, Spain & Berkman Center at Harvard, USA

COLLA Advisory Committee

Lasse Berntzen, University College of Southeast, Norway
Mohamed Eltoweissy, Virgina Military Institute/Virginia Tech, USA
Howard Spoelstra, Open University in the Netherlands, Netherlands
Pascal Salembier, University of Technology of Troyes, France
Atsuo Hazeyama, Tokyo Gakugei University, Japan
Henric Johnson, Blekinge Institute of Technology, Sweden
Christophe Thovex, University of Nantes, France
Alessandro Campi, Politecnico di Milano, Italy
Anna Kocurova, University of West London, United Kingdom

COLLA Industry/Research Chairs

Anna Divoli, Pingar Research, New Zealand
Jin-Hee Cho, U.S. Army Research Laboratory (USARL) - Adelphi, USA
Holger Kett, Fraunhofer IAO - Stuttgart, Germany
Raymond A Liuzzi, Raymond Technologies - Whitesboro, USA
Jérôme Dantan, Esitpa, France

COLLA Publicity Chairs

Dapeng Dong, University College Cork, Ireland
Benjamin Knoke, BIBA – Bremer Institut für Produktion und Logistik, Germany
Mateusz Adamczyk, University of Warsaw, Poland
Kenji Takagi, Tokyo Metropolitan University, Japan
Yann Veilleroy, Université Catholique de Lille, France

COLLA 2016

Committee

COLLA General Chair

Samer Hassan, Universidad Complutense de Madrid, Spain & Berkman Center at Harvard, USA

COLLA Advisory Committee

Lasse Berntzen, University College of Southeast, Norway
Mohamed Eltoweissy, Virgina Military Institute/Virginia Tech, USA
Howard Spoelstra, Open University in the Netherlands, Netherlands
Pascal Salembier, University of Technology of Troyes, France
Atsuo Hazeyama, Tokyo Gakugei University, Japan
Henric Johnson, Blekinge Institute of Technology, Sweden
Christophe Thovex, University of Nantes, France
Alessandro Campi, Politecnico di Milano, Italy
Anna Kocurova, University of West London, United Kingdom

COLLA Industry/Research Chairs

Anna Divoli, Pingar Research, New Zealand
Jin-Hee Cho, U.S. Army Research Laboratory (USARL) - Adelphi, USA
Holger Kett, Fraunhofer IAO - Stuttgart, Germany
Raymond A Liuzzi, Raymond Technologies - Whitesboro, USA
Jérôme Dantan, Esitpa, France

COLLA Publicity Chairs

Dapeng Dong, University College Cork, Ireland
Benjamin Knoke, BIBA – Bremer Institut für Produktion und Logistik, Germany
Mateusz Adamczyk, University of Warsaw, Poland
Kenji Takagi, Tokyo Metropolitan University, Japan
Yann Veilleroy, Université Catholique de Lille, France

COLLA 2016 Technical Program Committee

Imad Abugessaisa, Karolinska Institutet - Stockholm, Sweden
Marcelo Armentano, ISISTAN Research Institute (CONICET/UNICEN), Argentina
Patricia Arnold, Munich University of Applied Sciences, Germany
Liz Bacon, University of Greenwich, UK
Thierry Badard, Laval University, Canada
Mostafa Bassiouni, University of Central Florida, USA
Samia Ben Rajeb, LUCID - University of Liege, Belgium

Xiaoqing (Frank) Liu, Missouri University of Science and Technology, USA
Raymond A Liuzzi, Raymond Technologies - Whitesboro, USA
M. Antonia Martínez-Carreras, Universidad de Murcia, Spain
Célia Martinie, ICS-IRIT | University Toulouse 3 Paul Sabatier, France
Robert Matzinger, University of Applied Science Burgenland, Austria
Christoph Meinel, Hasso-Plattner-Institut GmbH - Potsdam, Germany
Klaus Moessner, University of Surrey, UK
Martin Molhanec, Czech Technical University in Prague, Czech Republic
Jennifer Murray, Edinburgh Napier University Sighthill Campus, Scotland
Surya Nepal, CSIRO, Australia
Eugénio Oliveira, University of Porto, Portugal
Simge Esin Orhun, Ozyegin University, Turkey
Felipe Ortega, Universidad Rey Juan Carlos, Spain
Mourad Chabane Oussalah, LINA - CNRS Faculté des Sciences de Nantes, France
Paolo Perego, Politecnico di Milano, Italy
Willy Picard, Poznan University of Economics, Poland
Agostino Poggi, University of Parma, Italy
Yann Pollet, Conservatoire National des Arts et Métiers, France
Enrico Pontelli, New Mexico State University, USA
Elaheh Pourabbas, National Research Council of Italy, Rome
Claudia Raibulet, University of Milano-Bicocca, Italy
Ling Rothrock, Pennsylvania State University, USA
Stuart Rubin, SSC-PAC, USA
Francesc Saiqi Rubió, Open University of Catalonia (UOC), Spain
Abdel-Badeeh M. Salem, Ain Shams University - Cairo, Egypt
Pascal Salembier, University of Technology of Troyes, France
Jaime Sánchez, University of Chile, Chile
Corrado Santoro, University of Catania, Italy
Marcello Sarini, University of Milano-Bicocca, Italy
Silvia Schiaffino, ISISTAN (CONICET - UNCPBA), Argentina
Thomas Schuster, Hochschule Pforzheim, Germany
Wolfgang Seiringer, Vienna University of Technology, Austria
Haifeng Shen, Flinders University, Australia
Dongwan Shin, New Mexico Tech, USA
Mohamed Shehab, University of North Carolina at Charlotte, USA
Alexander Smirnov, St. Petersburg Institute for Informatics & Automation of the Russian Academy of Sciences (SPIIRAS), Russia
Howard Spoelstra, Open University in the Netherlands, Netherlands
Hussein Suleman, University of Cape Town, South Africa
Julian Szymanski, Gdansk University of Technology, Poland
Yehia Taher, Université de Versailles Saint-Quentin-en-Yvelines – Versaille, France
Christophe Thovex, CNRS 6241 / University of Nantes, France
Katya Aries, Roehampton Online Education Programmes - Laureate International Universities, UK
Thrasyvoulos Tsiatsos, Aristotle University of Thessaloniki, Greece
Manolis Tzagarakis, University of Patras, Greece
Michael Vassilakopoulos, University of Thessaly, Greece
Claire Vishik, Intel Corporation, USA
Yi Wang, IBM Almaden Research Center, USA

Mudasser F. Wyne, National University, USA
Kevin X. Yang, Wolfson College / University of Cambridge, UK
Yi Yang, Fontbonne University, St Louis, USA
Ting Yu, University of Sydney, Australia
Weihai Yu, University of Tromsø, Norway
Roberto Yus, University of Zaragoza, Spain
Xiaokun Zhang, Athabasca University, Canada

Copyright Information

For your reference, this is the text governing the copyright release for material published by IARIA.

The copyright release is a transfer of publication rights, which allows IARIA and its partners to drive the dissemination of the published material. This allows IARIA to give articles increased visibility via distribution, inclusion in libraries, and arrangements for submission to indexes.

I, the undersigned, declare that the article is original, and that I represent the authors of this article in the copyright release matters. If this work has been done as work-for-hire, I have obtained all necessary clearances to execute a copyright release. I hereby irrevocably transfer exclusive copyright for this material to IARIA. I give IARIA permission or reproduce the work in any media format such as, but not limited to, print, digital, or electronic. I give IARIA permission to distribute the materials without restriction to any institutions or individuals. I give IARIA permission to submit the work for inclusion in article repositories as IARIA sees fit.

I, the undersigned, declare that to the best of my knowledge, the article is does not contain libelous or otherwise unlawful contents or invading the right of privacy or infringing on a proprietary right.

Following the copyright release, any circulated version of the article must bear the copyright notice and any header and footer information that IARIA applies to the published article.

IARIA grants royalty-free permission to the authors to disseminate the work, under the above provisions, for any academic, commercial, or industrial use. IARIA grants royalty-free permission to any individuals or institutions to make the article available electronically, online, or in print.

IARIA acknowledges that rights to any algorithm, process, procedure, apparatus, or articles of manufacture remain with the authors and their employers.

I, the undersigned, understand that IARIA will not be liable, in contract, tort (including, without limitation, negligence), pre-contract or other representations (other than fraudulent misrepresentations) or otherwise in connection with the publication of my work.

Exception to the above is made for work-for-hire performed while employed by the government. In that case, copyright to the material remains with the said government. The rightful owners (authors and government entity) grant unlimited and unrestricted permission to IARIA, IARIA's contractors, and IARIA's partners to further distribute the work.

Collaborative Mapping and the Reliability of Volunteered Data

Christian Voigt
Technology & Knowledge
Centre for Social Innovation
Vienna, Austria
voigt@zsi.at

Susanne Dobner
Technology & Knowledge
Centre for Social Innovation
Vienna, Austria
dobner@zsi.at

Manuela Schmidt
Research Group Cartography
Technical University Vienna
Vienna, Austria
manuela.schmidt@tuwien.ac.at

Abstract— **Participation platforms, such as OpenStreet Map.org or Wheelmap.org represent a shift from a world defined by the few to a world where almost everyone can participate voluntarily. Emerging cultures of participation offer powerful mechanisms to raise awareness of some of today's most pressing societal problems. However, just because citizens could contribute to these platforms, does not mean that they will actually do it. Engaging volunteers and offering straightforward means of participation whilst simultaneously ensuring that volunteers meet the necessary quality standards remains a known challenge. In this paper, we explore the robustness of a collaborative mapping process, specifically collecting accessibility data of cities' built environment. The paper combines theoretical considerations from the field of participatory design and actual data from the authors' recent experiences with crowdsourcing open accessibility information. Finally, the paper makes the case for enhancing a categorical approach to mapping with a stronger consideration of a map's purpose and a healthy scepticism towards overly simplified crowdsourcing mechanisms.**

Keywords- participation platforms; digital maps; volunteered geographic information; participatory design.

I. Introduction

Participation platforms, such as Wikipedia.com (creating knowledge collectively), Thingiverse.com (sharing digital designs) or Wheelmap.org (collecting accessibility information on a map) represent a shift from a world defined by the few to a world where almost everyone can participate [1]. Accompanying these platforms are emerging cultures of participation that offer powerful mechanisms to raise awareness of some of today's most pressing societal problems. For example, people have been successfully engaged through the volunteering of geo-referenced data about the scale of an environmental disaster or the level of noise pollution [2] [3].

Fischer [1] makes the point that improving participation platforms requires a shift from 'design for use' to continuously involving users in the development of a service, even if that service is already in use. Put differently, participation platforms depend on their ability to massively engage prosumers (i.e., people who provide parts of the services they consume for free) and deliver the aggregated results of participants in the needed quality [4]. A critical success factor in this effort are users as co-designers (i.e., users who directly participate in the design of the service so that emerging needs are met as soon as they are identified). The focus of our paper is on the design and use of participation platforms that are open source and create open data, thereby adding to the creation of informational commons.

Centerpiece of this paper is Wheelmap.org, a participatory platform and online map service to find and categorize wheelchair accessible places. However, just because citizens have the opportunity to actively contribute to this platforms, does not mean that they will actually do it. Ongoing engagement of existing and new citizens is a known challenge to participation platforms [5] and we cannot simply assume that our theories about interaction, group formation or motivation in the off-line world will also hold in virtual or hybrid worlds. The need for good engagement strategies is clear, more users and more long-term users increase not only the *quantity* of contributions (i.e., the number of places with accessibility attributes) but also the *quality and consistency* of contributions (i.e., the reliability of indicated accessibility conditions). This paper explores the potential of participatory design (PD) as a means to co-design *mapping criteria* in order to increase the quality of mapping initiatives. From its very beginnings, PD in organizations aimed at balancing power relations in order to ensure technology serves all stakeholders. Global participation systems, such as Wikipedia or OpenStreetMap, however, are not so much shaped by managerial, top down decisions but live and evolve through the active participation of those who use the systems. The open source equivalent to centralized management are democratic governance structures, which process users' critical reflections and comments. Nonetheless, the methods of PD are still applicable; interviews, user diaries and visual artifacts (photos or drawings) bring people in and make their voices heard.

Our paper is based on recent experiences with initiatives promoting the mapping of open accessibility information [ref. authors of this paper]. One of these initiatives involved 55 cartography students, who, over the course of three months, mapped places on wheelmap.org. Wheelmap, founded in 2010 by the German non-profit organisation 'Sozialhelden', is an online map service to find and categorize wheelchair accessible places based on a traffic light system: red (not wheelchair accessible), yellow (partly wheelchair accessible), green (wheelchair accessible). The service is based on OpenStreetMap (OSM) project, an open source digital map of the world. OSM contains, among many other things, information about the accessibility of specific points-of-interest, ranging from hospitals and train stations to playgrounds and bars. OSM's growth relies on the ongoing crowdsourcing effort of its community.

There are a number of issues that need to be investigated in order to better understand what influences the quality of collaborative mapping and to what extent participatory design can be a remedy.

- *Semantic issues:* Crowdsourcing physical attributes of geographic places is based on interpretation work, which is inherently plagued by ambiguity. Hence, common sense is an insufficient base for mapping and establishing protocols for action is one of the measures taken to limit ambiguity [2]. The question here is how far can these protocols go and what role can learning and community membership play to help with disambiguation.
- *Digital divide*: Technologies used during online mapping range from paper maps and Apps on Smartphones to Image Databases and more advanced OSM Editors. However, open-source mapping is only effective if people have the physical and social means to access the technology. For example, people need smartphones with appropriate data plans in order to connect to online groups where they can access the latest information and help [6].
- *Internet literacy issues:* Closely related to the issue of 'access to technology' is the fact that people need a minimum of knowledge in order to get connected and use online mapping services. This leads to the question of whether design can inscribe knowledge to minimize the required learning curve for using the technology. Yet, a minimum level of Internet literacy is needed, e.g., understanding the hypermedia structure of the Internet and having a basic orientation in order to navigate between the different sides and services [7].

'Semantic issues' and related quality issues with mapping results have been the main motivation to explore volunteer participation, participatory design, semantic issues and mutual learning as a possible solution. The potential role of PD is conceptualized by using Star and Griesemer's notion of 'boundary objects' [8], which conveys succinctly what we need from collaborative processes: consistency of results (i.e., the mapping of reliable accessibility information) and variability in utilizations (i.e., the ongoing refinement of our mapping criteria, co-evolving with our understanding of accessibility and barriers). The paper is organized as follows: In section 2, we discuss collaborative mapping platforms and the role participatory design could take to improve participation quantitatively as well as qualitatively. Section 3 continues with an in-depth discussion of a specific collaborative mapping case, focusing on the operational and conceptual dimensions of the mapping process. Finally, in section 4 we elaborate a non-trivial trade off between the need for a simple yet intuitively compelling categorization system for accessibility mapping. Section 5 concludes with a brief summary of findings and their implications for future crowd-based accessibility maps.

II. Collaborative Mapping Platforms

One way of creating engagement is letting users participate in the design or refinement of crowd-based data collections. In the case of volunteering geo-located accessibility data, co-design can have a double motivating aspect: (a) optimizing intuitive use increases mappers perceived self-efficacy and (b) improving the coherence of mapping categories makes a difference for everyone using the map, hence, mappers sense the importance of their actions [5]. It's clear that not every mapping activity can lead to changes in the design of the mapping application, but it can well entail a rethinking of how we design mapping events and what advice to give mappers along the way.

A. Participatory Design for Mapping Applications

We start with Simonsen and Robertson's [9] definition of participatory design as mutual learning situations based on collective reflection. The need to reflect on design decisions and learn from these reflections applies to participation platforms as well. Also DePaula's description of PD as a balancing effort between different actors' needs, motivations, and values in order to create "socio-technical-political conditions that reduce the gap between design practices and use practices" [10, p. 162], holds for participation platforms, at least to some extent. Eventually PD is also evaluated against the degree of empowerment people get from a process that takes on their goals and values. A process that is highly iterative, integrating feedback on design changes and their impacts [11].

B. Digital Maps

Digital maps as participation platforms have become enormously effective tools for raising awareness and influencing power relations [12]. Maps have shifted from representing stable knowledge about territories to data collection platforms enabling the creation of multiple maps on the fly. A trend supporting the uptake of digital maps is the steady increase of mobile communication, which enables completely new ways for citizens to engage with online services in an ad-hoc fashion, wherever they are. 85 per cent of touchscreen phones released from 2010 onwards can use the global navigation satellite system (GNSS) [13]. A well-known example is the *OpenStreetMap* project, founded in 2004 at the University College London with the goal to create a free database with geographic information of the entire world. A plethora of spatial data, such as roads, buildings, land use areas, or points of interest is entered into the project's database. Similar to other community-based projects on the Internet, any user can start contributing to the project and editing data after a short online registration.

III. Case Description

A. The Purpose of Collaborative Mapping: Open Accessibility Information

An increasingly aging population, as well as a change in awareness of the needs of people with mobility impairments raises the importance of having open information on accessibility. In Vienna alone, 24% of the city's population will be aged 65 plus by 2030 [14]. Open accessibility data include information about geo-located entrances, parking spots or toilets and their accessibility. However, in a wider context, the location of other points of interests (POIs), such as lifts or characteristics of pathways, e.g., their slope and width, also form part of an informational ecosystem that increases the mobility of people with mobility constraints. OpenStreetMap makes these data openly available and free of charge.

Over the last 4 years (2012 - 2015), over 8.800 places on average were tagged each month according to their accessibility using the wheelchair tag (wheelchair={yes, limited, no}) [15]. However, even major tourist destinations, such as London, Vienna or Paris show relatively low percentages (less than 8%) of accessibility related information in OSM like whether a street has sidewalks or not [16]. Hence, even though OSM has a rapidly growing community and has proven to deliver good spatial data quality, completeness of area coverage and longevity of volunteer engagement are remaining challenges for OSM [17].

Geographic information in terms of streets, buildings and other spaces is mostly complete in larger cities, however, this is not the case with open accessibility data. Multiple stakeholders have covert or explicit interests in the mapping of barriers. For example, there is some political brisance to exposing a city's lack of accessibility. This is not a concern if the platform is primarily driven by citizen activism, but gets problematic if a collaboration with city officials, e.g., urban planning or public transport departments, is sought after [18].

But apart from the political dimension of designing and using participation platforms addressing accessibility issues in cities, there is also the challenge of engaging a sufficiently large community that can carry the OSM mission to create a digital map of the world - we would add - including accessibility information. Crowdsourced or volunteer-based services depend on people's interest- and preference-driven decisions of where and when to spend their time. There is a rich body of literature dedicated to 'volunteerism in non-profit organizations', studying the decisions of volunteers in terms of 'engagement', 'commitment' and 'well-being' [19] or using similar concepts describing psychological empowerment of volunteers, including 'sense of community', 'perceived self-efficacy' (i.e., the possibility to master the task at hand) and 'causal importance' (i.e., the understanding that volunteering serves the common good) [5].

The following sections are describing a mapping action, which we organized in collaboration with a group of cartography students. The mapping action had a twofold objective: (a) gaining a better understanding of the current traffic light design for categorizing the accessibility of places and (b) boosting mapping engagement and create awareness around urban accessibility.

B. Collaborative Mapping Technology: Wheelmap

The specific application we used for accessibility mapping was Wheelmap.org, an open-source mapping application aiming to support the cause of better wheelchair-accessibility. Once the application is installed, everyone can contribute information about the accessibility of a point of interest (POI). Additionally, if mappers register, they can upload photos and add more specific comments on why a place is not or only partially wheelchair accessible. Registration is kept as simple as possible, only requiring a self-chosen user name and a password. No additional personal information is requested. The goal is to involve as many people as possible and avoid privacy issues or cumbersome registration procedures.

The tagging follows a traffic light metaphor (Fig. 1). Grey indicates places with an unknown status, that is we cannot say whether the place is wheelchair accessible or not. Places shown in green have been tagged as accessible, i.e., one can enter the building with wheelchairs, and for buildings where one would expect a public toilet to be available, the toilet would be accessible as well. Places in red are not wheelchair accessible, that would be the case if the entrance has a step higher than 7 cm and no ramp [20]. When viewing a map, the user will be shown all available POIs from a set of 12 categories, e.g., shopping, sport or tourism.

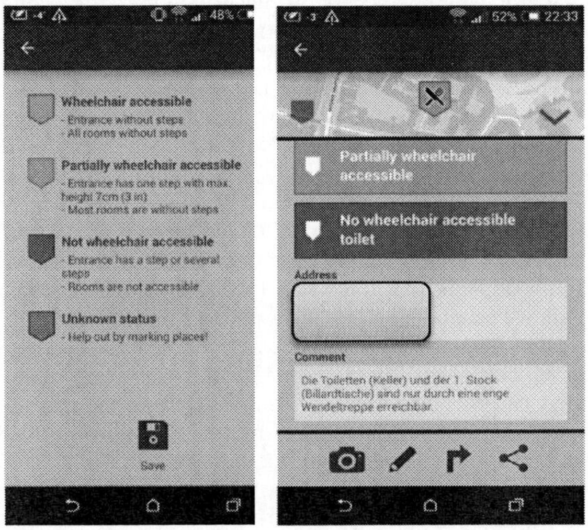

Figure 1. Mapping accessibility on the Wheelmap.

Clicking on the yellow icon for a restaurant (cf. Fig. 1) will open a pop-up window with the address and additional comments.

C. The collaborative mapping process

Together with a major university in Vienna, we organized a mapping action following a critical cartography approach [21]. Critical cartography implied that students reflected on the functionality of the digital map, as well as on ways in which the map influenced their views on accessibility. Altogether 55 students (about half of the class, 47%) participated in the voluntary task to map places on the Wheelmap. Two thirds were female students and one third male. We did not record the age of participants, but they resembled a typical, rather homogenous, group of students in their second year at university (approx. 20 - 25 years). The mapping action was introduced during a course called 'Thematic Cartography in Regional Planning' (October to December 2014). Students could obtain bonus points for their participation, those could be of help if they had missed the better grade by just a few points. Their task included (a) their feedback on their experience when using the Wheelmap and (b) their feedback on their mapping experience, specifically when deciding between the color codes of the mobile mapping application (cf. Fig. 1). In concrete terms, students were asked to:

- categorize at least five places without accessibility information. These places appeared in grey on the Wheelmap.
- revisit at least three places, which have been categorized as 'partially wheelchair accessible'. These places appeared yellow on the Wheelmap.
- consider the appropriateness of the place's categorization and change its status if necessary.

Additionally, we explained that the purpose was to address the non-trivial challenge inherent in a categorization system needed to be simple enough to engage as many volunteers as possible but also meaningful enough to be of help to people searching accessible places. Students recorded their experiences in a mapping protocol consisting of a discussion of places visited including a place's conditions that could explain a categorization (task 1) or a change in categorization (task 2). Almost all students included photographs of the places visited in their protocols and a reflection on how their mapping influenced their views on accessibility in the city of Vienna.

Further information was obtained by two of the authors analyzing the 55 mapping protocols we got. Primarily quantifying students' reasoning about their mapping decisions. All in all, we scanned the protocols for the following information (I) How many barriers had been considered when categorizing a place?; (II) What types of barriers had been considered when categorizing a place?; and (III) In what ways were photos helpful in understanding the categorization of a place? All three types of information were then analyzed in relation to specific mapping decisions, namely (i) changing the categorization of a place; (ii) leaving a place's categorization as is and (iii) categorizing a place for the first time. Options (i) and (ii) were most interesting as we were interested in the effects of considering more than one barrier, possibly broadening the range of barriers or taking a picture of a barrier.

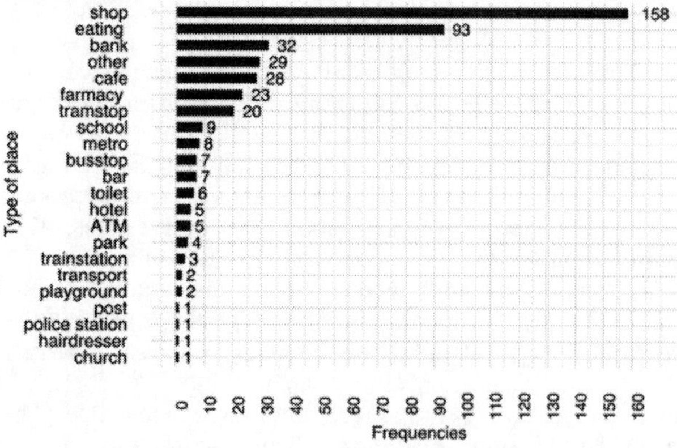

Figure 2. Type of mapped places (n=445).

However, some of our quantifications could be incomplete. For example, a mapper might have contemplated four types of barriers but reported only one in his or her mapping protocol. We believe that this is a limitation inherent to most self-reported data and difficult to prevent, if there is no other, more reliable data source to compare with.

Altogether, 279 new places had been categorized using the Wheelmap App and another 166 places had been reviewed and partly re-categorized (Fig. 2). Mappers found 168 completely accessible places and 277 places with barriers. Out of the 166 revisited places with limited accessibility, 51% remained unchanged and 49% changed, either to completely accessible or not accessible. Shops and restaurants were most prominent among the types of places that had been mapped. Access points to public transport received comparatively little attention.

IV. Case Discusison

An underlying issue of our case not yet discussed is the 'accountability aspect' when providing accessibility data. Put differently, the question is whether lay people, i.e., volunteers, can be trusted with providing this information and should not trained members of public authorities assume this task. In a review of the adoption of participatory geographic information systems (PGIS), Brown [18] lists several reasons for the fact, that participation in data collection has been promoted more by academics than by government agencies, including fear of the public, lack of experience in participatory processes and distrust in lay knowledge. At the core of these concerns is mostly a misunderstanding in that volunteers are not to be seen as a replacement for technically qualified experts but as a way to add local knowledge or lived experience. Both forms of knowledge, technical and experiential should be considered valuable sources of information to inform users of GIS.

Yet, our initial question was whether accessibility mapping done by lay people was problematic or controversial due to ambiguous or fuzzy classification systems. Since we did not want to compare the accuracy of lay mapping with expert mapping, we focused on the replicability of mapping results. In the end, we found two main conditions that triggered changes of mapped barriers: (1) a place contained multiple, aggregated barriers and (2) the mapper expanded his or her very notion of what a barrier is. The following discusses the mapping process on two different levels [22]:

- The *operational level*: How to apply mapping criteria to more complex buildings (shopping centers, train stations, museums, etc.)?
- The *conceptual level*: How can we make the concept of accessibility more tangible in order to ensure a sufficiently high quality of mapping outcomes?

These levels also reflect the semantic challenges of mapping categories outlined earlier in the introduction of the paper.

A. Operational Level: How many Barriers are there?

When assessing the accessibility of more complex structures, e.g., a supermarket, a train station or a bank, we will often find that multiple types of barriers exist. For example, there is an ongoing debate whether supermarkets are accessible if they have no steps at the entrance and sufficient space between shelves, but lack a payment option at the exit that is mounted at a height accessible for wheelchair users.

Hence, before starting the mapping project we emphasized the need to attempt a functional mapping rather than a categorical approach. Functional mapping would start with the question of 'What is the purpose of this place?' and could lead to a discovery of barriers not previously considered. On the contrary, the approach followed by the Wheelmap app (cf. Fig. 1) suggests a categorical approach (steps not higher than 7 cm and sufficient spaces within a location). The height of credit card readers, counters or door handles for example, is not explicitly mentioned.

We are aware that reducing a rather complex concept, such as 'accessibility' to a number of physical properties is a compromise a crowdsourcing platform has to make in order to keep things feasible and draw in as many volunteers as possible. But what consequences does it have if we switch from a categorical to a functional approach for mapping? Fig. 3 compares places with multiple, aggregated barriers with places that had been categorized taking a single barrier into account. As highlighted with the slightly darker bar, if mappers revisited a place already categorized, chances that they were to change the existing categorization were twice as high if they took into consideration multiple barriers (24% compared to 12%).

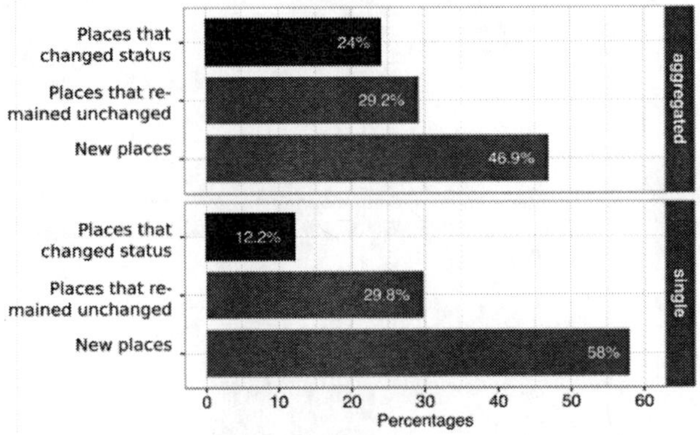

Figure 3. Mapping of aggregated or single barriers (n=277).

However, we cannot tell whether the places that changed their mapping status had already been mapped with multiple barriers in mind or whether the mappers revisiting the place simply saw a combination of barriers where previously only single barriers had been checked. Comments on changes from green to yellow (e.g., non-accessible toilet in a restaurant with an accessible entrance) or on changes from yellow to red (e.g., a movie theatre with accessible entrance but no wheelchair place in the cinema hall) seem to suggest that considering more possible barriers led to the changes.

Fig. 4 compares changes from yellow ('partially accessible') to red ('not accessible') depending on whether multiple or single barriers had been considered. Again the likelihood of a place to change to 'not accessible' is almost twice as high (25% versus 47%) if mappers take into account multiple barriers.

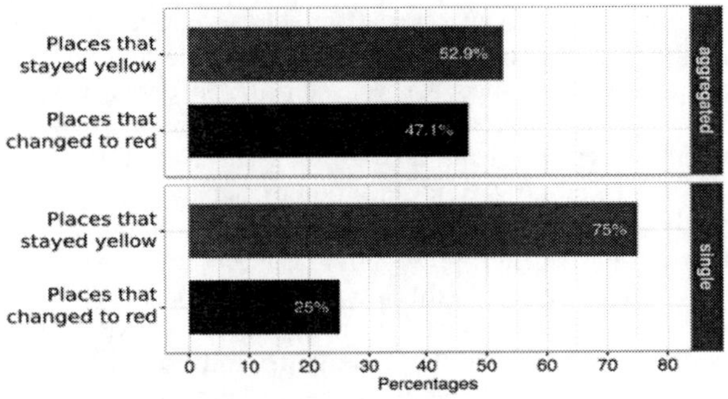

Figure 4. Impact of aggregated barriers on categorization changes (n=127).

Still, the objective of a categorization system cannot be to consider as many potential barriers as possible and thereby reduce the availability of accessible places if this is not absolutely necessary. Students became aware that striking a balance between mapping existing barriers, as well as producing useful accessibility information was a challenge not yet completely solved.

The relatively recent increase of Linked Open Data could provide a solution to his issue in the long term. Rather than trying to capture all accessibility related information through a single application, needed information could be combined accessing different sources. Ding et al. [23] conducted a survey of open accessible information, and found that different sources of similar accessibility information used different levels of aggregation. For example, whereas the accessibility of train stations in the Wheelmap is mostly based on tagged entrances and toilets, similar accessibility information included in the national rail station dataset (UK), is based on tags, such as 'ramp for train access' or 'accessible ticket machines'. Rather than trying to establish an all-embracing standard of tags, Ding and colleagues suggest to link open data. Linked data principles would allow for integrating data sets using different data structures, as ontology matching is a known approach to overcome semantic heterogeneity [23]. One possible first step in that direction could also be to direct users of the Wheelmap to another site, if that site offers additional information to the place the user had just inquired.

B. *Conceptual Level: Our Notions of Barriers and the Role of Photos*

The right to personal mobility is recognized globally as a human right, as reflected in the Convention on the Rights of Persons with Disabilities of the United Nations, which states that nations: "must take measures to ensure that persons with disabilities have equal access to the physical environment, to transportation, to information and communications, and to other facilities open or provided to the public" [24]. Following from this statement, it becomes clear that mobility and physical accessibility is a precondition to having choices in life, be it the school that is accessible or not, the workplace or the means of transport people with disabilities can or cannot use.

Matthews [25] surveyed different user groups (in regards to age and types of wheelchair) and listed the following most frequently mentioned barriers: steps, high curbs, deep gutters, gravel surfaces, lack of dropped curbs, narrow pavements, steep gradients and cobbled surfaces. Even though this might be already a fairly comprehensive list, given the methodology applied, types of barriers can be differentiated into normative (i.e., prescriptive) barriers and positive (i.e., descriptive) barriers [26]. Since we did not use an a-priori normative framework for our mapping action, we were particularly interested in the formulation and use of descriptive barriers. Fig. 5 shows the types of barriers that had been mapped. The most frequently mentioned barriers were steps (48.8%) and narrow spaces (22.8%). Next were barriers related to height (10.5%) and a category other (7.7%). 'Other barriers' included things like double doors, doors too heavy or ramp too steep.

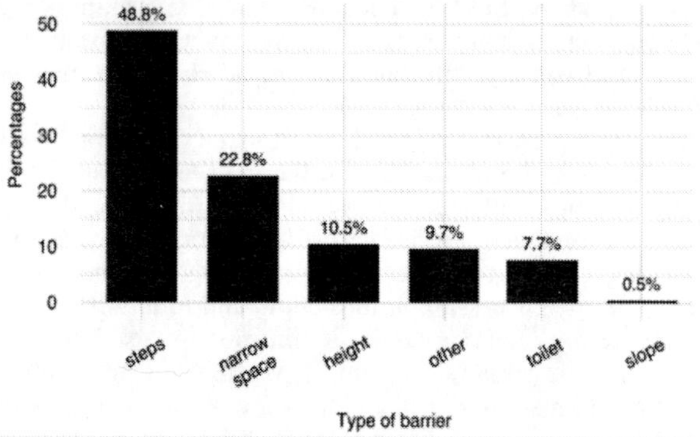

Figure 5. Types of barriers mapped (n=391)

Next, we wanted to see whether the explicit reference to a new type of barriers would influence the possibility that an existing categorization would change.

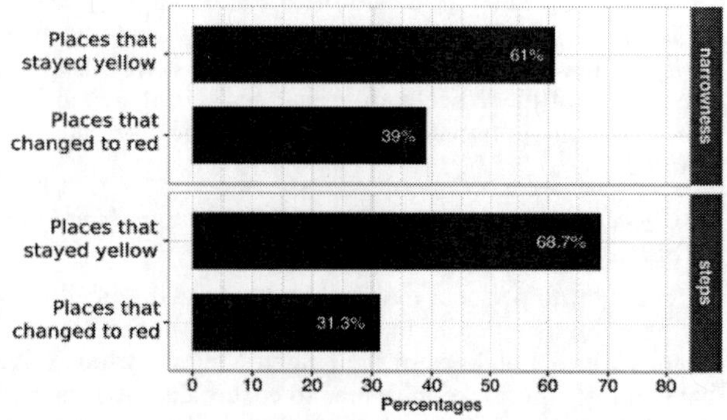

Figure 6. Impact of 'steps' and 'narrowness' on categorization changes (n=124).

For that, we compared 124 places that were tagged 'partially wheelchair accessible' either because they had steps or narrow spaces inside (Fig. 6). We would argue that 'steps' as it is mentioned on Wheelmap's mobile app interface is a prescriptive category and 'narrowness' an emerging, descriptive category. What we can see in Fig. 6 then, is that both categories have similar effects, in 39% of the cases the 'new', emerging category 'narrowness' co-occurred with changing a place into 'not accessible'. Since the majority of the places that changed into 'not accessible' were cafes, bars or restaurants, having emphasized the functional approach to mapping could be another reason for the relatively high impact of 'narrowness' as a new type of barriers.

Throughout the mapping action participants were encouraged to take pictures of the barriers they analyzed. Our initial hypothesis was that photos would help the specification of barriers and therefore enhance clarity and transparency of the mapping decisions. Hence, two of the authors looked through the 215 photos taken during the mapping project and classified them according to their effect on understanding mapping decisions (Fig. 7).

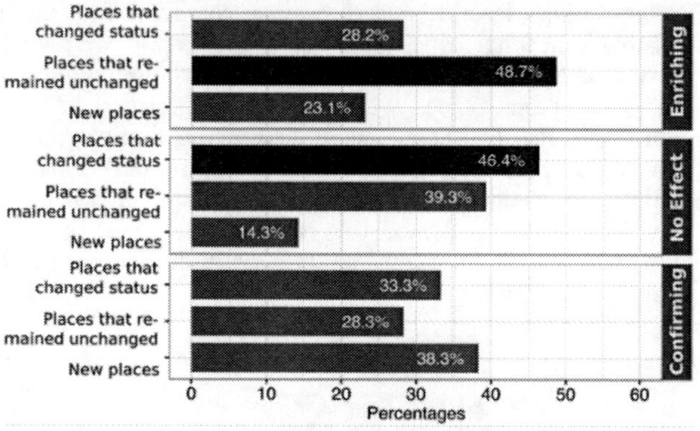

Figure 7. The effect of photos on status clarity (n=215).

A photo was said to be 'enriching' whenever the photo showed more then what was expressed in the verbal description of a barrier.

Figure 8. A clear picture of barriers

For example, rather than having to speculate whether double doors at the entrance might be a barrier that could be overcome, a photo such as in Fig. 8 supports the visualization and individual evaluation of a barrier, be it the shape of the curb or the steepness of the slope that can make a difference. If a photo just showed a panoramic view of a location without a clear focus on a barrier, we decided that the photo had 'no effect' on our understanding of the accessibility of a place. 'Confirming' photos were similar to Fig. 8, only that they represented less complex situations of single stairs or steps. They are still useful as they help to avoid surprises if users go by verbal descriptions only.

C. *Learning with Boundary Objects and Probabilistic Models*

One reason to go through a detailed evaluation of a mapping process on an operational and conceptual level was to make a case for learning the pros and cons of mapping categories, as well as learning when a good description of the place is more needed than a general debate about the 'right' mapping categories.

Spinuzzi suggests a methodology that aims to understand 'knowledge' by doing, i.e., "the traditional, tacit, and often invisible ways of how people perform their everyday activities and how those activities may be shaped productively" [11]. Categorization work of volunteer mappers can be researched under just the same premise: What are the often tacit perceptions that shape mapping decisions? Hence, a conceptual extension to PD is the notion that collaborative mapping involves learning, similar to communities-of-practice, where the transition from peripheral to genuine participation requires changes in doing, talking, thinking and feeling [4]. If we think of collaborative mapping as the production of socially constructed knowledge, i.e., a shared knowledge creation experience, then Star and Griesemer's 'boundary objects' [8] can be a useful paraphrase of 'flexible mapping categories'. Boundary objects are " objects which are both plastic enough to adapt to local needs and constraints of the several parties employing them, yet robust enough to maintain a common identity across sites. They are weakly structured in common use, and become strongly structured in individual-site use" [8].

If we continue with the metaphor of the 'robust core' of mapping decisions, a prescriptive set of barriers could serve just this purpose. However, Fig. 5 presented only a relatively small data set of 391 barriers and 'narrowness' became an example for a barrier, previously not much considered. What if we were to analyze the accessibility of thousands of places? How many additional types of barriers could we discover and how would we want to map them? We can assume that a very long list of barriers would be impractical in the context of crowdsourcing. When relying on volunteer contributions, we would suggest that the categorization of 'accessibility' couldn't be managed through a checklist of accessibility-defining attributes, no matter how comprehensive. We would rather aim for mappers to develop a mental model of accessibility in order to decide whether a place is accessible or not.

In such situations, mappers need to be able to adapt their categorization procedures and develop new categories of accessibility in accordance to the place they want to map. Barsalou [27] suggests two ways for how we acquire new categories: (a) we learn from exemplars (several objects have overlapping characteristics and therefore suggest a category) and (b) we learn by recombining features of existing categories. An example for the latter would be the combination of an attribute like 'width of passage' with 'available space in front of a door' to form a new category 'maneuvering space'. In a shop that has just one long corridor, wheelchair users should be able to turn around at the end of the corridor, especially if they use an electric wheelchair. The underlying idea would be that it is not enough if a wheelchair can move ahead, if in fact the user of a wheelchair needs to make a turn.

V. Conclusion: Co-Design Drives Engagement

The paper started with the claim that large scale participation platforms offer new possibilities for addressing long-standing societal problems, such as creating awareness for the accessibility of cities. We then presented collaborative mapping and digital maps as a typical instance of a participation platform which in many aspects is already a success story, offering an open source alternative to commercial products, such as Google Maps. Next, we linked collaborative mapping to the case of Wheelmap.org, an accessibility mapping platform built on top of the OSM. Using wheelmap.org as a case study, we concentrated on issues around the operational and conceptual foundations of the mapping process. The case discussion made clear that 'conceptualizations of barriers' and 'rules of mapping' are critical components of an application's design and impact the quality of the mapping done.

Being foremost concerned with ambiguities and reliability issues of accessibility mapping, we focused on identifying issues with mapping complex places and - often tacitly hold - concepts of accessibility and barriers. We found that efforts to raise awareness of accessibility barriers often faced the challenge that the public cannot relate to accessibility data if they are not able to relate to the meaning of accessibility, either because they think it does not apply to their lives or because they cannot make the link to the personal context of their daily experiences [28]. Yet, if we want people to challenge their believes and to contribute to improving the accessibility of their cities, we need mechanisms that allow people to contextually relate with accessibility. Research on awareness raising through crowd-based accessibility maps by Goncalves [28] has shown the effectiveness of contextual cues when people are asked to relate with past experiences or memories. Moreover, without implying causation, Goncalves showed that people who took pictures during an accessibility-mapping event reported considerably more places than those participants who did not take pictures.

Yet, the implicit engagement strategy in this paper has been to make crowdsourcing also a co-design and mutual learning activity. To summarize, this paper (a) highlighted the need for switching from a categorical to a functional approach for mapping; (b) demonstrated the value of involving volunteer mappers as co-designers in order to optimize designs at the operational and conceptual level; and (c) suggested an explicit learning component as part of the collaborative mapping process, using a boundary objects metaphor in order to balance flexibility and feasibility when collaboratively mapping accessibility.

ACKNOWLEDGMENT

This research has been supported by cap4access, a project funded by the European Commission in the 7th Framework Program.

REFERENCES

[1] G. Fischer, "Understanding, fostering, and supporting cultures of participation", *interactions*, vol. 18, no. 3, pp. 42–53, 2011.

[2] M. F. Goodchild, "Citizens as sensors: the world of volunteered geography", *GeoJournal*, vol. 69, no. 4, pp. 211–221, 2007.

[3] E. Hornecker et al., "UbiComp in opportunity spaces: challenges for participatory design", in *Proceedings of the ninth conference on Participatory design: Expanding boundaries in design-Volume 1*, pp. 47–56, 2006.

[4] P. Ehn, "Participation in design things", in *Proceedings of the Tenth Anniversary Conference on Participatory Design 2008*, pp. 92–101, 2008.

[5] J. Gonçalves et al., "Citizen motivation on the go: The role of psychological empowerment", *Interacting with Computers*, vol. 26, no. 3, p. 196-207, 2014.

[6] N. Selwyn, "Reconsidering political and popular understandings of the digital divide", *New Media & Society*, vol. 6, no. 3, pp. 341–362, 2004.

[7] A. J. Van Deursen and J. A. van Dijk, "Modeling traditional literacy, Internet skills and Internet usage: An empirical study", *Interacting with computers*, vol. 28, no. 1, p. 13-26, 2016.

[8] S. L. Star and J. R. Griesemer, "Institutional Ecology, `Translations' and Boundary Objects: Amateurs and Professionals in Berkeley's Museum of Vertebrate Zoology, 1907-39", *Social Studies of Science*, vol. 19, pp. 387–420, Aug. 1989.

[9] J. Simonsen and M. Hertzum, "Participative design and the challenges of large-scale systems: Extending the iterative PD approach", in *Proceedings of the tenth anniversary conference on participatory design 2008*, pp. 1–10, 2008.

[10] R. DePaula, "Lost in translation: a critical analysis of actors, artifacts, agendas, and arenas in participatory design", in *Proceedings of the eighth conference on Participatory design: Artful integration: interweaving media, materials and practices-Volume 1*, pp. 162–172, 2004.

[11] C. Spinuzzi, "The methodology of participatory design", *Technical Communication*, vol. 52, no. 2, pp. 163–174, 2005.

[12] J. W. Crampton, "Maps as social constructions: power, communication and visualization", *Progress in Human Geography*, vol. 25, no. 2, pp. 235–252, 2001.

[13] M. Schaefer and T. Woodyer, "Assessing absolute and relative accuracy of recreation-grade and mobile phone GNSS devices: a method for informing device choice", *Area*, vol. 47, no. 2, pp. 185–196, 2015.

[14] Statistics Austria, "Population census und structure", 2016. [Online]. Available: http://www.statistik.at/web_de/statistiken/menschen_und_gesellschaft/bevoelkerung/index.html. [Retrieved: September, 2016].

[15] R. Spindler, "OpenStreetMap Wheelchair History: A subset of wheelchair tagged nodes of a Planet OSM-Full-History", in *Unpublished Database*, 2015.

[16] M. Bakillah et al., "Toward a collective tagging Android application for gathering accessibility-related geospatial data in European cities", in *Agile Conference*, pp. 21-26, 2015.

[17] M. Haklay, "How good is volunteered geographical information? A comparative study of OpenStreetMap and Ordnance Survey datasets", *Environment and planning B: Planning and design*, vol. 37, no. 4, pp. 682–703, 2010.

[18] G. Brown, "Public Participation GIS (PPGIS) for regional and environmental planning: Reflections on a decade of empirical research", *Journal of Urban and Regional Information Systems Association*, vol. 25, no. 2, pp. 7–18, 2012.

[19] M. Snyder and A. M. Omoto, "Volunteerism: Social issues perspectives and social policy implications", *Social Issues and Policy Review*, vol. 2, no. 1, pp. 1–36, 2008.

[20] Hans Voss, "D3.2 Technical Design, Collective Awareness Platforms for Improving Accessibility in European Cities & Regions", in *7th Framework Programme*, 2015.

[21] J. W. Crampton and J. Krygier, "An introduction to critical cartography", *ACME: an International E-journal for Critical Geographies*, vol. 4, no. 1, pp. 11–33, 2005.

[22] F. Barcellini, L. Prost, and M. Cerf, "Designers' and users' roles in participatory design: What is actually co-designed by participants?", *Applied ergonomics*, vol. 50, pp. 31–40, 2015.

[23] C. Ding, M. Wald, and G. Wills, "A survey of open accessibility data", in *Proceedings of the 11th Web for All Conference*, pp. 37-40, 2014.

[24] United Nations, "Convention on the Rights of Persons with Disabilities", 2007. [Online]. Available: http://www.un.org/disabilities/default.asp?navid=15&pid=150. [Retrieved: September, 2016].

[25] H. Matthews, L. Beale, P. Picton, and D. Briggs, "Modelling Access with GIS in Urban Systems (MAGUS): capturing the experiences of wheelchair users", *Area*, vol. 35, no. 1, pp. 34–45, 2003.

[26] A. Páez, D. M. Scott, and C. Morency, "Measuring accessibility: positive and normative implementations of various accessibility indicators", *Journal of Transport Geography*, vol. 25, pp. 141–153, 2012.

[27] L. W. Barsalou, "Deriving categories to achieve goals", *Goal Directed Learning. MIT Press, Cambridge MA*, pp. 121–176, 1995.

[28] J. Goncalves, V. Kostakos, S. Hosio, E. Karapanos, and O. Lyra, "IncluCity: Using contextual cues to raise awareness on environmental accessibility", in Proceedings of the 15th International ACM SIGACCESS Conference on Computers and Accessibility, pp. 17-24, 2013.

The Engine node Mining Algorithm in Microblog Information Spreading

Jing Yang
College of Computer Science and Technology,
Harbin Engineering University,
Harbin, Heilongjiang 150001, China
yangjing@hrbeu.edu.cn

Pengfei Sun
College of Computer Science and Technology,
Harbin Normal University,
Harbin, Heilongjiang 150025, China
sunpengfei@hrbeu.edu.cn

Xueyan Zhou
College of Computer Science and Technology,
Harbin Engineering University,
Harbin Engineering University Science Park
College of Engineering, Harbin University,
Harbin, Heilongjiang 150086, China
zhouxueyan@hrbeu.edu.cn

Yongshi Zhang
College of Computer Science and Technology, Harbin Engineering University, Harbin, Heilongjiang 150001,
zhangyongshi@hrbeu.edu.cn

Jing Zhang
College of Computer Science and Technology,
Harbin Engineering University,
Harbin, Heilongjiang, China
zhangjing@hrbeu.edu.cn

***Abstract*—Retweeting is the main propagation mechanism in microblog platform. The information often spreads wider through some engine nodes. The paper proposes a new engine node mining algorithm. Firstly, the cascade (session tree) is built according to the retweeting of a microblog. Secondly the pruning strategy is used according to the timestamp. Thirdly, the cascade set (session forest) is clustered by topical relevance. Finally, the engine node with different precision can be extracted through computing the integrated diffusion capacity. We conduct an experiment to show the effective of the proposed algorithm.**

Keywords-Microblog; retweeting; engine node; generating; pruning

I. INTRODUCTION

In recent years, the microblog platform has developed rapidly; Sina microblog has more than 600 million users, among which the number of monthly active users reached 129.1 million[1][2]. The microblog platform has many characteristics such as the immediate information dissemination, the high propagation speed, the large transmission range. Since a user can share feelings and information at any time, so the information dissemination of microblog has more incomparable advantages than that of traditional media. The convenient way, however, makes the information more difficult to track and control.

Many researchers have studied microblogs, such as the microblog topic extraction and analysis, sentiment analysis, information retrieval and recommendation, the user relationship mining, information dissemination evolution and user influence analysis. The user influence analysis mainly mines the different types of nodes from different angles, such as high-impact nodes, active nodes, the nodes with high confidence, the core nodes, the source nodes and engines nodes, etc. Traditional researches of individual influence technologies include degree, closeness, betweenness, HITS, PageRank and extension methods. These studies are generally for a snapshot of the network topology, and no analysis of the specific topic. The other microblog information dissemination process is often due to the high influence of users and the rapid spread of retweeting.The basic idea is that these nodes will disseminate information more widely[3][4]. This paper proposes an engine node mining method based on topic. Engine node is the node with larger diffusion force. The mining method first builds a cascade according to the retweeting of a microblog, after which the pruning strategy is used according to the timestamp. The remainder of this paper is structured as follows. In Section II we review the related work and propose the engine node mining algorithm. In Section III, we conduct an experiment on real data. Section IV concludes the whole paper.

II. RELATED WORK

The microblog information dissemination mechanism and retweeting in microblog are introduced in this section, and then the engine node mining algorithm is proposed in detail.

A. Microblog Information Dissemination Mechanism

In recent years, lots of information diffusion algorithms on social network have been proposed. Among them, quite a number of algorithms extract information network from a group of most influential nodes. Their basic idea is that these nodes will make the information disseminate more widely, including information dissemination prediction by analyzing the blog information cascade [5][6].

Information dissemination speed on the microblog platform is much faster than that on the blog platform, and their propagate model are also different. Dabeer [7], analyzed the factors affecting the microblog information dissemination, including information characteristics and the activity, response and out-degree of fans nodes. He proposed a decision-making framework based on Markov to measure the effectiveness of information dissemination. Lehmann et al. [8] tracked the HashTag diffusion process in Twitter network, and discovered that the epidemic spread model played an important role. Yang et al. [9] predicted the microblog information dissemination speed, size and scope. Tsur et al. [10] employed a linear regression model to predict the diffusion of information within a given time according to the content and network topology. Wang [11] provided a network-traffic based web traffic computing technology for hot topic discovery, incident detection, real-time tracking and other applications. The "fission" engine node mining algorithms are rare, and these nodes which make the information "Second outbreak" or even "N times outbreak" have a great potential for application. On the one hand, grasping the engine node is helpful for the information control. On the other hand, seeking out the engine nodes is significant in the field of advertising and other commercial applications.)

B. *Retweeting in microblog*

Retweeting in microblog is the main object of data mining, because it is the base of information dissemination, influence analysis, sentiment analysis, topic discovery and evolution etc. Therefore, the study of microblog retweeting contributes to the understanding of the information diffusion mechanism. Macskassy et al. [12] showed that the majority of users do not necessarily retweet their familiar topic. Pal and Counts [13] assessed and sorted the user's authority using the number of the original tweeting, participated in the session and retweeting as primary index. They used a Gaussian mixture model to calculate the user's influence. Since the computation complexity of the model is very high, it is not suitable for traceability research. In addition, the user influence assessment based on information needs to deal with many insoluble problems, such as languages, dialects, pictures and videos. Therefore, we must use a simple way to get information as accurate as possible, such as only the cascade and the topology are used to study traceability research without semantic mining, and only the positive and negative emotions to assess the influence while ignoring the impact of information in different formats.

The microblog information propagation model can be described as G= (V, E), where V is a user and E is the retweeting or comment relationships. An information cascade is also known as a session tree, and the out-degree of its initiator is 0, the others link to the initiator or participators to form the information cascade through retweeting, sharing or commenting etc. So the influence is opposite to the direct edge. The information cascade may contain loops, and there are following relationships in microblog, so strictly speaking it is not a tree structure. The timestamps have been concerned to pruning and generating the cascade tree, and then the engine nodes can be digged out through attribute measuring.

C. *The Engine node Mining Algorithm*

Engine node mining algorithms are designed to extract nodes with high information diffusion ability. Firstly, the information is built according to the retweeting. Secondly the pruning strategy is used according to the timestamp. Thirdly, the cascade set is clustered by topical relevance. Finally, the engine node with different precision can be extracted through computing the integrated diffusion capacity. Algorithm 1 shows the main steps.

```
Algorithm 1: EngineNodes
Input: G (V, E)
Output: Mining Engine node ENT for each topic T
Begin
  C←ExtractCascade (G);
  C←PruningStrategy(C);
  IF C is context-aware then
        ←ExtractSubgraph(C);
  else
        ={C}
  for each GT∈  do
   if GT is not a tree then
      {GT ←GeneratingStrategy(GT);
      GT ←PruningStrategy(GT);}
      ENT← EngineNodes(GT);
End
```

The GeneratingStrategy and PruningStrategy are used to amend the cascades to the tree structure. The PruningStrategy will delete certain retweeting edges according to the timestamp to remove the circle structure, and the GeneratingStrategy will add certain retweeting edges according to the timestamp and following factor to form a larger cascade tree. The PruningStrategy is shown in Figure 1.

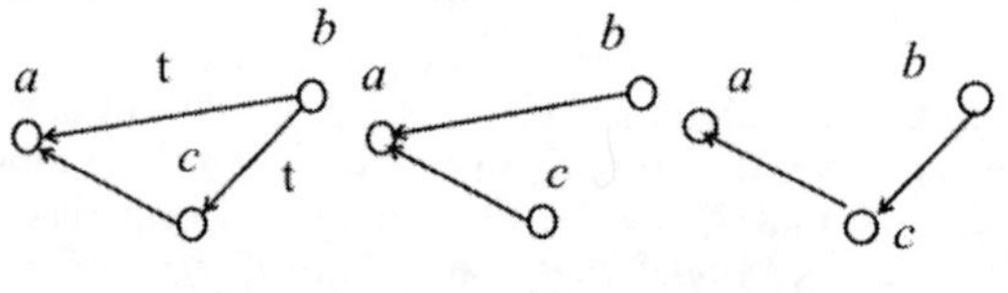

(a) Retweeting with circle structure (b) PruningStrategy while t1<t2 (c) GeneratingStrategy while t1>t2

Figure 1. PruningStrategy Schematic Diagram

PruningStrategy eliminates loops based on the first retweeting. User b forwards the same message from a and c to form a loop, then the PruningStrategy is used according to the time stamp, such as the edge b to c will be cut off while t1<t2, and vice versa.

At the same time, GeneratingStrategy adds virtual edges combine scattered information to cascade into larger information cascade tree. The GeneratingStrategy is shown in Figure 2.

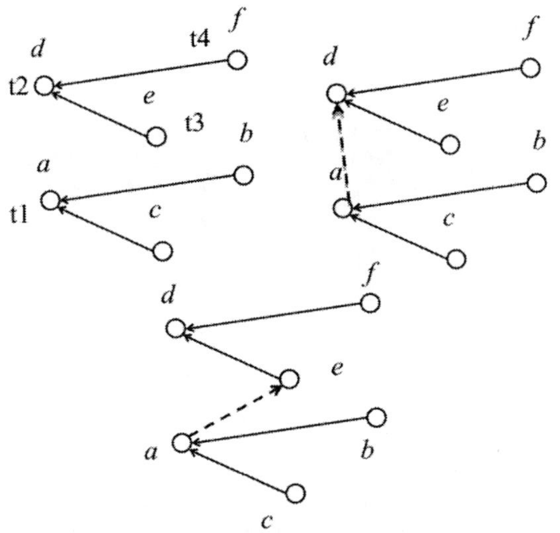

(a)Two independent cascade tree(b)while d,e,f follow a and t2<t1(c)while e,f follow a,t3<t4 and t3<t1

Figure 2. GeneratingStrategy Schematic Diagram

The basic principle of GeneratingStrategy regards the user who post the same message later than ones' friends, and then adds virtual edges. Specific steps are as following: (1) for the root node, look for its friends with the earliest timestamp within the cascade; (2) regarding the root node as children of the friend with earliest timestamp by adding virtual edges, which will increase the size of the cascade; (3) if the GeneratingStrategy brings in some loops, the PruningStrategy should be used.

Diffusion coefficient α in formula (1) is used to measure the information diffusion force of the node. For example, each node of information cascade tree in Figure 3. has a different diffusion coefficient.

$$\alpha = \frac{O_i}{O_i - N_{i1} + \sum_{k=1}^{N_{i1}} O_k} \qquad (1)$$

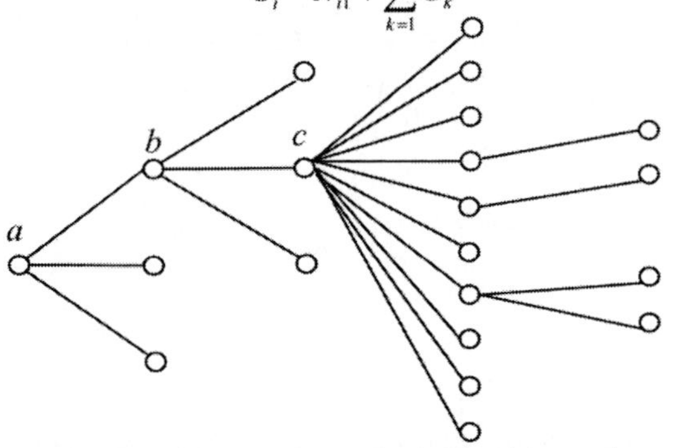

Figure 3. The diffusion coefficient of an information cascade tree

Where, diffusion coefficient α denotes the information diffusion force of node i, Oi is the outdegree of node i, and Ni1 is the number of the one-hop non-leaf of node i. The denominator of the diffusion coefficient is equal to the number of the leaf nodes. For example, the diffusion coefficient of node a, b and c respectively are 3/15, 3/13 and 10/11, and the node c is the maximum one. So the diffusion coefficient can be applied to mine the engine node.

III. EXPERIMENTS

The data set is taken from a well-known China microblog site - Sina microblog, which was opened to the public in Oct. 2009. It has nearly 600 million registered users, among which nearly 100 million are daily active users. Microblog information has strong timeliness, and most topics will fade in a short time. The experiment data take partial data in Oct. 2014(including 75,526,147 posts) for analysis. The proposed algorithm is mainly to extract the engine node in the information propagation.

A. *Cascade extraction*

Cascade can be divided into two categories, namely chain and star. The chain has only one node in each layer, focusing on depth propagation, and the star has multiple nodes in a layer, focusing on breadth propagation. In the database, the frequency of the star is higher than that of the chain under the same cascade size. According to the definition of engine node, namely the "nuclear fission" central node, these nodes are more likely to exist in the star cascade. In fact, most of the cascades are between the two cases, for the complex shape of chain and star. In addition, due to the special nature of microblog retweeting, it will not appear in the case of multiple initiators, namely there is only one root in the topology. And a user can forward the message many times, so there may be a loop in a cascade. Figure 4 shows six basic high frequency cascade topology structures, and it can be seen that most cascades are too short to mine the engine node, so the GeneratingStrategy and PruningStrategy are used to amend the cascades to the tree structure.

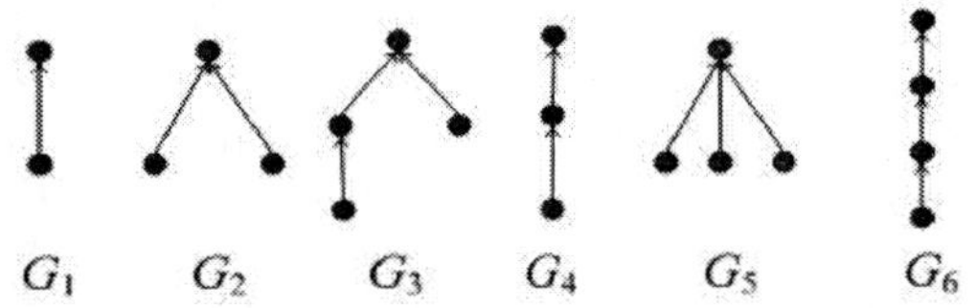

Figure 4. The basic high frequency cascade topology structure

B. *Engine node mining*

To calculate the diffusion coefficient of all nodes in all topics is not necessary, and the computation complexity is high, so the algorithm analyzes the diffusion capacity of nodes in a certain topic. The keyword matching algorithm is used to extract the sub graph based on topic, and the core idea is to put the cascades with same keywords into a collection. The topic T has the keyword {k1, k2, k3}, and GT is the cascade set with same keywords of topic T. The GeneratingStrategy and PruningStrategy are used to amend the cascades to cascade sets based on topics, and then the largest connected component is the main data for analysis. The largest connected component may contain more engine nodes. Assuming that the branch contains n nodes, n-1 retweeting edges and m leaf nodes, according to the definition of diffusion coefficient, we can get $\alpha = 0$ on the leaf nodes and $\alpha = 1$ on the nodes whose one-hop nodes are leaf nodes. Diffusion capacity of these two nodes is limited. But the diffusion coefficient of other nodes in cascade tree is between 0 and 1. Taking the "Lanxiang" event with duration of 11 days and "persistent haze" event with duration of 12 days as an example, in the topic-based cascade, the diffusion capacity of three largest branches are analyzed respectively. TABLE I shows the nodes analysis of each cascade branch. A high engine node percent means topology structure is closer to the star topology.

TABLE I. THE NODES ANALYSIS OF EACH CASCADE BRANCH

Event	**Lanxiang**			**Haze**		
Branch No.	1	2	3	4	5	6
nodes	8065	7619	5210	7324	4301	3847
edges	8064	7618	5209	7323	4300	3846
Leaf nodes	2516	2734	1837	3519	1042	1566
Leaf-to-be	1027	1804	1094	1249	841	931
Engine node	4522	3081	2279	2556	2418	1350
Percent	56.1	40.4	43.7	34.9	56.2	35.1

The node diffusion coefficient in each branch is calculated, and the nodes with $\alpha > 0.9$ should be labeled as engine node. The distribution is shown in Figure 5.The red section represents the nodes size with $\alpha > 0.9$, whose proportion is small in each branch. The highest proportion is 16% in No.4, and the lowest proportion is 10% in No.2. It is obvious that the proportion of high coefficient diffusion nodes is low. The result set is beneficial for the network public opinion analysis, and the engine nodes are very important for the advertising and other applications.

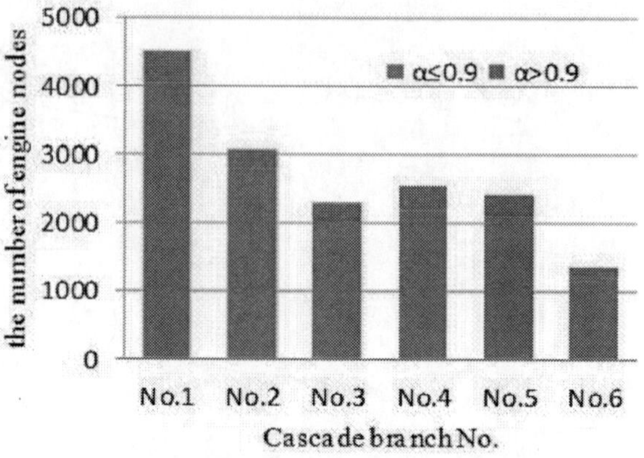

Figure 5. The nodes with $\alpha > 0.9$ in the diffusion nodes

Determining the engine node in different network topology according to the nodes ($\alpha > 0.9$) is unreasonable. In order to control the number of engine nodes, our experiment usually chooses a certain percentage. As there are 8065 nodes in No.1 cascade branch, if 2% nodes are required to be advertised, the engine node is 161 with $\alpha > 0.937$, which is far less than the red section of 477 nodes in Figure 5. Therefore, the engine node set is a variable data field based on actual demands. By manual verification, the resulting engine node has many fans and retweeting. They are always celebrities or grassroots heroes.

IV. CONCLUSIONS

The paper proposes an algorithm to extract the engine node with high information diffusion capacity on the microblog data. The algorithm combines knowledge of information cascade, the time factor, the topic factors and graph theory, and the engine node set is variably based on the actual demands. On one hand, these nodes have reasonable size to be used for public opinion analysis and early warning. On the other hand, the advertising has broad prospects. Therefore the research of marketing strategy based on engine nodes computation will be our future work.

ACKNOWLEDGMENT

This paper is supported by (1) the National Natural Science Foundation of China under Grant nos. 61672179, 61370083 and 61402126, (2) the Research Fund for the Doctoral Program of Higher Education of China under Grant nos. 20122304110012, (3) the Natural Science Foundation of Heilongjiang Province of China under Grant no. F201320.(4) 2017-2020 The National Natural Science Fund (Project No.51679058). (5) 2013-2016 China Higher Specialized Research Fund (PhD supervisor category) (20132304110018). (6) Heilongjiang social science research Fund (16XWB01, 16TQD03). (7) Harbin

University Young Doctor start-up fund scientific research projects.

REFERENCES

[1] Ding Zhaoyun, Jia Yan, Zhou Bin.Survey of Data Mining for Microblog. Journal of Computer Research and Development. 51(4): pp.691-706.2014.

[2] Hu Q, GAO Y, Ma P, et al. A new approach to identify influential spreaders in complex networks. In: Web-Age Information Management 2013. New York: Springer, pp.99-104.2013.

[3] Chen D B, Lü L, Shang M S, et al. Identifying influential nodes in complex networks. Physica A, 391: pp.1777-1787.2012.

[4] Yang J, Counts S. Predicting the Speed, Scale, and Range of Information Diffusion in Twitter. ICWSM,10:pp.355-358P.2010.

[5] Leskovec, Jurel. "Cascading Behavior in Large Blog Graphs." Trials15. pp.1-11, 2007.

[6] Li, Hui. "Affinity-driven blog cascade analysis and prediction." Data Mining & Knowledge Discovery 28.2. pp.442-474,2014.

[7] Dabeer, Onkar. "Timing Tweets to Increase Effectiveness of Information Campaigns." International Conference on Weblogs & Social Media 2011.

[8] Janette Lehmann, et al. "Dynamical classes of collective attention in twitter". Computer Science . pp.251-260.2011.

[9] Yang, Jiang, S. Counts. "Predicting the Speed, Scale, and Range of Information Diffusion in Twitter". International Conference on Weblogs & Social Media 2010.

[10] Tsur, Oren, A. Rappoport. "What's in a hashtag?: content based prediction of the spread of ideas in microblogging communities". International Conference on Web Search & Web Data Mining . pp..643-652. 2015

[11] Wang, Bai Ling, et al. "Research on Network-Traffic Based Web Traffic Computing Technology." Acta Electronica Sinica 41.4.pp.751-756. 2013.

[12] Macskassy, Sofus A., M. Michelson. "Why do People Retweet? Anti-Homophily Wins the Day!." International Conference on Weblogs & Social Media 2015.

[13] Pal, Aditya, and S. Counts. "Identifying topical authorities in microblogs." ACM International Conference on Web Search & Data Mining. pp.:45-54.2011.

The Support for the Integration of BIM Through Collaborative Action Research: ShareLab

Charlène Naville[1], Pierre Leclercq[1] and Samia Ben Rajeb[1,2]
[1]LUCID - Lab for User Cognition & Innovative Design, University of Liège, Belgium
[2]COLLAeB - Lab of Collaborative Design and Digital Mediations, University of Bruxelles, Belgium
e-mail: charlene.naville @ student.ulg.ac.be, samia.benrajeb / pierre.leclercq @ ulg.ac.be

Abstract— **Building Information Modeling (BIM) deals with building technologies and techniques that cover the entire lifespan of a building or structure. It allows for building design and documentation (information modelling), as well as the coordination and management of information (information management) that describes the building, its limitations and its performance objectives. This article questions the integration of BIM in the integrated design processes of major architectural and engineering firms. It proposes collaborative action research: ShareLab as a new approach to the appropriation of BIM paradigms. Equipped with various methods of reflection and information collection, the goal of ShareLab use is to collaboratively construct a common understanding of various issues and a shared vision of the stakes at play. This is done in an effort to push businesses into the BIM integration process.**

Keywords-BIM; collaboration; action research; change management; the science of design; the performance of a design project: time and tools.

I. Introduction

This section describes the BIM context and issues as well as the notion of ShareLab..

A. BIM: a response to current industrial and societal stake

In today's world, collaboration plays an integral part in design especially in the public domain. There is an ever growing number of players who, as early as the initial stages, intervene in the layout of a project. This number continues to grow due to more stringent performance demands and shorter deadlines.

In this context, Building Information Modeling (BIM) methods and technology allow for integrated "teamwork" during the entire design, construction and life cycle of the building. BIM uses numerical models to design and represent the data relating to the building, its limitations and its performance objectives. This information is managed and coordinated by a collaborative process called the BIM, whose integration is yet to be concocted [1].

This innovative collaborative approach calls upon the participation of all the players involved in the construction project (architects, engineers, entrepreneurs, contracting authorities, managers and clients) and it covers the project's entire lifespan. While the management, sharing and synchronisation of information remains a major challenge in the process, the numerical templates of the building represent a fundamental evolution in the field and are effecting changes worldwide.

The results of BIM pilot projects demonstrate the many advantages of its implementation [2]: the meeting of delivery deadlines and the reduction of construction costs through decreasing human design errors. In contrast to other fields in the manufacturing sector, the construction industry has evolved very little in its methods and its work efficiency. The positive BIM performance results are revelatory of its potential. As a result of increased dialogue between various players who hope to improve project performance and overall productivity, construction projects have become more elaborate. The use of these integrated technologies and processes are seen as a promising way to respond to this increase in project complexity [3].

There are two main reasons why businesses have switched to BIM: 1) the every growing demands on the performance of buildings on a technical, environmental ad budgetary level, and 2) the legislative constraints that increasingly recommend the use of BIM technologies and methods to answer public requests for tender. For example, European Union member countries have progressively begun implementing the January 15, 2014 European Union directive, which encourages the use of BIMs for the financing of public projects. Since 2016, Norway, Denmark, Finland, Great Britain and the Netherlands have committed to managing these types of major projects through collaborative BIM processes.

B. Issues

Through the use of data sharing models, businesses can efficiently use new procedures and technologies to create projects that are more environmentally and economically friendly throughout their entire life cycle. However, this requires both internal and external action. Internally, it necessitates a review of current practices and workflows, and externally, a response to the new realities of competitivity and innovation [4]. Thus, the implementation of a BIM work process calls for significant change on an organizational, technical and even legal level.

The switch from a sequential organization, organization by "batches", to a BIM collective, where players work concurrently in order to achieve a common goal, entails the integration of complex organizational processes [5] . There is ever growing need to manage change in way that helps professionals and firms adapt to their changing environment and coordinate their market vision with that of present operational realities.

The goal of this study is to develop, experiment and validate a new participatory approach for understanding the implementation of BIM in the integrated design process. This study proposes collaborative action research as a means to achieve this end. This new method is structured in order to be applied in large construction firms and as a same time to take into consideration the specificity of each actors and its function in the organization of a building project.

C. Structure of the paper

The state of the art presents different studies and methods developed to guide the change to BIM work practices and technologies. The section following expound the structure of a new approach to deals with this issue: the Sharelab. Then, methodological tools used for the Sharelab are broached before demonstrating the interest of the method for BIM integration. The conclusion proposes a summary, with limitations and perspectives of the research.

II. STATE OF THE ART

There have been many recent studies on the interoperability of objects in 3D and on the advantages that BIM can bring to the optimization of construction deadlines [6]. In order to increase productivity through the use of BIM, businesses must implement specialised technologies from software providers and computer consultants. That being said, to fully benefit from the use of BIM, businesses need to go beyond this technocentric view and organize around their own company and management.

A. International Studies

On an international level, a Canadian study by Staub-French, [2] focuses on two primary objectives: the first, the analysis of the usage of BIM in a variety of professions and projects; the second, the study of best practices in real cases that cover different levels of the business. Among the recently developed methods and tools, Penn State University's [7] approach is at the forefront. The goal of this approach is twofold: 1) the identification of BIM objectives and the tasks and steps that need to be taken for their attainment, and 2) globally defining and coordinating BIM project requirements by involving all players. The study is based on the idea that BIM serves a large database of uses and that it is primarily suited for comparing user objectives and capabilities.

TABLE I. COMPARATIVE TABLE OF DIFFERENT BIM INTEGRATION GUIDES ' APPLICATION FRAMEWORK

	Author / Editor	Target audience	Objective announced	Field of application
PAS 1192-2 (UK, 2013)	BSI (British Standard Institution)	Every actor of building industry, BIM qualified and experimented.	To propose a set of tools to apply rapidly to support BIM integration	The whole life cycle of a construction project
Statsbygg BIM Manual 1.2.1 (Norway, 2013)	Statsbygg, buildingSMART member	Every actor involved in a BIM process	To guide the use of BIM software	The whole life cycle of a construction project
Singapore BIM Guide (2013)	Building and Construction Authority	A global document is addressed to the whole building trade and specific ones target every actor	To demystify the BIM and to give keys for the use of BIM at each stage of a project	The whole life cycle of a construction project with specific approach according to the different building trades.
Planning Guide for Facility Owners (US, 2013)	CIC, Computer Integrated Construction	Contractor	To help contractors implementing BIM in construction projects	Preliminary studies to prepare a project, from the definition of needs to execution deals
The Guide to BIM (Belgium, 2015)	ADEB-VBA	Every actwor of building industry	To propose a support for collaboration and digital information exchange	The whole life cycle of a construction project
Methodological Guide for BIM project convention (France, 2016)	Mediaconstruct, buildingSMART member	Every actor of building industry	To guide professionals in the formalization of a BIM convention in their projects	The whole life cycle of a construction project, vocabulary adapted for conception and construction stages

B. European Studies

There has been much recent research in Europe concerning the development of tools for the evaluation of BIM practices in the construction industry. These research initiatives include the BIMetric method, which is the product of the collaboration of three research laboratories (LIST Luxembourg, LRA Toulouse and MAACC Paris) [8]. These laboratories developed this approach for "Plan Urbanisme Construction et Architecture" (PUCA), an interministerial French organization. It was inspired by two goals in the aforementioned Penn State University approach: 1) the evaluation of the maturity of the organization of the industry with regards to BIM and 2) the identification of investment return for the implementation of BIM processes on the project level. Today, many architectural agencies in France and Luxembourg have already implemented this type of evaluation.

C. Project Positioning

In parallel to international and European studies, many BIM guides and standards have recently emerged throughout the world, such as the *BIM Guide of Singapore* [9], the *Statsbygg BIM manual of Norway* [10], the *Guide to BIM* [11], *the British Standard Institution PAS* [12], and *the Methodological Guide for BIM project convention of France* [13]. These primarily technocentric methods allow for the standardization and guidance in the use of BIM technologies.

Table I proposes a synthetic comparison between a selection of guides frequently mentioned in conferences and used by professionals. These methodologies refer to the global project organization and aim to guide the interaction between the different building trade actors. The BIM integration at the scale of individual firm, internal change management, is not mentioned much. The Penn State University approach [7] distinguish itself to the extent that a specific maturity matrix is proposed in order to help contractors forming a project team in accordance to professional's competences. But the goal remains evaluating BIM expertise and not guiding professional to improve it.

For the purpose of our study, we hope to satisfy the need for a global collaborative approach that is user oriented. We adapt the tools developed in the Penn State University study to consider social issues of BIM implementation, that is to say the change management to new technologies and work practices. It is this that will propel businesses to go beyond the evaluation stage of BIM integration to demanding industry change and support in their technological implementation of collaborative processes between various players in the construction sector.

III. Proposed Methodology: ShareLab

The novelty of our research resides in the fact that it is based on a collaborative research approach. In this approach, borrowed from social sciences, actions are at the heart of the research and they aim to understand and transform practices. The individuals involved in the observed processes are thus both players and collaborators in the research [14]. In order to measure the weight of the effects of each action, the researcher is required to observe the tasks, attitudes and the language used, as well as quantitative data that resulted from the action. This method is well-developed in the field of social and human sciences and should prove to be of great interest in this new context. In the short term, collaborative action research yields a better understanding of the evolving organizational and technological implementations, thus aiding businesses in their improvement and mastery. The long-term goal is "learning how to learn" by to enabling companies to progressively develop their own processes and workshops.

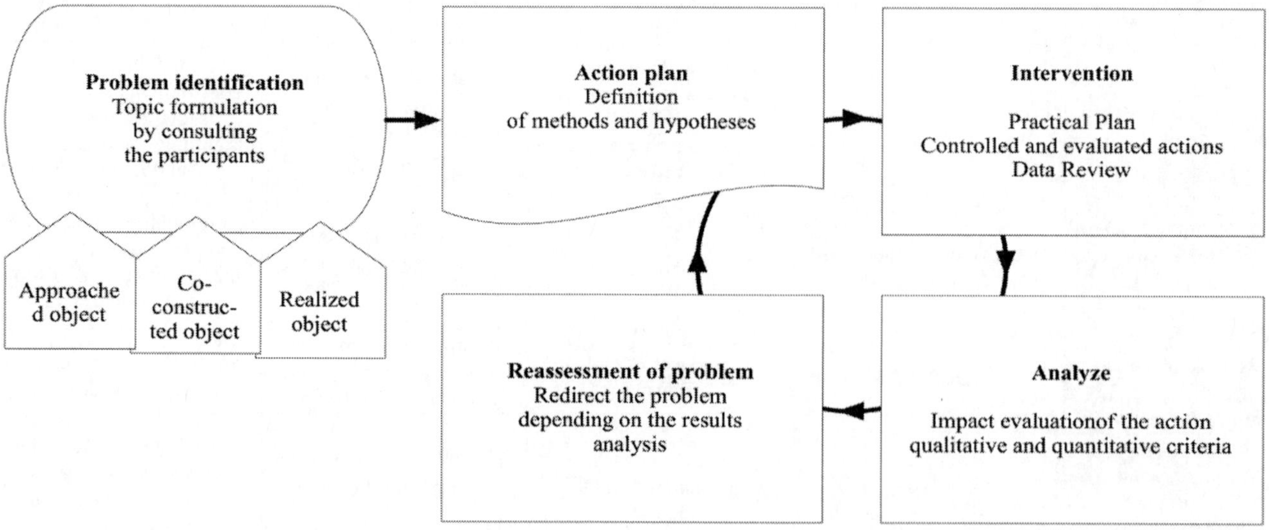

Figure 1. The cyclical approach to Action Research, inspired by [16].

In order to better monitor the evolution of BIM in various firms, we advocate ShareLab, an approach based on collaborative action research and adapted to the realm of design and construction. ShareLab [15] unites partners from various levels in the industry. With the assistance of a researcher, the collaborators are able to create a common understanding of the issues. This shared perspective helps them advance in their reflection on and their creation of a common vision and of a shared short- and long-term strategy for the implementation of a BIM process at the heart of the business. In this immersive process, researchers and industry players have an equal role to play in the design of the various stages of the research. This grants us access to information that is useful to understanding complex situations. Applications are conducted in the various types of multidisciplinary businesses and multi-sites of professionals in building construction and design.

More precisely, this action research approach, adapted to the building domain, is conducted by means of a series of cycles that are composed of the following five steps (Fig. 1).

To complete the description of the cycle that is described in Fig. 1, here are a few precisions on the initial step for the identification of the problem. The basis for these precisions is a threefold concept:

- the definition of the object related to the preliminary work carried out by the researcher, as well as the researcher's understanding of the subject, its logic, impact and scope. It is from this starting point that the researcher can propose the general direction of the research to the collaborators;
- the formulation of the subject and its validation (goal co-constructed), architects and engineers involved in the company management are requested at this stage in order to integrate the research project to the firm objectives;
- the elaboration of hypotheses, that are based on a depth study of the issues, allows for the development of an initial action plan (goal accomplished) [17].

The second step of the cycle is to define the action plan: the researcher formulates hypotheses and develops, with the collaboration of the change project's supervisors on site, different scientific methods and protocols.

The following step is the intervention phase, during which the action plan is put in place. Actions are measured, controlled and examined gradually through data collection. Afterwards, the effects of the actions are quantitatively and qualitatively analysed, with tools and indicators presented in the next section. This step, like the entire cycle is achieved collaboratively: each player contributes to the evolution of the process.

Lastly, the initial question is re-evaluated with the whole change project's actors and the results of the analysis are kept in mind in order to draft the subject of the research. The subsequent cycle will, therefore, begin on the basis of this new definition of the problem.

IV. ShareLab's Methodological tools

In order to have a complete understanding of BIM implementation on the business level, one must begin by describing the actual situation. This description must reflect a vision shared by each of the participants. This new approach that we are proposing by means of ShareLab plays a role in change management and helps brings about transformation at the centre of the organization. This is achieved through a common understanding of the problem's main issues and goals. As a process for change, our hypothesis is more effective and less disruptive if each player is aware of the stakes and the issues at hand, and when they each contribute to the definition of the project's objectives. Furthermore, this method involves groundworkers in the research process. Their involvement allows for the consolidation of a shared business consciousness, which facilitates the creation of a common vision. This, in turn, moves the change process toward the desired craftsmanship.

The first stage of analysis of BIM integration is observation by means of an analysis chart, based on the Penn State University study, defined and readjusted according to the circumstances as presented in the next paragraph. This phase serves to define BIM's operational capacity in the selected fields of study.

Researchers use observations, partially guided interviews, self-confrontation and other participatory practices, within agencies and design offices, to map out the various situations and attitudes that can help businesses better define their processes and expertise. These maps represent a common point of reference for all the players involved in the design process. These results are then used to define and implement an action plan (corporate governance). This plan is key in guiding the integration process toward the realization of the efficiency goals defined in the previous stage.

An interactive heuristic chart will then provide users with a tool that is adaptable and suitable to reflection. Inspired by *design thinking*, this method provides support to the conception phase of the process. Its objective is to stimulate cognitive processes of design in order to re-examine work methods, practices and strategies [18].

A. Maturity Chart

The maturity chart developed by our team was inspired by the American Penn State University study [7]. As mentioned in the state of the art, this study participates in the production of reference documents in the United States. The purpose of these documents is to help contracting authorities implement BIM in the management of their projects. Here, we have adapted this tool to the process of design. The chart that we use in our study has the following six main categories: (1) strategy, (2) the uses of BIM, (3) processes, (4) information, (5) infrastructure, (6) operational. These categories are divided into subcategories, ranging from 0 to 5, that detail their level of maturity. Fig. 2 is an example of our "Infrastructure" chart.

Researchers can take a variety of situations into consideration in order to fill in the analysis chart. The Penn

State University Study [7] suggests that researchers must examine two conditions to complete this maturity matrix:

- the maturity of the BIM in the business at the moment of the study.
- the maturity desired by the business.

In order to apply this tool on site, we propose that researchers make a distinction between the "perceived" and the "real" situation so to define the current level of maturity (Fig. 3).

TABLE II. AN EXAMPLE OF THE ELABORATED SUBCATEGORIES OF THE "INFRASTRUCTURE" CATEGORY.

Infrastructure	Level of maturity					
	0 Non-existent	**1 Initial**	**2 Defined**	**3 Managed / Shared**	**4 Formalized**	**5 Optimized**
Software The programs and IT architecture used in BIM implementation	No BIM compatible software	Object-oriented software (BIM software)	BIM software database	Advanced software systems compatible with BIM	The use of software systems compatible with other participants	A program created to evolve with the BIM software market
Hardware The technical equipment and information used in BIM implementation	Inadequate hardware	Some hardware that ensures the use of BIM software	All hardware is BIM software compatible	Some hardware can support advanced BIM software systems	All hardware can support the use of advanced BIM software systems	The program is developed to ensure that the hardware adapts to changes in market requirements.
Software and Hardware Management The management of the transition between old and new infrastructure	No BIM infrastructure	The business has initiated a BIM infrastructure through various pilot projects without changing its former infrastructure	The business has defined a hybrid infrastructure between the old and the new	The business applies the new infrastructure in certain departments / satellite offices	The business applies the new infrastructure to each of its departments / satellite offices	The business develops its own API* in order to work with its external partners

[box] Example of modification from Penn State University matrix

* An API (Application Programming Interface) is a programming interface that grants access to a selected piece of program data.

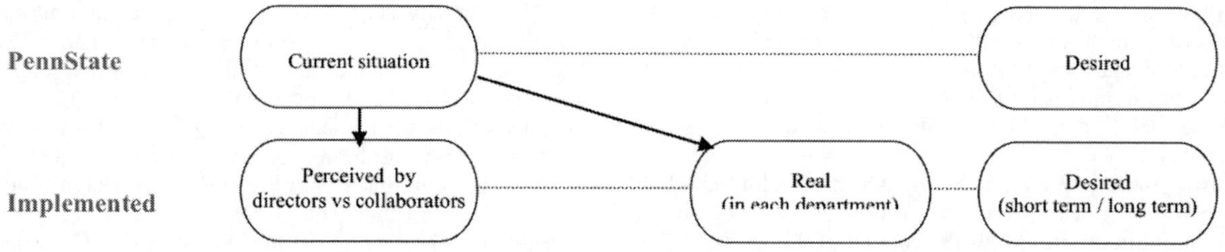

Figure 2. Taking different situations, specified by actors, into consideration for charting BIM maturity levels.

B. *Self-confrontation*

Our research team applied this analysis chart to pluridisciplinary and multi-site design agencies and construction firms. We adapted this method to define the level of BIM implementation in various agencies based on the perceptions of employees and upper management. In order to collect this data, we combined self-confrontation techniques with partially directed interviews and observations on site. Self-confrontation is vital to our approach, as it uses collaborative action, to characterize and chart the flow of data and work in the project. Self-confrontation is composed of the following six steps:

- use introductory questions to appeal to short-term memory. The researcher asks the participant general questions about the project on which the participant has worked by way of BIM. The researcher encourages the participant to speak about concrete project components (the schedule, teams affected, libraries consulted, the tools used, his or her role, his or her use of BIM in the project, the level of detail that he or she managed etc.). The answers to these questions can either serve as new examples for the maturity chart, or they can help the researcher to better conduct the remainder of the interview and formalize the process;
- begin to work on the groundwork for the layout of the project (supported by a legend created by the researcher). The researcher asks participants to sequentially draw the main phases of the process and to list, in the order of importance, the various players involved. Only the participant draws in this step. The researcher is permitted to accompany the participant in parallel;
- detail each phase by describing the main actions that were taken in the process. It is important to explicitly highlight the start and finish of each phase, as well as the main decisions that were taken;
- review and supplement the actions in each stage (by way of a tracing paper placed on the outline of the actions that have been successfully carried out). In an effort to verify the interoperability between various documents/ models used/ produced, specify the input documents/ models, the software used and the output of each player and describe the transition from one document or model to another;
- detect the problem areas and provide a description for them (by placing another piece of tracing paper placed on top of the former). This is done in an effort to understand their source, to glean expertise and feedback regarding participants' experience and to potentially optimize the process;
- define and standardize the different workflows that were discussed during the sum of the interviews. After a couple of days, ask the participants to evaluate them.

This approach removes the researcher from his or her traditional role in data collection, treatment and analysis. In the traditional model the creator relies completely on the researcher's interpretation of the information collected, observed, treated and analyzed. In compliance to the principles of collaborative action research, through our approach, the creator is also one of the actors and she or he contributes to the creation of his or her own workflow. This type of research method not only fosters a shared understanding of the role of each player in the design process, but it also helps chart the different steps. The charting of these stages helps standardize, manage and optimize them.

C. *The heuristic card*

Our team used an interactive heuristic card to focus the discussion on the skills that were developed at the heart of an agency in relation to BIM. This was done in an effort to highlight internal expertise, as well as the difficulties and disappointments encountered during the implementation of BIM. This card has a two input approach: (1) the expertise applied to support the implementation of BIM in the business, (2) the skills devoted to the creation of a design project. For each of the aforementioned inputs, researchers suggest and define various fields of action on the heuristic card. This is done in an effort to encourage contemplation on the part of the participants with regard to their own practices. Fig. 4 illustrates an example of the proposed field, with the definitions of the terms used.

The application of a heuristic card is characterized by a two-step process:

- understanding the proposed sites and questioning the way in which actions are implemented in the agency - do they use a BIM, classic or hybrid method;
- concretely describe the practices used, by answering the questions: "why?", "with what?", "with whom?".

V. SHARELAB AT THE SERVICE OF IMPLEMENTATION

A. *On site use: building a context for exchange*

The Sharelab, based on collaboration and interaction, requires confrontation between the results of actions and the participants (Fig. 1), so the practical use of this approach on site requires a minimum of two cycles. The first allows for exchange, the creation of a collective consciousness and a shared understanding of the context and the issues at hand. This first cycle permits participants to work together to create a shared vision of the realities on site.

A second interventionary cycle is then necessary to construct a common goal. The synchronisation of the various players with regards to the present context serves as support for the definition of the project's aim and of the steps required to be taken in order to solve the problem at hand.

1) The involvement of different partners

The choice of ShareLab partners and players is a question in its own right. The same issue can be broached in each level of the organization through the participation of players with differing views and roles. With regards to the types of questions asked and the subjects discussed, the presence of members from the upper echelons of the company can greatly influence the direction of the conversation.

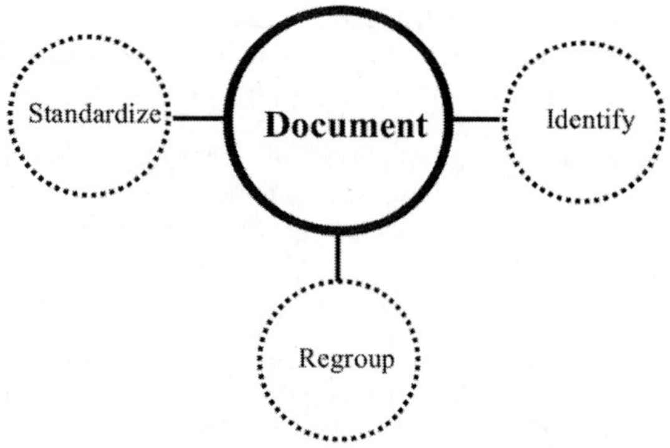

Document: use a physical or numerical way of expression that is both transferable and shareable, in order to express a decision or a piece information.

Standardize	create a single model to represent information related to different entities (the same object database for different projects, a framework for process mapping …).
Identify	indicate the nature, the category and the characteristics of a decision or a piece of information.
Regroup	assemble the information that has been produced separately in order to optimize and facilitate their access.

Figure 3. An example of the field of reflection of a heuristic card.

Figure 4. Photos showing the situations for the application of ShareLab.

In the goal of promoting collective awareness of the realities on site and of elaborating a goal for the future, the presence of these actors is fundamental. Therefore, the various players can participate in the research process at any one of the many steps of the cycle with the knowledge that it is the researcher who secures the transmission of information and assures participants' anonymity.

In the context of pluridisciplinary professionals, the involvement of participants from various backgrounds in the research process creates an environment that is ripe for exchange. The interaction of different types of industry professionals from various sectors fosters in depth discussions regarding the realities on site. Moreover, it promotes cooperation of services that often work toward the same goal through different approaches and/ or project timelines (Fig. 5).

2) Restitution as a foundation for research

The systematic planning of a minimum of two phases of intervention allows for feedback, in the second meeting with the participants, regarding the analysis made during the first meeting. The restitution step is one of the "methodological commitments" that frames players in the interactive research process [19]. Restitution allows ShareLab participants to confirm the analysis that the researcher proposed at the beginning of the intervention. This validation is key in preparing results and in ensuring conformity in the data that ShareLab participants provided. While the second cycle presents an interesting opportunity for return, each ShareLab should have a restitution phase so to corroborate the researcher's analysis and to respect his or her commitments.

Furthermore, restitution is in and of itself an object of analysis for the researcher. Not only do participant responses contribute to adjusting the intentions of the study, but they also bolster them. In fact, participants see restitution as a possibility to give feedback on the entire situation, and this new perspective can bring about many different types of reactions among the participants. As Beaujolin-Bellet note [19], the observation and the collection of this return is highly useful in the development of a plan for the comprehension of the subject, and it can also challenge to the initial version of the researcher's analysis.

If restitution is fundamental in the course of action-research in preparing and reinforcing data analysis, it is all the more necessary at the end of the process to bring a close to the intervention. Restitution at the end of the research protects the researcher from the "temptation of a hasty conclusion" [20] and it ensures the continuity of the work performed during the research phase by encouraging professionals' ownership and autonomy.

3) Equip and organize the context for exchange

In order to respect professional time constraints and in the spirit of efficiency in the discussion of key issues, moments of sharing and discussion are moderated by the researcher. The research team prepares the proposed ShareLab methods beforehand, and the individual researcher allots the time that he or she deems necessary for the completion of each step. The researcher is, therefore, the master of his or her own time during the intervention phase.

During the discussions, the researcher's goal is to guide the topics of conversation with a dual objective in mind: 1) to collect sufficiently elaborated data for analysis and validation and 2) to compile varying points of view in order to highlight controversial, as well as agreed upon topics. To properly execute this mission, the researcher must relaunch certain topics during the discussion. There are two ways to relaunch a discussion in order to comply to both of the aforementioned goals: 1) ask for precisions with regard to a specific subject that is discussed by one of the participants. Questions such as "why?", "with whom?", "with what?" allow the researcher to better define the comments' intention. 2) Go back to the remark of one of participants and ask the other participants to comment on them.

4) Participant Feedback at the end of each ShareLab

Participant feedback with regard to ShareLab is an important step in the process. The assessment of the participants allows the researcher to discern their opinion and understanding of the methodological tools that the researcher used (such as the maturity chart or the heuristic card that was presented in paragraph IV). It also helps the researcher understand the participants' opinion on the relevance of the intervention of an external researcher in internal business issues. In fact, in the interest of the business, ShareLab's goal is to help professionals in change management and in periods of transition, where traditional work practices and methods are put into question. In this context it is essential to evaluate the impact of the use of ShareLab during the course of the research in order to glean answers to the issues facing BIM implementation.

This evaluation helps justify (or not) the need for and the intervention of a research team on site. The reciprocal interest of the research team and the group of professionals is a motivating factor for participants, and it can positively influence their involvement and dialogue.

B. The possibilities and difficulties of ShareLab: the position and the involvement of the researcher

The participation of different players in the ShareLab project allows for the creation of an environment of exchange. The participants are accompanied by the researcher through the evaluation of the level of maturity of BIM in the company or through the use of interactive heuristic cards. These moments of communication create the ideal environment for the collection of data that is related to participants' experiences and daily practices. The spontaneous sharing of this information and its subsequent analysis promotes the creation of a common consciousness to support the process of change.

A multi-participant dialogue about an issue that puts into question customary work practices will inevitably generate heated debates [19], where a social or sensitive issue may come into play. It is imperative that the researcher clearly defines his or her role so to avoid any confusion on the part of the participants regarding his or her opinion on the subject matter. The researcher's adoption of a non-judgemental approach and his or her assurance of participant anonymity is vital to encouraging participants to speak freely without feeling evaluated and without the fear of negative repercussions outside the ShareLab. Furthermore, by attentively listening to each participant, researchers are able to maintain their neutrality and to guide participants in their thought process in order to help them find the words to describe their frustrations.

In the spirit of encouraging participants to define their objectives and to elaborate on different solutions, the expression of individual frustrations and points of contention can prove helpful in the development and the conception of vectors of change.

C. Participant feedback: what are the next steps in ShareLab?

Participant feedback regarding ShareLab use gives researchers the opportunity to collect data regarding participants' perception of ShareLab's contribution to the implementation of BIM in the business.

The initial ShareLabs examine the issue at large. This is done by way of a maturity matrix at the agency level or through heuristic cards at the project level. This allows the researchers to define the primary factors for crisis and the areas for development. With the goal of proposing more and more concrete solutions for the problem, once the initial phase is complete, ShareLabs can target more specific problems and focus on specific questions, such as the integration of BIM on the building site, the creation of an agency specific BIM chart or even the elaboration of a BIM offer suggested to a contracting authority.

VI. Conclusion: Summary, Contributions and Limitations

The implementation of ShareLabs through collaborative action research is a new way of finding solutions to the issues that construction companies face in their application of BIM technology. Contrary to a technocratic view regarding the implementation of BIM tools and practices, the ShareLab approach takes into consideration societal and individual stakes with regard to change. Actual studies led on site gave significant results. Following our intervention in a large company of engineering and architecture, the firm developed different actions to structure the change to BIM with its collaborators: working groups to solve specific questions, a BIM day to share the progress with the whole team.

The immersion of the researcher in the professional environment can give rise to concern regarding his or her position on the topic and his or her relationship with the various players. By remaining neutral and objective throughout the entire process, the researcher promotes an environment of exchange among all players on site.

Businesses may consider the time that participants dedicate to ShareLabs as unproductive. Moreover, the professional environment makes it difficult for all staff to participate in such research. These factors oblige researchers to use test groups that may not be entirely representative of all levels of the organization. Moreover, involvement and motivation of actors on site are essential and these parameters still have to be included in the structure of the ShareLab method. That being said, if BIM methods and technologies are to succeed in improving the efficiency of the organization of a construction project, businesses must optimise the time it takes to synchronize and coordinate the implementation of BIM. This way, businesses are able to reduce the time it takes between making a decision and its execution. This optimization of the time needed to synchronise between stakeholders requires a discussion and exchange phase in order to build a common understanding of the stakes within companies and agencies.

The actual perspectives relate to the relation between the building designer, the contracting authority and the builder. That why our research will go on larger intervention, involving more actors with different function at the scale of the construction project.

References

[1] S. Azhar, M. Khalfan, and T. Maqsood, "Building Information Modeling (BIM) : Now and Beyond." Australasian Journal of Construction Economics and Building, vol. 12, pp. 15-28, Dec 2012, doi: 10.5130/ajceb.v12i4.3032.

[2] S. Staub-French, *Building Information Modeling (BIM) 'Best Practices' Project Report,* 2011. [Online]. Available from: bim-civil.sites.olt.ubc.ca/files/2014/06/BIMBestPractices2011.pdf [retrieved: october, 2016].

[3] NSCSC, Nova Scotia Construction Sector Council, *Functional Information Technology Phase 1: Detailed Analysis*. Construction Engineering and Management Group, Université du Nouveau Brunswick, 2010. [Online] Available from:http://www.nscsc.ca/Documents/FIT_Final_Report_Part_I-v7_web_copy.pdf [retrieved: july, 2016].

[4] J. Taylor and P. Bernstein, "Paradigm Trajectories of Building Information Modeling Practice in Project Networks." In Journal of Management in engineering, vol. 25, pp. 69-76, April 2009, doi: 10.1061/(ASCE)0742-597X(2009)25:2(69).

[5] R. Deutsch, BIM integrated design : strategies for architectural practice. John Wiley & Sons, 2011.

[6] S. Azhar, "Building Information Modeling (BIM): Trends, Benefits, Risks and Challenges for the AEC Industry", In ASCE Journal of Leadership and Management in Engineering, vol. 11, pp 241-252, July 2011, doi: 10.1061/(ASCE)LM.1943-5630.0000127.

[7] CIC (Computer Intergated Construction Research Program). *Planning Guide for Facility Owners*. The Pennsylvania State University, 2013. [Online] Available from: http://bim.psu.edu/resources/owner/bim_planning_guide_for_facility_owners-version_2.0.pdf [retrieved: october, 2016].

[8] LIST, LRA, MAACC, *La méthode BIMétric*, 2015. [Online] Available from: http://bimetric.list.lu/ [retrieved: september, 2016].

[9] BCA, (Building and Construction Authority), *BIM Essential Guide for Architectural Consultants*. Singapour Government, 2013. [Online] Available from: https://www.corenet.gov.sg/media/586146/Essential-Guide-Archi.pdf [retrieved: september, 2016].

[10] Statsbygg. *Statsbygg BIM Manual 1.2.1*. 2013. [Online] Available from: http://www.statsbygg.no/Files/publikasjoner/manualer/StatsbyggBIM-manual-ver1-2-1eng-2013-12-17.pdf [retrieved: october, 2016].

[11] ADEB-VBA. (2015). *The Guide to BIM*, 2015. [Online] Available from: http://adeb-vba.be/the-guide-to-bim.pdf [retrieved: october, 2016].

[12] BSI (British Standard Institution). (2013). P*AS 1192-2:2013 Specification for information management for the capital/delivery phase of construction projects using building information modelling.* [Online] Available from: http://shop.bsigroup.com/navigate-by/pas/pas- 1192-22013/ [retrieved: june, 2016].

[13] MediaConstruct. (2016). *Methodological Guide for BIM project convention*. [Online] Available from: //www.mediaconstruct.fr/sinformer/le-blog-du-bim/post/4730 [retrieved: october, 2016].

[14] G. Monceau, "La recherche-action en France : histoire récente et usages actuels." In Les recherches-actions collaboratives, Presses de l'EHESP, pp 21-31, 2015.

[15] S. Ben Rajeb, A. Senciuc, and I. Pluchinotta, "ShareLab, Support for Collective Intelligence." In Proceedings of the Fifth International Conference on Advanced Collaborative Networks, Systems and Applications. COLLA'15, Malta, 2015, pp 152-161.

[16] M. Catroux, "Introduction à la recherche-action : modalités d'une démarche théorique centrée sur la pratique." In Recherche et pratiques pédagogiques en langues de spécialité, 21, 8-20, 2002.

[17] F. Saint-Luc, *La recherche-action : une recherche à visée formatrice et transformatrice,* 2014. [Online] Available http://www.icem-pedagogie-freinet.org/sites/default/files/la_recherche-action.pdf [retrieved: september, 2016].

[18] T. Brown, Design Thinking, *Harvard Business Review,* June 2008.

[19] R. Beaujolin-Bellet, "Recherches interactives sur les restructurations : quels engagements du chercheur ?" In La recherche-intervention peut-elle être socialement responsable *?* Paris : Vuibert, pp 85-102, 2008.

[20] F. Pichault, O. Lisein, G. Rondeaux, and V. Xhauflaire, "La recherche-intervention face à ses tentations." In La recherche-intervention peut-elle être socialement responsable ? Paris : Vuibert, pp 7-25, 2008.

This page intentionally left blank.

Collaborative Multi-Perspective Urban Knowledge and Civic Media

A Never-Ending Design Challenge

Alessio Antonini, Lucia Lupi, Guido Boella, Stefania Buccoliero, Claudio Schifanella
Dept. of Computer Science
University of Turin
Turin, Italy
{antonini, lupi, boella, buccolie, schi}@di.unito.it

Abstract—**Developing a civic social network requires to consider users meeting in real life, collaborating on digital entries related to real urban entities. This makes necessary to think about collaboration tools in a new perspective: ensuring the participation of users with different levels and forms of legitimacy to represent complex relations among entities, and ensuring the accountability of each contributor. We present a set of technical solutions allowing the collaboration on complex entities, keeping interactions simple, and representing multiple perspectives about shared entities.**

Keywords-urban informatics; civic media; collaborative network; urban entities; participatory design.

I. Introduction

The knowledge about the city can be seen as a coherent system of social and geographical information about urban entities, ranging from street furniture to buildings, from the neighbourhood life to city services systems. Each entity and each place is defined by perception and uses of a multitude of local players involved in ongoing activities and projects in those spaces at the same time.

Nowadays, new challenges arise from social media and map-based applications where the focus is not just on mapping a place indicating its position, but on sharing social information aimed to support new forms of citizen engagement. This kind of information is not only about physical components, but also about intangible and un-representable elements that define the corpus of the urban knowledge. In this scenario, spatial attribution of contents is a mandatory requirement because digital entities correspond to real places, actual events, and active groups. In general, real life dynamics occurring in real environments can be potentially expressed and documented in a virtual space.

Finding new intuitive solutions to gather and visualise multiple contributions about same urban entities from heterogeneous sources and different perspectives is a challenging task: it is crucial to represent the operational context acting in the city by representing the coexistence of networks, flows, initiatives, minimizing conflict situations, and without forcing a simplification of reality.

We are working on designing a Civic Social Network (CSN) [2][3][4], intended to address this issue by establishing a collaborative framework based on citizenship and public engagement at local and urban level.

In our opinion, a CSN aimed to represent urban and local reality avoiding the fragmentation of information should not host multiple parallel-unconnected entities, but it should rebuild the social context integrating different contributions, without discriminating in favour of one of many parties' position. This is the premise to design a collaborative platform to promote collaboration in real life among different players (with concurrent perspectives and goals) interacting in the same physical space. User legitimacy and responsibility over contents are the key problems to be addressed in this kind of platform.

During a participatory design process involving 1500 people in 70 meetings, workshops and living labs, we engaged potential users in a first cycle about assessing the requisite for collaboration on digital platforms in their real context. Considering their inputs, we designed and developed a set of solutions [13] oriented to the following goals:

a) Providing a mechanism to contribute in contents creation regardless their initiators, in order to taking into account different forms and levels of legitimacy of local players, and let various sources coexist without forcing a common position or a unilateral perspective;
b) Providing a mechanism to share the responsibility of moderation over contents about the same urban entity;
c) Ensuring a clear accountability of users even in case of multiple contributors, relying on non-anonymity of users, and on identification of collective users such as organizations, local authorities or businesses.

The result is a system capable to represent a network of digital entities corresponding to real urban and local objects.

New issues are related to the fact that relationships among users in a CSN are based on spatial proximity and on collaboration on the same urban entities, both in real world and virtual space. The main interaction is about and through contents describing places, activities, projects and groups. Define clear policies to enhance all contributions and preventing abuses is the precondition to create a positive virtual work environment for civic engagement.

In this contribution, we present the extension of this design process, proposing the solutions we implemented to answer to the following questions:

1. Can we define a category system able to classify places and other urban entities in an objective way?
2. Which policies are socially acceptable to extend moderation mechanisms over contents on the same entity from the first author (initiator) to multiple contributors?
3. How to support a daily use of a platform and common sense interactions?

The structure of the paper is the following: Section II includes a brief analysis about the main approaches used by the most successful digital platforms based on users' collaboration for the content production. In Section III, we describe the general approach we followed in relation to the issues regarding legitimacy and responsibilities. We describe the technical solutions we implemented in Section IV. Then, we present the evaluation and the open issues. Lastly, we synthesize our conclusions and the future developments of our CSN.

II. State of the Art

We introduce an emblematic real use case emerged during our workshops with potential users in order to compare the approaches used in collaborative digital platforms and the related outputs for the example.

We need to map a school in a neighbourhood. Who is legitimate to describe the school? The dean, the school board, school employees, teachers, students' parents, former or current students? The school board and the dean can describe the school in term of educational vision and methods, or syllabus and training paths; employees are qualified to write about the public services offered by the school; students and parents can share their experience lived in the school environment.

What if the school is hosted in an historical building? What is more prominent? The historical or the educational aspects? Therefore, who is legitimated to describe the historical aspects? Historians, architects, local experts, students, neighbourhood inhabitants, cultural heritage authorities, or local administrations? The local administration can motivate the change of destination of a monumental place to a public facility in order to revitalize the local area. Historians can describe the significance of that building in the city history. Architects and local experts can describe stylistic and technical characteristics and why the building is worth to be preserved. The cultural heritage authority can place the building into the local cultural assets. For neighbours, a public building as a school is an important focal point in the place where they live over time.

The example can become even more complex. What if the school gym is used by sport organizations for their activities? What if the school is managed by a religious organization?

The school is a complex urban entity that lends itself to be represented by a multiplicity of descriptions, all fitting a specific aspect of the reality, with different forms and levels of legitimacy.

We consider this scenario in order to study the problem of defining a suitable category system for complex urban entities and the solution implemented so far as moderation mechanisms.

A. *Category systems*

A platform category system can be addressed by top down or bottom up design approaches.

An example of a bottom up approach can be found in OpenStreetMap (OSM) [17]: the community of users raise proposals and decide the category system, which is a folksonomy supported by a wiki documentation [18] collecting motivations, examples, pictures about the interpretation and correct use of categories. In this case, there are well-known issues regarding the locality-based semantic of categories, the small number of active contributors engaged in category definition, and the resulting low quality of data. In a bottom-up project such as OSM, the school in our example would be flattened into a physical Point of Interest on a map defined by shape, name, address and function. Activities, social relations and uses of spaces will not be represented.

Following, GeoKey [19] enables the definition of categories at "community level": each group can setup a project with their own data types and features. This bottom-up approach presents interoperability issues and hardship in interpreting and reasoning with data. On this platform, the same urban entity could be included in several different community maps with their own categorization, without fostering for a mutual exchange of information among groups working on the same place.

On the other hand, the stability given by top-down approaches have as counterpart the loss of flexibility in terms of representation of heterogeneous point of views. For instance, Pinterest as world ideas catalogue defined 34 categories [20] for all possible ideas; Foursquare provides a category tree for all possible places [21]; Twitter defined recently ten categories of streams to cluster all tweets, such as "music" [22]. In these social network, the school in our example would be fragmented in multiple unconnected entities and entry points, making impossible to merge several contents actually related to the same complex entity. Each content, even if related to the same real place or object, would fit in one of the categories set by the system.

B. *Moderation policies: common goal and owership*

If we consider to use Wikipedia in our scenario, the result will be two interlinked pages addressing the school and the historical building. Homogenous groups of experts, with the supervision on Wikipedia editors [6], will develop each one of them [5]. Personal experience will not be allowed and contingent activities will not be documented.

Considering Facebook groups [9], the result will be a parents group about sharing personal experiences as students' parents or former students. The dean or other authorities will not be included in this kind of group or they may participate as individuals and not as in charge of institutional authority.

In both cases, the problem of plurality is simplified involving users in something of very specific where it is possible to assume the collaboration of users toward a common goal. Indeed, contents in an encyclopaedia page are general and acceptable for a large majority of people without representing multiple perspectives. In a parents group on Facebook, users share a set of characteristics and interests, and their involvement is limited. Potential conflicts about attribution and legitimacy are solved addressing the compliance of each contribution to the common goal. This overall guide is done by editors in the case of Wikipedia, and group owners or moderators in Facebook, but in a working environment where interactions among users are strictly regulated by explicit and implicit rules.

When expressing the identity is more prominent than other goals, the legitimacy issue is solved in an ownership assessment. In other words, if the goal is to represent an entity in an official way the problem is to identify who has the rights on this entity. Collaboration on defining the entity can be done, but under the owner's supervision and permission. In some cases, owners may allow contrasting opinions if the draw-back of censuring is bigger than the contrast itself, but contributors have no rights to demand a fair acknowledgement of their positions. This is the approach of Facebook and Google+ pages, of Google maps about places and of websites integrating social media features. The collaboration mechanisms are meant to mediate the asymmetric relation between one owner and many contributors with no rights.

Considering Facebook applied to our example, the dean will open an official Facebook page [8] of the school, giving the responsibility of managing contents to an employee that will publish only general information and official announcements. If the dean wants, the page can collect comments, which will be moderated by the same employee, or simply ignored. It will result in parents and students opening their own groups about specific topics or even fake or unofficial pages about the school in order to express other positions than the official one.

Considering Wikipedia, a contrast of opinions will be resolved asking for sources such as the official school website or the school board documents. The hierarchy of sources leads to the users' hierarchy.

Anyone can add information on Google maps, but in order to claim the ownership of a place [7], a postal card is sent to the declared address in order to verify the owner identity. But then, once a place is mapped, also anonymous users can indiscriminately post comments, ratings and pictures which the owner has to keep in check in order to avoid attacks from rivals.

In any case, the perspective is unique and limited by the tool. The result is the multiplication of entry points, which is not a problem for Google and Facebook but it is for users that must know where to search information. In these systems, interactions among users are simple and clear but mostly left to the good will of the owner, which has actually no obligations toward others. The acceptability is very low for the excluded users that are the large majority.

Self-regulating communities such as tech forum are basing the moderation system on users' reputation gained by contributing to the system. These approaches have many limitations based on the implicit assumption that users are experts of the whole domain which can be more or less true in domain forums but definitely it is not true on a generalist platform. In other words, a user may spend his/her reputation outside their expertise field. Furthermore, voting system leads to a result which can be right or wrong, more or less favourite by the community, but in general a result which is quite difficult to overrule in the future. This is not a problem in tech forums because a new question can always be open (in particular regarding a new version of a problem) but in our scenario the goal is to keep an entity dynamic and alive preventing the definitive establishment of a position.

III. General Approach

In this Section, we address the issues we identified as key points in building the civic platform as a trustworthy environment.

A. Legitimacy

The evaluation of legitimacy is left to users that can make their own evaluation about the relevance of the contribution shared on the platform w.r.t. to their authors, their context and their area or theme of interest. On the platform, users can be registered as single citizen or as collective bodies like organizations, associations, institutions, local authorities, business, etc. Non-anonymity is one of the principle assumed as prerequisite to model and design interactions and functionalities.

While a citizen could be not entitled to provide an official representation of an urban entity, his/her experience could be valuable for other users. Following our running example, the experience expressed by former students may be much more relevant than a dean statement about how the school experience will be for your children.

On the contrary, the level of accountability of information shared by local administrative offices about services or public programmes is stronger than a general contribution shared by citizens.

In real life, people perform this kind of evaluation all the time making assumptions based on their goal and perspective, and on the official role and competences of other subjects they interact with. In our platform, we let users decide the relevance of contents in relation to their experience without relying on recommendation systems based on popularity or user profile, since a CSN is oriented only to the public dimension and exclude any form of user profiling [13].

B. Sharing responsibilities over contents

Non-anonymity is the first step to take responsibility about contents. The relation between the platform and shared urban spaces, or the connection between virtual space and real space, reinforces the awareness of consequences related to personal actions and statement in the public sphere, containing incorrect and uncooperative behaviours. Experimental evidences we collected during our participatory workshops confirmed that associating identity and actions at local scale discourage inappropriate conduct.

In addition, the responsibility over contents should be shared among the interested parties in order to ensure plurality and cooperation on building common urban entities. We can define users investing enough energy as those recognized worth of responsibility as proactive contributors. Proactiveness is not related to the production of digital contents in general, but is related to the documentation of real actions having an effect at local level using the platform functionalities to enhance processes and outcomes. On the contrary, sharing opinions does not mean be proactive, because not necessarily an opinion is related to an active involvement in local initiatives and projects.

We decided to structure entities (places, events, groups, insights, news) as complex objects. Each of them have a single evident entry point giving access to all point of views and sub entities, rather than multiplying the entity for each point of view. Structuring entities can still enable the chance of having different responsible groups for different purposes. In other terms, we propose content driven solutions to represent shared responsibilities among players acting on the same places.

IV. TECHNICAL SOLUTIONS

In this Section, we introduce the solutions we developed to build entities as shared workplace for heterogeneous local actors.

A. First-order Entities and Second-order Entities

Our platform has a map-based main interface. In other words, we separate the mapping activity from the interpretation of a place and the documentation of activities and project carried out from users, because we are interested in collecting social information rather than geographical entities.

Technically speaking, we make a distinction between entity properties and description properties: we have first order entities working as shared entry points and second order entities. We define a shared set of primary properties belonging to the entity and that must be defined in the creation process (sandbox [15]): title, valid time interval, categories, tags, external URL, coordinates (latitude and longitude). Each primary entity may have specific primary properties, for instance: events have door time, duration, organizer, attendees and performer (The entity properties are mostly inspired to entities of schema.org specifications [16]). Primary properties should be more or less objective in order to avoid the proliferation of homonymous entities. Following the example, we want to avoid many parallel entries about the same school letting the first one defining a "place" school without having the concern of making a general or official description.

Then, we defined a set of second order entities describing a primary entity. The second order entities are available for any primary order entity as its complement and to any user, except into groups where the content creation is reserved only to the group members. The second order entities are meant to be fast to create. As today, we implemented: descriptions requiring a title and a text (Figure 1 (b)), comments requiring just text and images.

Light-weighted entities enriched with secondary-order entities as properties result in sharable entry points for collecting different perspectives by different users, as second-order entities Figure 1 (c).

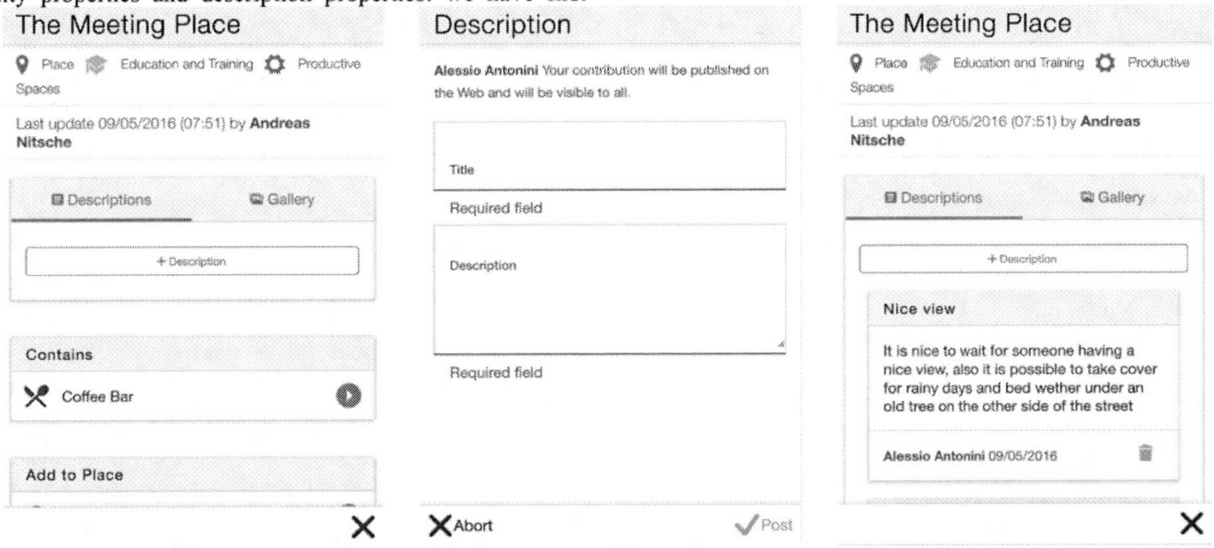

(a) (b) (c)

Figure 1. A place containing an event (a). The description for (b), and a description added to a place created by a different author (c).

B. Relations Among Entities

Managing typed single entry points is not enough to catch the complexity of real life entities. In general, we consider part of relations among entities of the same type:

1. A place can contain sub-places, such as office rooms
2. An event can be composed by several sub events
3. Articles can have sub-topics
4. Groups can be spliced in operative or thematic sub-groups.

Moreover, we introduced additional relations:

1. *"location"*, from an event to a place
2. *"news of"* from news to an entity that is not a news *"group of"* from a group toward an entity
3. *"group from"* an entity to a group

Adding relations among entities results in enabling the possibility to build complex structures from a single entry point from different users' contributions.

For instance, following the running example, the "place" school can host events, organized in many sub-events, and groups, structured around a class or a type of activity. An event organized by a sport organization can be independent from the school context, but it can be hosted in the school and the same for the news related to this event (registration, updates, etc.)

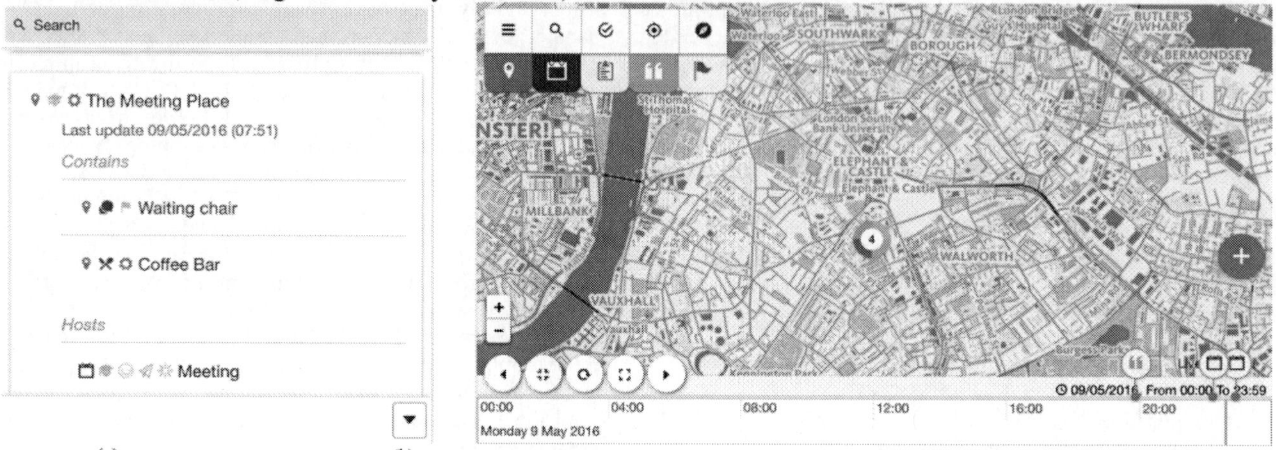

(a) (b)

Figure 2. A place two sub places and an event in FirstLife wall (a). A map view with the first version of the timeline (b).

C. *Relations Among Authors, Moderators and Contributors*

An entry point is the result of one user action but one user, even if legitimate, cannot cover all points of view about an urban entity. Moreover, one user should not have the monopoly of an entity for many reasons:

1. Lack of perspective, as we just stated he/she cannot pretend to express everything can be said about an entity;
2. Dynamic reality: things change and so users' commitments toward taking care of a piece of information can change;
3. Excess of responsibility: the burden is too heavy from the user perspective, and the risk of missing an important and vital piece of the puzzle is too high from the community perspective;
4. Coproduction of social reality: nothing social is made by one person but everything requires others, and thus their representation.

We do not recognize the role of owner, but the greatest importance is referred to contributors. Each first level entity has one initiator (the first contributor) and a set of contributors. Starting from an entry point, in parallel with the graph of entities, we defined a network of collaborations replacing the standard friendship/following-relations of social networks. Users are connected through contents and so they share the responsibility of taking care of contents, by acting at content level.

The initiators still play an important role at the beginning, but on the contrary of other web 2.0 and social network mechanisms, the burden is released as the entities becomes more complex relying on collective moderation. Contributors are engaged in self moderating themselves, being notified about activities and comments added to the entity they contribute to create, and they can comment, report abuses or eventually delete a contribution.

A user can always be identified by playing the contributor or the moderator role resulting in exposing yourself and your own reputation. Contributor and moderators conduct must be compliant with the guidelines included in the ethical code of the platform. Moreover, they can always report abuses to the platform administrators.

V. Evaluation and Open Issues

In this section we present results of the first design- phase where we tested the considering scenario. In particular, we held a specific series of workshops involving local stakeholders such as organised citizens, organisations, local authorities, local institutions, universities, schools, traders associations, etc. (about 70 meetings with a total of 1500 participants) to collect and testing scenarios, which where formalized as object diagrams and user stories. Moreover, we involved a full class of prospective geographers from the University of Turin in order to test the mechanisms we designed and implemented from a domain-expert point of view.

As result, some open issues have arisen:

1. Categorization fallacy: the first user still has a huge impact in defining an entity category;
2. Events stickiness: events and other timed entities tend to stick together; the timeline is not used in its extend
3. Unused comments: comments at entity level are not used as expected, on the other hand comments can be used to notify issues at description level. The right level of comments is too bounded to the type of entity but, in general, enabling comments for second level entities is a need

4. Balancing moderator power: the problem in finding a suitable policy to extend the moderator role from author to contributors is due the power of moderator itself. In order to establish a policy, we need to balance the moderator power with a double check from the crowd.

In the following, we analyse those four open issues using user stories and use cases in order to revise the solutions we implemented.

A. Categorization Fallacy

Extracting descriptions from entities was a solution to limit the authors' responsibility in defining entities and make the creation process faster. In particular, we decided to open entities to different contributors and to enable the creation of multi-facet entities. Considering the categorization fallacy, we did not accomplish the latter objective completely. Considering the lesson learned from experimentations with university students, we found that the categorization task is strongly influenced by the current user goal, even when there is no room for misunderstandings.

An emblematic example is the supermarket categorization. Since university students do not go to supermarkets for common shopping like anyone else, but for lunch, we found many grocery stores categorized as "restaurants" rather than "market".

This issue can be addressed through many strategies, but we may revise the constraints collected so far:

1. We want to avoid conflicts
2. We wish to avoid multiple categorization, without a proper justification
3. We do not want to take sides

The solution we came to require to relax a "wish to have" constraint, or in other words, we need multiple categories to be defined by different users. On the other hand, losing a crisp classification of entities may result in a foggy definition of entities, it would be nice to bind categories to proper justifications.

For this reason, we decided to split categories in functional categories and properties. We found that the most objective categories can be considered as entity properties (i.e. the event cost). Moreover, we also moved functional categories to second-order entities in order to bound a categorization to a visual or textual context.

Revising the previous example: now a student can classify a grocery store as supermarket because connecting the category to a description about having lunch there.

B. Events stickiness

In a first prototype, we introduced a timeline as time filtering control and as an exploration tool for timed entities [14]. The timeline was continuous ranging from centuries to seconds, giving to users total control in defining the period of interest. What we did not realize was that most of daily activities take place at the same time. For instance, we sleep 1/3 of day hours and the work activities are mostly condensed from 8 a.m. to 8 p.m. The result was having few spots of the timeline condensed with events and most of the timeline useless.

Furthermore, the "freedom" of the previous timeline resulted in scaring users: they did not get what they were doing and which was the connection between map and timeline.

Since the timeline goal was to give an idea of the presence or not of timed entities on the map, we decided to rebuild the timeline from scratch following few principles:

1. It is not possible to access to entity through the timeline
2. The timeline need to provide a qualitative (entity type) and qualitative (ratio) evaluation of what is currently visualized on the map;
3. The timeline should be support human interpretation.

In order to support user interpretation, we first split the timeline in time steps: months, weeks, days, night, morning, afternoon and evening. Each step was enriched with a qualitative and quantitative bar displaying the ratio of timed entities for each entity type, avoiding any direct reference to the single entities (Figure 3 , Figure 2 (b)).

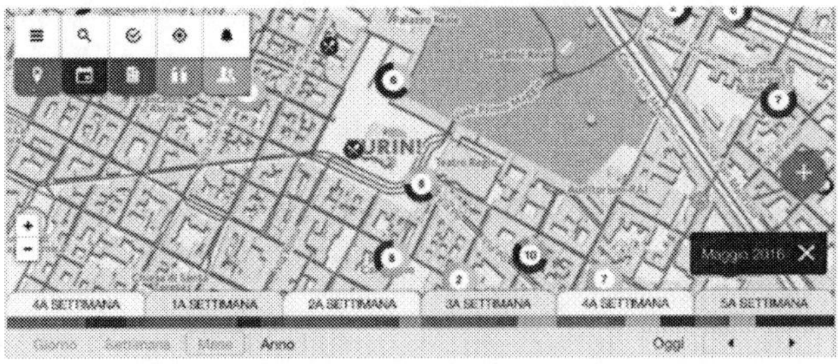

Figure 3. The timeline is slit in steps easy making it easier to read for users, i.e. weeks in a month. Each step shows the ratio of timed entity types.

With this new setup, users can consider much more intuitive the interaction with the time-line clicking on a step to zoom in and focus the map on the timeframe they wanted.

C. Unused comments

The general platform setup should engage users in be useful to others leaving the "guts" to other social networks. It worked so well that users ignored the comment feature completely. We thought deep about providing or not comments but in the end, we integrated comments because we knew we were missing a method to ask questions or pointing errors. The transformation of description and pictures from simple properties to second-order entities had the drawback of making comments mostly unused.

Starting from the original goal, we extended comments to pictures and descriptions, restoring their original purpose.

D. Balancing moderator power

We spent a large amount of time trying to define a policy to extend moderator privileges from authors to moderators. Despite our effort, we did not come up to any general solution, which can consider different lifecycles of entities. The problem lies on the definition of "contributor": what a user should do and how long we need to wait until promoting a user from the role of contributor to the moderator level?

Each policy required an assumption about the original author will to check contributors in an objective way, or having contributes being checked by the crowd fast enough to rise eventual complains in time. Are those strategies general enough?

We found plenty of counterexamples based on different lifecycles of information. For instance, there are entities, which are mostly used in very short time and others that are not used much. In this second case, how long should we wait? Furthermore, an author can leave FirstLife without checking contribution or prevent any contribution at all deleting systematically everything. This is a wicked problem [24].

After evaluating social and technical constraints, we decided to bind content moderation in a double check mechanism: a moderator can delete or modify a content if there is a "report" from a different user. This solution reduces the impact of the policy we are trying to define, lowering users' expectations and concerns about it.

We found the moderation mechanism be the main problem. The common pattern gives the power to delete or modify contents without control or justification. This is not compatible with the multi perspective collaborative environment we are trying to build. Moreover, it was forcing the introduction of a mechanism to require the intervention of an external editor, which is something we really wish to avoid.

We still need to define in detail a suitable policy, but nevertheless we reduced expectations and make the impact of this policy less critical since we expect the policy definition process a never-ending challenge.

VI. Conclusions and Future Works

Designing a collaborative civic social network is a huge challenge itself, stressing common solutions in scenario where users are engaged both online and offline, and in which different point of view need to coexist. In this contribution, we revised the solutions we developed during one year of participatory design. In particular, we focused on three specific aspects related to the construction of a model:

1. Supporting interactions on shared use of entities,
2. Supporting common sense interpretation about urban entities,
3. Defining a mechanism to share responsibilities over contents among multiple contributors.

Categorization was one of the few top-down features we had in order to support the map-based visualization system. Moving the category attribution from first order to second order entities, we managed to build a richer description system avoiding the introduction of moderation mechanisms. Finally, we enabled comments for second order entities, in order to support users' self-moderation and self-aid in maintaining entities correctness.

Having a shared environment with contributions of different types and for different purposes makes the CSN quite complex. We found very important to simplify the mechanisms where possible, and in particular we designed a hybrid timeline based on the classical calendar views: year, month, week, day.

The most challenging task was to tackle an impossible problem such as making contributors trust each other on a web platform sharing the moderator role. Studying the problem, we found that we needed a less powerful role of "moderator". A light moderation requiring a double check from a second user resulted to be much more acceptable and easy to understand rather than sophisticate policies based on time intervals and users' visualizations.

As partial conclusion, this process did not end yet and it will most likely not end because, as society changes, technology needs to follow and be updated, in particular in term of addressing new needs and facing new requirements and expectations.

Currently, we are developing a new set of features for supporting group coordination and process patterns. The new solutions will be tested in the next months in three trial sites within the H2020 project "WeGovNow!" [23].

References

[1] A. Ray. Reviewing the Author-Function in the Age of Wikipedia Amit Ray and Erhardt Graeff. Originality, imitation, and plagiarism: teaching writing in the digital age, 39, 2008.

[2] A. M. Kaplan, and M. Haenlein. Users of the world, unite! The challenges and opportunities of Social Media. Business horizons 53.1, 59-68, 2010.

[3] J. H. Kietzmann, K. Hermkens, I. P. McCarthy, and B. S. Silvestre. Social media? Get serious! Understanding the functional building blocks of social media. *Business horizons*, *54*(3), 241-251, 2011.

[4] E. Gordon, and P. Mihailidis. Civic Media: Technology, Design, Practice. MIT Press, 2016.

[5] https://en.wikipedia.org/wiki/Wikipedia:Reviewing [retrieved June 2016]

[6] https://en.wikipedia.org/wiki/Wikipedia:Editorial_oversight_and_control [retrieved June 2016]

[7] https://support.google.com/business/#topic=4539639 [retrieved June 2016]

[8] https://www.facebook.com/page_guidelines.php [retrieved June 2016]

[9] https://www.facebook.com/help/162866443847527/ [retrieved June 2016]

[10] J. Pasek, E. More, and D. Romer. Realizing the social Internet? Online social networking meets offline civic engagement." Journal of Information Technology & Politics 6.3-4, 197-215, 2009.

[11] http://wegovnow.firstlife.di.unito.it [retrieved June 2016]

[12] http://schema.org [retrieved June 2016]

[13] A. Antonini, G. Boella, L. Lupi, C. Schifanella. Civic social network: a challenge for co- production of contents about common urban entities. CollabTech 2016, accepted paper.

[14] https://almende.github.io/chap-links-library/timeline.html [retrieved June 2016]

[15] http://test.firstlife.di.unito.it/ [retrieved June 2016]

[16] http://schema.org/ [retrieved June 2016]

[17] http://www.openstreetmap.org/ [retrieved October 2016]

[18] https://wiki.openstreetmap.org/ [retrieved October 2016]

[19] http://geokey.org.uk/ [retrieved October 2016]

[20] https://pinterest.com/categories/ [retrieved October 2016]

[21] https://developer.foursquare.com/categorytree [retrieved October 2016]

[22] https://twitter.com/i/streams/category/687094907350036504 [retrieved October 2016]

[23] http://wegovnow.eu [retrieved October 2016]

[24] B. Richard. Wicked problems in design thinking. *Design issues* 8.2 (1992): 5-2

We Built Our Own Worlds - Story Canonicity and Indirect Collaboration in a Shared Story World

Alan Tapscott[1], Joaquim Colás[2], Valeria Righi[2], Carlos León[1] and Josep Blat[2]

{alan.tapscott,cleon}@ucm.es - joaquim.colas,valeria.righi,josep.blat}@upf.edu
[1]Facultad de Informática, Universidad Complutense de Madrid
[2]Grup de Tecnologies Interactives, Universitat Pompeu Fabra

***Abstract*—In this work, we conducted a longitudinal study to understand better how authors collaborate when building shared story worlds. To accomplish this goal we deployed Chronoverse, a tool specifically designed for this purpose that provides authors with a common story timeline and character faction tags. The study had three distinct phases. In the first phase, undergraduate students (the authors we study) used Chronoverse to develop their stories in a common context during a lab that lasted four weeks. In the second phase, a jury rated the authors' contributions in terms of coherence and consistency, attempting to measure the integrity of the shared story world. In the third phase, a larger crowd of readers rated the stories according to their preferences and shared their opinion of what stories belong to a common overarching story. The results suggested that the initial story, introduced by the researchers, was given priority and considered more canonical or "official" by the authors, jury and readers. Author groups did not reference each other's contributions directly, but achieved consistent and coherent results indirectly by adhering to the initial story in terms of plot and tone. The usage of tags in the design of Chronoverse was positively received by authors and enhanced the plot and tone consistency perceived by readers.**

***Keywords*—collaborative story worlds;story canonicity;indirect collaboration.**

I. Introduction

Collaborative writing is a challenging task. However, the potential benefits of collaboration are motivating enough to encourage studies that seek to understand and improve the co-authoring of all sorts of texts. Writing fiction collaboratively using a shared story world represents a specific kind of challenge. Authors must share their conceptions of the story world's contents to write consistently, maintaining the impression that all media belongs to the same continuity. For the most part, story worlds do not exist explicitly; they emerge from the facts established by the author or authors in the story. Large fiction franchises, often involving multiple authors, solve this through the usage of internal documents that keep track of the plot developments, documenting the past, present and even future of the fiction, along with relevant character biographies and other fictional encyclopedic content. For instance, TV shows often rely on a confidential bible maintained and used by all screenwriters as reference to collaborate consistently. This seeks to avoid alienating the audience with inconsistencies and incoherences. While this kind of solution has been successfully used in scenarios with over a dozen authors, there is a clear challenge in a hypothetical large-scale online, crowdsourced scenario.

In creative writing, authorial style and artistic vision are important, as well as the capability to build interesting fictional worlds, especially for fantastic genres. Facts contained in the narrated story deviate from our reality up to some degree, presenting landscapes and characters that only exist in our imagination. For the current study, we consider the story world the set of elements (e.g., characters, locations, plots, motivations, rules) that constitute the world implicitly defined by a story along with the relationships between each other. According to Tolkien and his conception of secondary world [1] (a definition we believe to be close to our story world), all the elements (i.e., geography, characters, language and timeline) are interdependent and require internal consistency to suspend disbelief, becoming credible to the reader. Schmidt and Bannon have an extensive publication track that introduces the Common Information Space [2][3], defined as "...a central archive of organizational information with some level of 'shared' agreement as to the meaning of this information (locally constructed), despite the marked differences concerning the origins and context of these information items." We believe that this definition is conceptually aligned with our conception of a shared story world in the sense that it contains relevant data introduced by distinct authors and despite being potentially different, it must agree or be coherent to some degree. Bannon and Bødker discuss the dialectical nature of common information spaces and the challenge of putting information in common and interpreting it [4]. Despite presenting distinct scenarios, most of the considerations for common information spaces are very likely to appear in a shared story world and must be addressed. Mainly, Bannon and Bødker insist on the need for a common information space to be accessible and malleable while providing reliable information. Most of the relevant literature focuses either on the technical implementation of concurrent writing systems or on the narratological study of story worlds. Despite the emerging relevance of fiction transmedia story worlds, both in commercial and amateur contexts, to our best knowledge there is no formal study focused on collaborative authoring and story worlds published. This work aims to understand better the dynamics of collaborating authors when contributing to a shared story world, using computer-assisted collaboration to monitor and measure relevant aspects, such as cross-referencing, coherence and plot/tone consistency.

The study is structured in the following way. In Section

2, we provide a brief discussion of works that deal with relevant problems. Next, in Section 3, we describe our three months' longitudinal study where lab students contributed into a shared story world using Chronoverse, a prototype tool we designed and deployed to support the co-authoring of shared story worlds. Also in Section 3 we describe the jury and reader evaluation of the results from the longitudinal study. We present the results of the evaluation in terms of consistency, coherence and co-existence of an overarching story. Finally, in Section 4, we discuss the implications of the results and conclude with the insight learned from the whole study, along with potential directions for hypothetical subsequent research.

II. Related Work

There have been many works that have studied the usage of computer-based platforms to support collaboration. ShrEdit by Olson et al. [5] was a shared collaborative text editor meant to aid designers in brainstorming ideas. According to the authors, groups that used the editor produced less ideas ranked as more creative. This might imply that in a similar context, the usage of a digital platform for collaboration might prioritize quality over quantity. Posner and Baecker [6] present a taxonomy based on interviews that describes joint writing in the following terms: roles played in the collaboration, activities performed in the writing process, document control methods used, and writing strategies employed. This was later expanded by Lowry et al. [7] with collaborative writing activities, document control modes, roles, tools and work modes, a categorization that could be helpful in designing an adapted user experience. Google Docs, the popular collaborative word processor, has been studied in some works from the educational perspective [8], the longitudinal perspective of a large, diverse organization [9] and a tool to write educational papers [10] amongst others. Overall the design of Google Docs seems very appropriate for collaborative work in a computer platform.

Some other published works deal with similar scenarios such as Robinson's exploration of collaboration in authoring multimedia stories through specific devices [11]. Krowne and Bazaz discuss authority and territoriality in a study of collaborative editing systems [12], this is especially relevant in collaborative systems that deal with creativity and authoring. In the context of a shared story world and multiple collaborating authors, territoriality could be a very important factor to take into account. Likarish and Winet attempted to reproduce the surrealist Exquisite Corpse writing game on Twitter [13], attempting to "... understand the practical pitfalls of synchronous community-based authorship and to recommend methods of avoiding them." Besides reporting successful participation, Likarish concludes by acknowledging the need for "...providing structure via a wiki or suit of tools to enable authors to track details as well as the importance of community self-policing..." We share the belief for tools that introduce structure into the creative process. Thomas and Mason bravely attempted to write a novel in an open process [14] using a wiki platform. The wiki proved to be a competent and useful tool for structuring the narrative thanks to its familiar and accessible nature. According to the authors inter-author collaboration dynamics were challenging, citing content deletions or major restructuring performed by a single author as the source of conflicts. Among the other relevant remarks from the authors, there seems to be a dichotomy between contribution order and creativity, highlighting the importance of contribution sequence and timing when building this kind of systems.

Relevant works that seek to explore collaboration have resorted to the usage of timelines to provide adequate user experiences. Thiry et al. use a timeline in Project Greenwich [15], a tool meant for people to author their own personal digital timelines. In their work, Thiry et al. study the usage of the timeline as a vehicle that helps multiple authors in connecting past and present contributions. The capability to collaborate over time seems to be especially desirable in the context of an evolving shared story world. Some other interesting usages of a timeline include a programming interface by Cardoso et al. [16], medical records overviews by Reddy and Dourish [17], an adaptive timeline interface to personal history data by Ajanki et al. [18] and as an aid for history learning by Pyshkin and Bogdanov [19].

III. Study

The following section describes the longitudinal study, including its motivation, the prototype used and the methodology and results for each of its phases.

A. Context and motivation

Since the academic course of 2012-2013, Computer Science and Audiovisual Engineering undergraduates have attended the Audiovisual Language and Interactive Storytelling subject at UPF, participating in the lab and creating their own visual novels. Participants are distributed in groups of three to four students. Over two months, each of the groups creates a visual novel, including its design, script and implementation. The teachers were surprised by the convergence of the plots and tones of the stories, even though they never encouraged collaboration. Despite the lack of hard evidence to support the claim, informal observations suggested some students were collaborating indirectly, using common elements in their stories. Social and cultural trends had an impact in the creative process, as well as the university environment. For instance, every year featured multiple post-apocalyptic stories (a popular recurring theme in current popular fiction) and roughly half of the plots happened in the student's university (UPF). This observation served as motivation for the deployment of Chronoverse, a digital collaborative tool meant to reinforce the collaborative dynamics and the consistency of their collaborations.

B. Chronoverse

Our prototype, Chronovese, was an online tool meant to help authors in collaborating to produce media based in a shared story world.

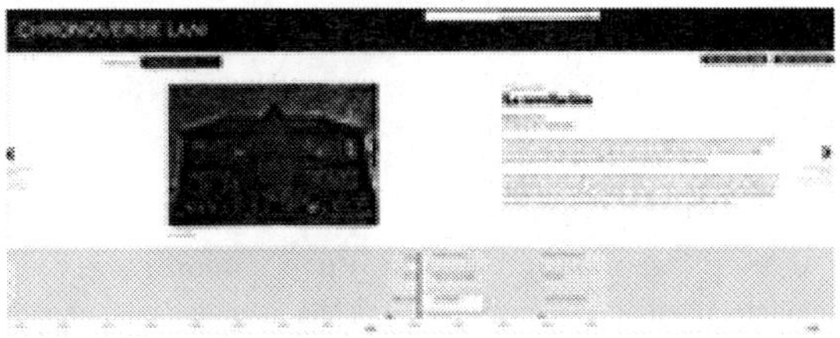

Figure 1: Chronoverse interface

Chronoverse allowed authorized users to introduce their own original scenes. As seen in Fig. 1, every scene contained a title, a short description, a date, an optional picture and optional tags describing the involved factions or groups of interest. On the bottom of the screen users could see a timeline with all the existing scenes. The usage of a timeline metaphor for the chronology of all scenes was meant to reinforce, for every contribution, the sense of belonging to the same continuity. Since all scenes had a date and were rendered inside the same timeline, we expected to provide an enhanced sense of coexistence in the same story world for all scenes. Also, as seen in the previous section, timelines are useful to connect past and present resources [15]. We made authors split their stories into scenes to promote the intertwining of plotlines. By providing a common canvas for contributions that took place inside the shared story world, with its content visible to all users, we expected to promote inter-author story awareness. This was partially validated by our evaluation.

Chronoverse's timeline stacked scenes vertically, in up to three lanes, allowing scenes to be placed close in the horizontal axis without much overlapping. Also the splitting of the story into scenes was favorable for the timeline, allowing users to perceive the story progression over time. The provided initial scenes in Chronoverse (described more in depth later) included factions. We chose to use factions as the main actors of the story instead of characters to avoid the problem of author territoriality mentioned in the previous section [12], preventing conflicts and promoting indirect collaboration. Contributors could create their own original characters and integrate them into the story world more easily via faction membership without necessarily conflicting with other authors and their characters. Other potential organizations (e.g., nations, clubs, nobiliary houses) are perfectly valid to achieve the same results. Users could filter the timeline to see scenes that only involve a specific faction, providing a navigational mechanism closely linked to the story world. This mechanism helps in establishing thematic links between scenes created by distinct authors who are not necessarily collaborating directly. We also introduced a pop-up that displays the relationship between the distinct initial factions in a graph.

C. Study structure and settings

As in the previous years, the 2014-2015 Audiovisual Language and Interactive Narrative subject lab took place. We decided to deploy Chronoverse and measure how did it impact on the results. The following phases were planned:

1) Authoring phase: Conduct the lab with the author students, having every group introduce the story plan for their visual novel into Chronoverse over four weeks. Conduct a short questionnaire to rank the usage of Chronoverse, according to its users.
2) Jury evaluation phase: A small jury ranks the contributions, rating coherence and plot/tone consistency. Comparisons include each contribution against each other and each contribution against the initial story.
3) Reader evaluation phase: A larger crowd reads all the stories and ranks their preferred ones. In order to validate the scores from the jury evaluation, they are also guess what stories belong to a common overarching story.

D. Authoring phase

We provided access to Chronoverse to all student groups and asked them to introduce the outline of their stories in it. The goal was to have every group plan their visual novel's plot before writing the final, extended script, encouraging collaboration and convergence. Since the platform was hosted in a public web server, every group could see other groups' work and potentially reference each other directly or indirectly. The resulting story plans, described by the scenes introduced into Chronoverse, would then be adapted into scripts for the visual novels. Ideally, this would allow authors to develop their story in a common frame and influence each other before being tied to the cumbersome work of developing a whole script.

Chronoverse had six initial story scenes (ISS) created by the teachers. The scenes told a single post-apocalyptic story in the university were several factions struggled for power. The first scene explained very vaguely the downfall of civilization for an unknown reason. Each of the following five weeks contained one scene narrating how each of the three fictional student factions attempted to rule the university until a tense and unstable peace is reached in the end. The results section details how the initial story and factions influenced author contributions. The story contained some of the most frequent elements from previous years' contributions, such as a post-apocalyptic world, the students' university, politics and mysterious factions. This story world was very open and purposefully vague, providing flexibility to allow the groups to fully develop their own ideas.

Overall, 22 groups composed by between three and four undergraduates participated. Each group received a textual description of a story world or setting in a brief text document that described the main characters, factions, events and also included some mysteries and "plot hooks" that could be freely developed or used at the authors' discretion. Groups were asked to create at least three scenes in the timeline that represented their visual novel's plot. For every weekly lab and during three weeks, the teacher told them to add at least one scene. This was done to provide groups with enough time to read existing contributions. Reading or even referencing existing material was always optional. No amount of contribution or collaboration was enforced. Three months after the lab sessions ended and each group had produced their

Chronoverse scenes along with the final visual novel, we asked the author students to take a short questionnaire aimed to get some feedback on their user experience. Specifically, we were interested in learning about their opinion on the usage of a default story world and the Chronoverse platform.

E. Authoring phase results

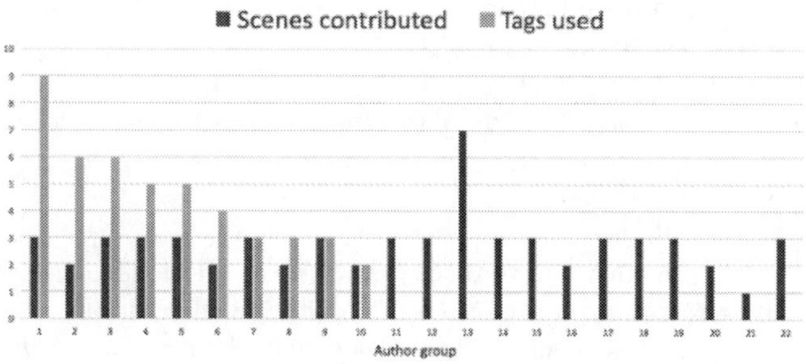

Figure 2: Author group scene and tag amount

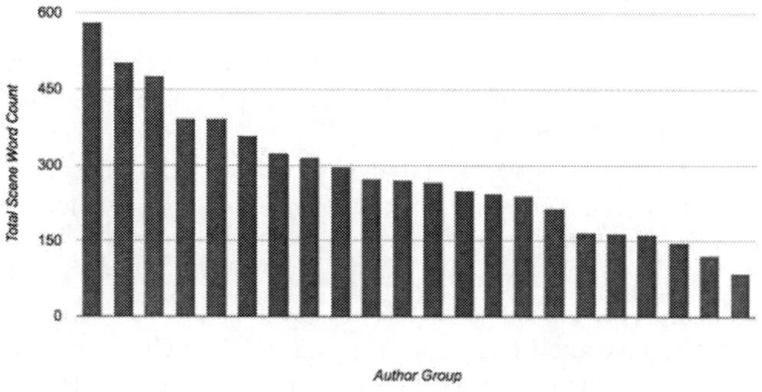

Figure 3: Total word count per group

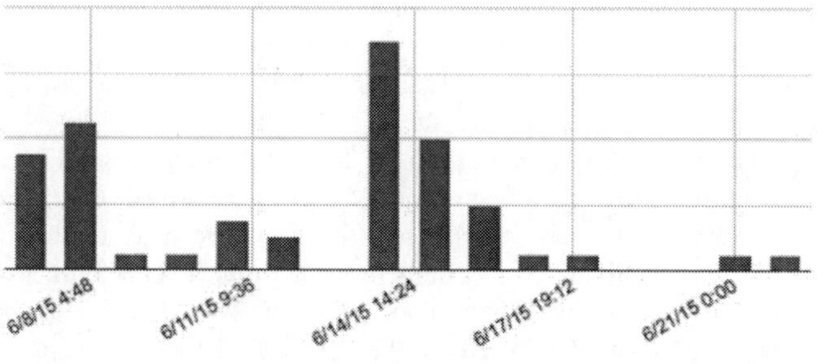

Figure 4: Total scene contributions by date

Table I, Fig. 2 and Fig. 3 show an overview of the results. Groups contributed an average of 2,8 scenes, 2 tags and 283,7 total words. Half of the groups did not use any tag at all and there were a couple of significant outliers (one groups used 9 tags and another group introduced 7 scenes). Fig. 4 shows when author groups introduced scenes into Chronoverse. All contributions were introduced between the 7th and the 22nd of June. The main contribution peaks are around the lab deadlines (8th and 14th of June).

F. Author questionnaires results

Due to the optional nature of the questionnaire only 17 of the 84 participating authors submitted answers. Results, rated from 1 to 5, are summarized in Tables II and III. Subjects found easy to read and write ($\bar{x}$=3,87 with σ=0,83 and $\bar{x}$=3,59 with σ=1,18 respectively). The provided initial story world (scenes and deliverable text document) scored as moderately useful to write $\bar{x}$=3,65 with σ=0,70, followed by images $\bar{x}$=3,53 with σ=0,68, and finally dates $\bar{x}$=2,76 with σ=1,18. Explicit dates are the less useful and less enjoyed part of the initial story. Some of the open answers provided corroborate this. Amongst all the results from the questionnaire we found a few worth mentioning. 88% of the subjects read some scenes and 12% none. Most of the subjects explicitly were not bothered by contradictions and state they did not influence their writing at all. 94% of the users claimed to have used the initial scenes provided in Chronoverse as inspiration for their contribution.

G. Jury evaluation phase

Once the lab was finished and we gathered all the contributions, we were interested in evaluating the results in terms of consistency and coherence. These measures were meant to determine the integrity of the set of stories as a story world. In order to rate the stories, we created a jury made of three members. Two were teachers who actively designed and supervised the labs and the third was a Ph.D. student who was unfamiliar with the subject or the lab. We were especially interested in determining the relationship between each group's contributions and the initial scenes. Each groups' Chronoverse scenes (previously described) were joined to create an author group scene set (AGSS). The initial scenes created by us were joined into an initial scene set (ISS). The jury ranked every AGSS after the following measures:

- AGSS unitary coherence (is the scene set contributed by the author group coherent?)
- AGSS unitary image coherence (are the images used coherent?)
- AGSS tonal consistency with the ISS (is the author group scene set tonally consistent with the initial scene set from Chronoverse?)
- AGSS plot consistency with the ISS (is the author group scene set consistent with the initial scene set from Chronoverse in terms of plot?)
- AGSS tonal consistency with other AGSSs (is the author group scene set tonally consistent with other authors' scene sets?)
- AGSS plot consistency with other AGSSs (is the author group scene set consistent with other authors' scene sets in terms of plot?)

Coherence of a text referred to the internal logic of its discourse and image. Consistency referred to the text's similarity, in terms of narrative plot and tone, to another text. To ensure the jury evaluation criteria was unified, the measures were discussed informally and we conducted a pre-evaluation with some random Chronoverse contributions. We found no significant differences on the evaluations. Despite the fact that a member of the jury who was not involved in the lab experiment, the criteria for their ranking apparently was uniform. For the main jury evaluation, instead of comparing every AGSS to the rest of the set, each AGSS was compared to the ISS and 6 random AGSSs more. This cut was necessary to reduce the cost of the jury evaluation.

H. Jury evaluation phase results

Results, with the factors evaluated in a 1 to 4 scale, are summarized in Table IV. AGSS unitary plot coherence was somewhat high (average 3,02) while AGSS images were considered coherent with the story created by authors (average 3,45). AGSSs were moderately consistent with the ISS in terms of plot and tone (average 2,55 and 2,89). Inter-AGSS tonal consistency was also moderate (2,44/4) while inter-AGSS plot consistency was low (1,86/4). Next, we run a Pearson correlation analysis on the measures. Specifically, we wanted to find potential AGSS inter-relationships and between the 22 AGSSs and the ISS. The jury's measures of consistency should provide some insight on the collaboration dynamics of the participating groups. The results can be seen in Table V. There is not a significant correlation between AGSS-ISS plot consistency and unitary AGSS coherence, suggesting that adhering to the initial story world elements did not lead to either more or less coherent stories. AGSS unitary coherence was usually high, independently of their consistency with the ISS. There is a significant correlation ($r(N) = 0.63, \rho(N) = 0.002, r^2(N) = 0.4$) between AGSS-ISS plot consistency and inter-AGSS average plot consistency. The same happens with AGSS-ISS tone consistency and inter-AGSS average tone consistency ($r(N) = 0.62, \rho(N) = 0.002, r^2(N) = 0.4$). So groups trying to remain consistent with the initial story world in terms of plot and tone scored also high tonal and plot consistency with other author group contributions. It seems that there is also a strong correlation ($r(N) = 0.66, \rho(N) = 0.0008, r^2(N) = 0.4$) between AGSS-ISS plot consistency and AGSS-ISS tone consistency. Therefore, according to the jury, tonal and plot consistency with the ISS seem to imply each other to some degree. An interesting observation by our jury suggested that AGSS contributions consistent with other AGSSs referenced factions, places and events provided by the ISS, but never elements created by other author groups. AGSSs were ranked as consistent with each other due to their usage of initial ISS elements, not new AGSS elements introduced by other author contributions.

I. Reader evaluation phase

We conducted an evaluation to determine each scene perceived co-existence to the same overarching story and overall preference, according to external readers. We displayed the contributions in pairs and asked whether or not each pair of displayed texts belonged to the same story. We expected this to reflect the integrity of a hypothetical story world described by the crossover of both stories. Text pairings marked as belonging to the same story would argue in favor of the contributing authors collaborating in a shared story world. 40 volunteers participated in an online questionnaire, with ages ranging from 18 to 63 and a gender distribution of 43% females and 57% males. The volunteers were not author students from the first phase or juries from the second phase. The questionnaire was a simple website we developed using basic HTML and a Django backend. The questionnaire presented 10 pairs of texts, displaying only two at a time. To reduce the cost of the evaluation, pairings included i) the three AGSS that the jury ranked as more consistent with the initial story, ii) the three AGSS ranked as the less consistent with the initial story, and iii) two AGSS set in the middle range. The initial scene set (ISS) was also added to the questionnaire. Each volunteer was asked to rank the stories from 1 to 5 on a Likert scale where 1 meant "I do not like the story" and 5 was "I like the story a lot". We then asked them if paired texts belonged to the same story (only yes or no, closed reply). The simple web questionnaire can be seen in Fig. 5.

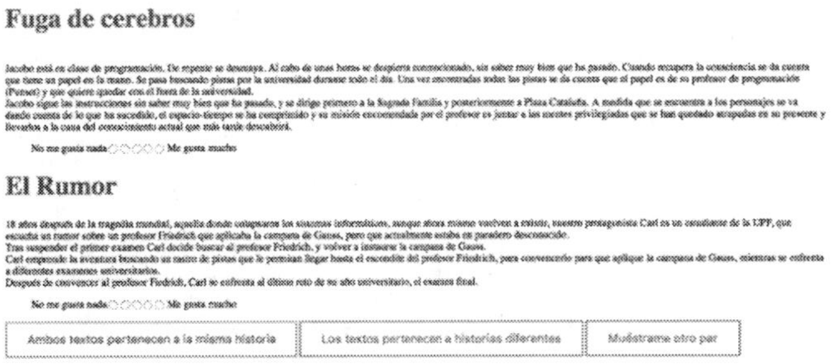

Figure 5: Online reader questionnaire

J. Reader evaluation phase results

Table VII shows how what stories were marked by readers as belonging to a common story. AGSSs marked by readers as belonging to the same story than the ISS tended to be also marked as belonging to a common story among each other. This result seems to be in line with our jury evaluation, where AGSSs that were consistent with the ISS were also consistent with each other and once again suggests indirect collaboration.

K. Global results comparison

After conducting the three phases of our study, we can compare each of the AGSSs metrics to each other. This should allow us to validate the distinct evaluations by finding correlations. Table VII summarizes the whole study and contains all the relevant comparisons with the resulting Pearson coefficient. Pearson correlations revealed a moderate correlation between the AGSSs previously ranked by the jury as highly consistent (both, in terms of plot and tone) with the ISS and the tendency to be marked by readers as belonging to the same story than the ISS ($r(N) = 0.52, \rho(N) = 0.01, r^2(N) = 0.27$ for both cases). This suggest the jury's consistency measures and the reader similarity measures are relatively aligned. There is also a moderate correlation between reader score of the AGGs and AGG-ISS plot consistency and AGG-ISS tone consistency (respectively $r(N)_{rv-pc} = 0.61, \rho(N)_{rv-pc} = 0.002, r^2(N)_{rv-pc} = 0.37$ and $r(N)_{rv-tc} = 0.47, \rho(N)_{rv-tc} = 0.02, r^2(N)_{rv-tc} = 0.22$). Apparently readers liked more stories consistent with the initial story world in terms of plot and tone. There is a moderate correlation between reader score of the AGGSs and tonal consistency with other AGGs ($r(N) = 0.53, \rho(N) = 0.01, r^2(N) = 0.28$). Being tonally consistent with other author contributions was liked by readers (according to the provided scores). Unlike the previous case, this is not extensible to plot consistency. There is a moderate-high correlation between the usage of tags and reader score ($r(N) = 0.54, \rho(N) = 0.001, r^2(N) = 0.29$) and a high correlation between the reader score and the tendency to be marked by readers as belonging to the same story than the ISS ($r(N) = 0.82, \rho(N) = 3\text{e}{-6}, r^2(N) = 0.67$). Also, AGSSs that used more tags revealed high correlations with plot consistency and tone consistency with other AGSSs (respectively $r(N)_{atpc-apc} = 0.78, \rho(N)_{atpc-apc} = 3\text{e}{-5}, r^2(N)_{atpc-apc} = 0.6$ and $r(N)_{attc-atc} = 0.65, \rho(N)_{attc-atc} = 0.001, r^2(N)_{attc-atc} = 0.42$) and the ISS (respectively $r(N)_{atpc-ipc} = 0.92, \rho(N)_{atpc-ipc} = 0, r^2(N)_{atpc-ipc} = 0.84$ and $r(N)_{attc-itc} = 0.77, \rho(N)_{attc-itc} = 2\text{e}{-5}, r^2(N)_{attc-itc} = 0.59$). According to the jury, people contributing closer to other scenes in terms of plot and tone felt more inclined to label their usage of existing character factions with tags.

IV. Discussion

Our goal was to understand better the dynamics of collaborating authors when contributing to a shared story world. Overall, despite giving freedom to our authors, we believe there have been two main outcomes. Some author groups (the majority) have followed and extended the initial story, while others have ignored completely the initial stories and their author colleagues. This means that there is collaboration happening, but it is not the collaboration we were expecting. Author groups that have followed the initial story collaborate indirectly with other author groups that have done the same, creating consistent stories with each other in terms of plot and tone. According to our readers, consistent contributions to Chronoverse are enjoyable and belong to a common shared story. Results have been extensively documented in the previous sections and annex, however there are a few key aspects we believe worth discussing in depth.

A. One story canon

Our main finding implies readers (and perhaps writers) have one single canonical or "official" version of facts. Most authors contributed consistently with the initial story and most readers marked stories consistent to the initial content as belonging to the same overarching story. Overall, it seems the initial scenes were considered more "official" or canonical than those introduced by the contributing author groups. Contributors seem to embrace the notion of an initial explicit story world and integrate its plot hooks and elements into their own creations. Our authors did not read many of the other authors' contributions and they never explicitly integrated them into their own contributions. The tone, however, was considered consistent between all authors' contributions. Perhaps the initial content, being written by the teachers, was given a special consideration. Maybe timing is the key factor, contributing authors might not feel confident or comfortable referencing and intertwining their content with the unfinished and ongoing contributions of other authors. The sequence in which the contributions occur might be key to determine what parts of the shared story world are perceived as more central or canonical.

This might explain the problems faced by Thomas and Mason [14] in their Wikinovel, with authors colliding as they attempt to impose a main plot structure. When compared to our own research it seems this phenomenon is similar to previous results [20] in which authors converged, establishing a main continuity or central interpretation of the story. The joint conception of a story world might require some information hierarchy, providing new contributors some solid narrative background or baseline from which to start. Information canonicity should be central in any further study of this nature, that is, finding mechanism for authors not only to contribute to a common story world, but also to ensure those ideas are well integrated and accessible. This should make possible that subsequent contributions by other authors are perceived as consistent, something positive for a shared story world according to our own results and by other works on collaborative information spaces [3].

B. Tags and inclusive character groups

The usage of character group or faction tags seems to increase story world consistency. Stories that included tags seem to be more consistent with all the rest of stories in terms of plot and tone. Also stories that used tags have been ranked better by readers. Overall, tags seem to be a good explicit mechanism to structure content in a shared story world. This somewhat implies a benefit in using inclusive groups or categories with an active role in the story contained in a story world (such as the ones found in Chronoverse). Our goal was to avoid author territoriality [12] or the lack of structure in a collaborative environment described by Likarish [13]. This kind of collaborative meta-data, often found in collaborative platforms such as wikis, might be beneficial for integrating original characters from multiple authors while enhancing the global consistency.

C. The usage of Chronoverse

The author questionnaire informal results seem to point towards a positive user experience. The usage of a timeline seems to be favorable for the construction of a shared story world, similarly to some related works [21]. Regarding other author contributions, authors did not read many other group's contributions before writing and did not care about contradictions. Coping with other authors' stories is apparently not a priority. We believe the authors were fairly motivated students, but this is not necessarily the average user in a shared story world-building scenario. We suspect the most common profile might be one or more professional writers. On one hand, writers might be more proficient at writing stories and building story worlds, potentially being more motivated to contribute more due to the professional background. On the other hand, students might be more open to novel scenarios, such as collaborating in an online platform to build a story world together. Still, we believe replicating the experiment with a professional audience would be paramount to generalize the results to a more common scenario, such as a team of scriptwriters writing a TV show season or a story anthology.

V. Conclusions and Future Work

Our main conclusion from this study is that authors who collaborate in a shared story world are conditioned by the pre-existing material. Contributions are more likely to reference and connect to pre-existing content than to ongoing contributions by other authors. In a shared story world, the sequence of the contributions seems to be critical in establishing information canonicity. Older contributions are more referenced than newer or unfinished ones. Our results and observations also point towards the aptness of timeline visualizations, scene tags and inclusive character factions for collaborative story world building scenarios. There are two main directions for this research to continue, generalizing its findings and extending its applications. On one hand, we are already trying to replicate these observations in a large-scale real scenario, a successful online community that builds and maintains a rich story world. On the other hand, these findings could be used to build a cognitive model or architecture of a collaborative story world.

Acknowledgment

Supported by WHIM (611560) and PROSECCO (600653), funded by the European Commission, Framework Program 7, the ICT theme, and the Future Emerging Technologies FET program. This research is partly funded by the Spanish Ministry of Economy and Competitiveness under RESET (TIN2014-53199-C3-3-R) and the Maria de Maeztu Units of Excellence Programme (MDM-2015- 0502). This work would not have been possible without the invaluable collaboration of the students from the Audiovisual Language and Interactive Storytelling lab, the volunteer reader crowd and the Ph.D. student jury collaborator.

References

[1] J. R. R. Tolkien, "Beowulf: The Monsters and the Critics," *Interpretations of Beowulf: A Critical Anthology*, p. 31, 1991.

[2] L. J. Bannon and K. Schmidt, "CSCW: Four characters in search of a context," *Studies in Computer-Supported Cooperative Work*, pp. 3–16, 1991.

[3] K. Schmidt and L. J. Bannon, "Taking CSCW seriously - Supporting articulation work," *Computer Supported Cooperative Work*, vol. 1, no. 1-2, pp. 7–40, 1992.

[4] L. J. Bannon and S. Bødker, "Constructing Common Information Spaces," *Proceedings of the Fifth European Conference on Computer Supported Cooperative Work*, pp. 81–96, 1997.

[5] J. S. Olson, G. M. Olson, M. Storrøsten, and M. Carter, "Groupwork close up: a comparison of the group design process with and without a simple group editor," *ACM Transactions on Information Systems*, vol. 11, no. 4, pp. 321–348, 1993.

[6] I. R. Posner and R. M. Baecker, "How People Write Together," *Proceedings of the Twenty-fifth Annual Hawaii International Conference on System Sciences*, vol. 4, pp. 127–138, 1992.

[7] P. B. Lowry, A. Curtis, and M. R. Lowry, "Building a taxonomy and nomenclature of collaborative writing to improve interdisciplinary research and practice," *Journal of Business Communication*, vol. 41, no. 1, pp. 66–99, 2004.

[8] I. Blau and A. Caspi, "What Type of Collaboration Helps? Psychological Ownership , Perceived Learning and Outcome Quality of Collaboration Using Google Docs," *Quality*, pp. 48–55, 2009.

[9] Y. Sun, D. Lambert, M. Uchida, and N. Remy, "Collaboration in the cloud at Google," *Proceedings of the 2014 ACM conference on Web science - WebSci '14*, pp. 239–240, 2014.

[10] R. Watson, "Extending Google Docs to Collaborate on Research Papers," *The University of Southern Queensland, Australia*, pp. 1–11, 2006.

[11] S. Robinson, M. Jones, E. Vartiainen, and G. Marsden, "PicoTales: collaborative authoring of animated stories using handheld projectors," *Proceedings of the ACM 2012 conference on Computer Supported Cooperative Work - CSCW '12*, p. 671, 2012.

[12] A. Krowne and A. Bazaz, "Authority Models for Collaborative Authoring," *Proceedings of the 37th Annual Hawaii International Conference on System Sciences*, vol. 00, pp. 18–24, 2004.

[13] P. Likarish and J. Winet, "Exquisite Corpse 2.0," *Proceedings of the Designing Interactive Systems Conference*, pp. 564–567, 2012.

[14] B. Mason and S. Thomas, "A Million Penguins Research Report," Institute of Creative Technologies, De Montfort University, Leicester, United Kingdom, pp. 1–36, 2008.

[15] E. Thiry, S. Lindley, R. Banks, and T. Regan, "Authoring personal histories: Exploring the timeline as a framework for meaning making," *Proceedings of the 2013 SIGCHI conference on Human Factors in computing systems (CHI 2013)*, pp. 1619–1628, 2013.

[16] B. Cardoso and T. Romão, "The timeline as a programming interface," *Conference on Human Factors in Computing Systems*, pp. 1423–1428, 2014.

[17] M. Reddy and P. Dourish, "A finger on the pulse: temporal rhythms and information seeking in medical work," *Proceedings of the ACM Conference on Computer Supported Collaborative Work CSCW*, pp. 344–353, 2002.

[18] A. Ajanki, M. Koskela, J. Laaksonen, and S. Kaski, "Adaptive timeline interface to personal history data," *Proceedings of the 15th ACM on International conference on multimodal interaction*, pp. 229–236, 2013.

[19] E. Pyshkin and N. Bogdanov, "Learning history with timelines: Use cases, requirements and design," *Computer Science and Information Systems (FedCSIS), 2014 Federated Conference on*, pp. 273–280, 2014.

[20] A. Tapscott, J. Colás, A. Moghnieh, and J. Blat, "Writing Consistent Stories based on Structured Multi-Authored Narrative Spaces," *Proceedings of the 4th Workshop on Computational Models of Narrative*, vol. 32, pp. 277–292, 2013.

[21] M. Bohøj, N. G. Borchorst, N. O. Bouvin, S. Bødker, and P.-O. Zander, "Timeline collaboration," *Proceedings of the 28th international conference on Human factors in computing systems CHI 10*, pp. 523–532, 2010.

APPENDIX

TABLE I: AUTHORING PHASE DESCRIPTIVE STATISTICS

	Scenes	Tags Used	Total Word Count
Sample Size:	22	22	22
Mean:	2.81	2.09	283.77
Median	3	0	268
Minimum:	1	0	87
Maximum:	7	9	581

TABLE II: AUTHOR QUESTIONNAIRE RANK QUESTION RESULTS

	Initial story was helpful in writing	Dates helped to write	Images helped in writing	Liked using dates	Liked using images	Reading from Chronoverse was easy	Contributing to Chronoverse was easy
AVG	3,65	2,47	3,53	2,76	3,71	3,87	3,59
STDEV	0,7	1,01	0,99	1,03	1,14	0,24	0,06

TABLE III: DETAILED AUTHOR QUESTIONNAIRE PERCENTAGE QUESTION RESULTS

	1 to 5 existing scenes	5 to 10 existing scenes	No existing scene	
I read...	53%	35%	12%	
	randomly	chronologically	guided by title	guided by images
My reading order was...	33%	27%	33%	7%
	before writing	after writing	during the whole experience	
I read existing scenes...	33%	53%	13%	
	fun	inspiring	typical	
Initial story was...	25%	31%	38%	
	were a minor annoyance	I didn't care	didn't bothered me at all	I liked them
Contradictions in the story...	24%	35%	29%	12%
	made writing difficult	didn't influence me	inspired me	
Those contradictions...	6%	88%	6%	
	based on existing story world	from scratch		
Wrote our story...	94%	6%		

TABLE IV: JURY EVALUATION PHASE RESULTS

	Plot coherence	Image coherence	Plot consistency with other AGSSs	Tone consistency with other AGSSs	Plot consistency with ISS	Tone consistency with ISS
AVG	3,02	3,45	1,86	2,44	2,55	2,89
STDEV	0,87	0,69	0,47	0,56	0,95	0,69

TABLE V: JURY EVALUATION PHASE RESULTS PEARSON CORRELATION COEFFICIENTS

	Plot coherence	Image coherence	Plot consistency with other AGSSs	Tone consistency with other AGSSs	Plot consistency with ISS	Tone consistency with ISS
Plot coherence	1	0,23	-0,01	-0,01	0,09	0,16
Image coherence	0,23	1	-0,16	0,16	-0,3	-0,18
Plot consistency with other AGSSs	-0,01	-0,16	1	0,23	0,63	0,33
Tone consistency with other AGSSs	-0,01	0,16	0,23	1	0,28	0,62
Plot consistency with ISS	0,09	-0,3	0,63	0,28	1	0,66
Tone consistency with ISS	0,16	-0,18	0,33	0,62	0,66	1

TABLE VI: READER EVALUATION PHASE AGSSs DESCRIPTIVE STATISTICS

	Reader Score	Same story than ISS?
Sample Size:	8	8
Mean:	3.10625	0.498125
Median:	3.08	0.52
Minimum:	2.75	0.08
Maximum:	3.4	875

TABLE VII: AGSS/ISS AVERAGE SIMILARITY

Same story?	AGSS1	AGSS2	AGSS3	AGSS4	AGSS5	AGSS6	AGSS7	AGSS8	ISS
AGSS1	1	0,4	1	0	0,22	0	0,4	0,42	0,71
AGSS2	0,4	1	0,3	0,29	0	0,14	0	0,33	0,08
AGSS3	1	0,3	1	0,36	0	0	0,67	0,4	0,88
AGSS4	0	0,29	0,36	1	0,38	0,13	0,6	0,2	0,33
AGSS5	0,22	0	0	0,38	1	0,33	0	0	0,14
AGSS6	0	0,14	0	0,13	0,33	1	0	0,14	0,15
AGSS7	0,4	0	0,67	0,6	0	0	1	1	0,83
AGSS8	0,42	0,33	0,4	0,2	0	0,14	1	1	0,88
ISS	0,71	0,08	0,88	0,33	0,14	0,15	0,83	0,88	1

TABLE VIII: GLOBAL PEARSON CORRELATION COEFFICIENTS PER AUTHOR GROUP

	Reader evaluation phase		Jury evaluation phase						Authoring phase		
	Reader score	Same story than ISS	Plot coherence	Image coherence	Plot consistency with other AGSSs	Tone consistency with other AGSSs	Plot consistency with ISS	Tone consistency with ISS	Average word count	Total word count	Total tags
Reader Score	1										
Same story than ISS	0,27	1									
Plot coherence	-0,16	0,19	1								
Image Coherence	0,35	0,19	-0,08	1							
Plot consistency with other AGSSs	0,37	0,52	0,62	-0,01	1						
Tone consistency with other AGSSs	0,53	0,52	0,04	0,16	0,74	1					
Plot consistency with ISS	0,61	0,47	-0,05	-0,24	0,66	0,82	1				
Tone consistency with ISS	0,47	0,36	-0,03	-0,04	0,64	-0,33	0,06	1			
Average word count	0,21	-0,45	-0,52	-0,04	-0,33	-0,33	0,06	-0,07	1		
Total word count	0,2	0,77	-0,38	-0,14	-0,28	-0,4	0,07	0,73	0,98	1	
Total tags	0,54	0,62	0,14	-0,15	0,78	0,65	0,92	0,77	0,19	0,22	1

Design and Implementation of Support System for Network Testing with Whitebox Switches

Megumi Shibuya[†], Hidehiko Kawakami[†], Teruyuki Hasegawa[†] and Hirozumi Yamaguchi[‡]
[†]KDDI Research, Inc.
Saitama, JAPAN
e-mail: {shibuya, hi-kawakami, teru}@kddi-research.jp
[‡]Osaka University
Osaka, JAPAN
e-mail: h-yamagu@ist.osaka-u.ac.jp

Abstract—**In this paper, we design and implement an automated network testing system that enables network testing operators to observe the behavior of networks under a variety of failures. We aim at automating the network failure testing of commercial networks, which is often time consuming since much effort is needed for network configuration, test scenario execution, evaluation report creation, and cause analysis of erroneous behavior. Moreover, we consider such an environment where whitebox switches and legacy switches co-exist. Whitebox switches are composed of commodity-based hardware components where Open Source Software (OSS), such as Chef can be used to manage them, while legacy switches are usually operated by vendor-dependent tools. Our system hides such difference and provides a seamless and automated management scheme in such heterogeneous environment. We have implemented the proposed system to confirm its effectiveness and feasibility.**

Keywords – Whitebox Switch; Chef; Automated Verification; OSS; DevOps

I. INTRODUCTION

Network providers need to assure a certain level of services in providing commercial networks. Such assurance would be necessary every time their elements (e.g., links and routers) are added, removed, updated, or replaced. As testing methodologies for IP networks, interconnect testing, stress testing, and failure testing are well-known and have been utilized. Those testing procedures contain test scenario generation, network testing environment preparation, test result analysis, and many other tasks.

In particular, failure testing is significant as a failure of network component often occurs. However, failure testing for commercial networks has several issues to be addressed. Firstly, it requires a large amount of time and efforts that should be dedicated to network equipment preparation, network cabling, network configuration including connectivity assessment, execution of a huge number of testing items, and analysis of the evaluation results. Furthermore, with increased size and complexity of commercial networks in recent years, cabling and setting errors are prone to occur when the network to be tested is constructed. This is because the man-hours for the testing has increased and testing is often manually undertaken by operators. Consequently, there are many cases in which a few months' work is required until they become ready for use [1][2]. This might be an obstacle to rapid deployment of the services.

In order to support network testing operators engaged in such time- and effort-consuming tasks of network failure testing, many network testers [3][4] and network simulators [5]-[7], which serve as automated network testing tools, have been manufactured. However, they are very costly and operations differ from each other. Thus, efficiency depends on the network testing environment of network equipment.

Recently, in contrast to legacy switches (denoted by *Legacy-SW*) where hardware and network OS are manufactured by conventional network equipment vendors, whitebox switches (denoted by *WB-SW*), which are composed of commodity-based hardware components and selectable network OSs, are becoming increasingly widespread [8]-[10]. As these network OSs are generally based on Linux OS, various testing processes can be automated by utilizing Open Source Software (OSS), such as Chef [11]. DevOps [12]-[15] is an emerging paradigm for fostering collaboration among system development and operations and it can improve the life cycle of software deployment and management processes. Besides, Chef and some other tools enable automated configuration of servers and clouds.

From a standpoint of network providers focusing on carrier-grade networks, we expect that Linux-based innovative WB-SWs will co-exist with Legacy-SWs in commercial networks. However, as the network OS of Legacy-SWs is not usually Linux-based, different automation techniques are necessary if these different SWs are co-used. Even in such heterogeneous environment containing both WB-SWs and Legacy-SWs, automation should be available to mitigate the workload of networking testing operators (*operational workload*).

In this paper, we assume future-generation commercial networks where Linux-based WB-SWs and Legacy-SWs co-exist. Then, we design an automated network testing system. The system is able to observe the behavior of the networks to be tested under given intended failures, collect testing results, and analyze them automatically. Heterogeneity due to different types of SWs is completely hidden and seamless testing operations are provided. The designed system has been implemented to confirm its effectiveness and feasibility. Specifically, we have implemented the automated network testing system that can automatically construct and configure the test target network containing both WB-SWs and Legacy-SWs, and have observed how the target network behaves in failure scenarios.

Since Legacy-SWs do not allow execution of OSS, a proxy to translate the Chef commands into Legacy-SW's is newly introduced. The proposed system automatically executes the testing procedure to confirm the influence of link failure and path switching on end-to-end communications. In addition, the system has a function to apply randomly-generated failures that occur in different times and locations. The results of such random tests are informative to find potential risks that may violate the fault tolerance of the target networks.

The contributions of this work are two-fold. Firstly, our system can deal with such an environment that contains both WB-SWs and Legacy-SWs. Although this is considerably important in assuring robustness and trustworthiness of carrier-grade commercial networks with lesser amount of human effort, no existing approach has explicitly and formally addressed this issue. Secondly, we show the effectiveness and feasibility of such a system by real implementation.

This paper is organized as follows. Section II summarizes related works and Section III explains the proposed automated network testing system. Section IV presents the experimental results of the proposed system. We conclude this work in Section V.

II. Related Work

Recently, the concept of DevOps, which is an emerging paradigm to actively foster collaboration between system development and operations, is becoming popular. In order to speed up the improvement in the development quality, some automated tools, such as Chef, Puppet [16], and Ansible [17], have emerged for realizing DevOps, which are able to construct a server- and/or cloud-based infrastructure environment [2][12][13]. Using these tools, a testing environment is constructed automatically, which saves time and effort for testing operations.

As related work of automated network testing, the L1 patch [18], where whole OpenFlow switches are virtually seen as a single L1 patch panel using an OpenFlow technique [19], is proposed. By combining this approach with Mininet [20], an OSS-based network testing tool, the operational workload was mitigated and the dedicated time was just a few minutes per operator, while a half or an hour by two operators was necessary in the conventional work procedure. Reference [18] also reports that the number of test types was increased to 194, which had been just 90 in the conventional approach. Reference [21] proposes a method of constructing an automated test platform for Virtual Network Functions (VNF). In such an environment where virtual machines from different vendors are controlled by different virtual infrastructure managers, such as OpenStack and VMware Esxi, a network testing tool that automatically performs a series of tasks, such as test scenario selection and verification testing, is implemented using the commercial products CloudShell and TestShell [22]. Such comprehensive tests, which had required a lot of manual operations so far, can be automatically performed by using the tool, and 2,736 types of tests can be completed in 40 hours. However, this approach does not support Legacy-SWs, and thus applicability is rather limited until the ISP completely migrates into the NFV environment as described above.

WB-SWs have recently become increasingly prominent, and they are less expensive than Legacy-SWs. In addition, unlike the software-based virtual SWs, WB-SWs are generally implemented with ASICs in order to transfer the packets at high speed. Since most of the network OSs [8][23] for WB-SWs are based on Linux, it is expected that various types of tasks are automated using OSS. For example, Chef can be used to construct the environment automatically. In addition, Zabbix [24] and iperf [25] are known as a network monitoring tool and a traffic generator, respectively. However, considering such a situation where WB-SWs and Legacy-SWs co-exist, we also need to support Legacy-SWs that cannot execute OSS. Therefore, it is crucial that WB-SWs and Legacy-SWs can be operated seamlessly.

For these reasons, we assume that Legacy-SWs are still used with WB-SWs during the migration period. We also assume that there is a growing demand for automated network testing to mitigate management costs. Therefore, we design the automated network testing system enabling seamless operations with heterogeneous SWs. The system can create the network to be tested (denoted as *NtbT* hereinafter) and execute the failure scenarios automatically. In addition, as the size of the networks is still growing and configurations are becoming more complicated, comprehensive failure testing should also be supported where network problems are found by random failure generations with testing.

III. Automated Network Testing System

In this section, we explain how our proposed automated network testing system is designed for commercial networks with WB-SWs and Legacy-SWs.

A. Design Principle

In general, a conventional test procedure consists of four steps as shown in Fig. 1 (a); create test items, construct NtbT, conduct tests, and confirm test results. Here, in order to reduce the operational workload, our proposed system automatically executes the following steps as shown in Fig. 1 (b); construct NtbT other than physical network cabling as step 2-2), conduct tests as step 3), and collect and analyze the results as step 4-1).

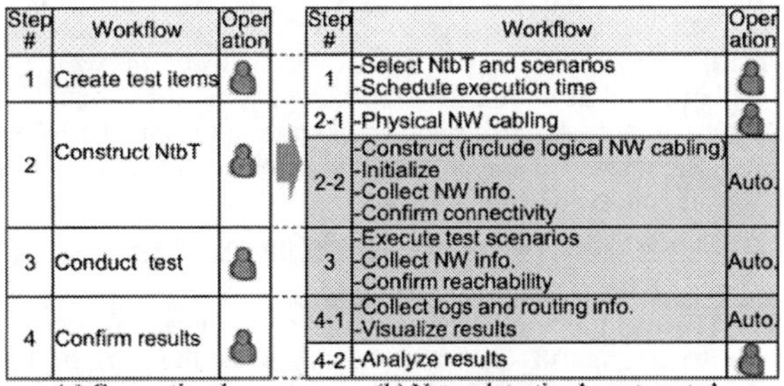

(a) Conventional network testing. (b) Network testing by automated network testing system.

Figure 1. Comparative defintions of network testing procedures.

Figure 2 shows our proposed automated network testing system that consists of (1) NtbT with network equipment (WB-SWs (physical and/or virtual), Legacy-SWs, and hosts), and (2) a network testing control server (NW-CS) that sends to NtbT instructions, such as "construct NtbT" and "occurrence of failure". NtbT and NW-CS are connected via Control Plane (C-Plane), and SWs and hosts forward the traffic via Data Plane (D-Plane).

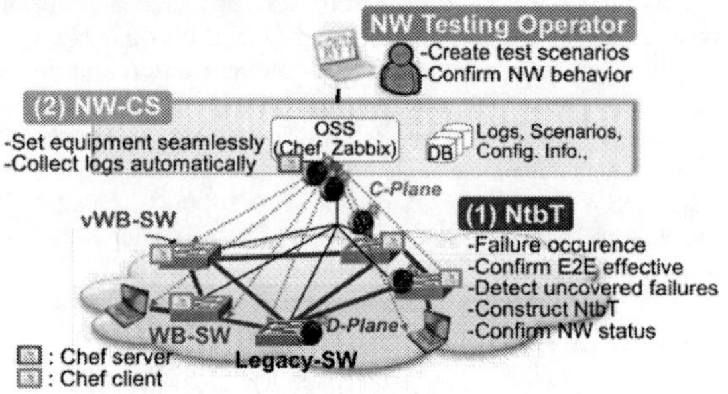

Figure 2. Automated network testing system.

We describe the design principles for each function below.

1) Automatic Construction of NtbT (for Step 2-2)

In order to construct NtbT automatically, Chef, which is an OSS infrastructure environment construction tool, is used. After completing the physical network cabling on NtbT, the Chef server instructs the Chef clients (i) to create the virtual WB-SWs (vWB-SWs) if necessary, (ii) to initialize and configure NtbT, and (iii) to start the routing protocol. This instruction is called *NtbT construction scenario*. To confirm the connectivity of the constructed NtbT, the Chef server conducts bidirectional reachability assessment on every link and between every host pair using *ping*.

2) Automatic failure occurrence (for Step 3)

The *failure scenario* specifies a series of failures in network testing. More concretely, the failure scenario consists of multiple *failure recipes*. A failure recipe corresponds to failure occurrence (e.g., link down and/or up). The location of failure in a recipe can be specified by the network testing operator (e.g., failures occur at SW#1) or can be randomly chosen. Then, the failure scenario specifies the execution ordering of those recipes. Network testing can be conducted repeatedly according to this failure scenario with the NtbT construction scenario. Both scenarios are stored in the database (DB). This is called *testing scenario*, which is explained in Section III-B. Furthermore, by the scheduling function, the testing scenario is executed at a specified time and date. Hence, it can be executed automatically at any time (e.g., nighttime or holidays).

3) Provisioning seamless operation of WB-SWs and Legacy-SWs (for Steps 1, 2-2 and 3)

To avoid complicated settings and operations due to coexistence of WB-SWs and Legacy-SWs, the settings and executing commands are made uniform for both types of SWs. However, Legacy-SWs cannot execute the Chef client because the network OS for Legacy-SWs is not Linux-based. Therefore, the proxy to translate the Chef commands to Legacy-SW's is prepared. We describe this in detail in Section III-C.

4) Network connectivity assessment (for Steps 2-2, 3 and 4-1)

In order to confirm bidirectional connectivity between adjacent equipment pair (via a certain link), Link Layer Discovery Protocol (LLDP) is used to collect the address information of the equipment pair, such as IP and MAC addresses. If LLDP is not applied to the target network, Address Resolution Protocol (ARP) is used instead.

5) Visualization of network behavior during and after network testing (for Steps 3 and 4-1)

To simplify the confirmation, the network behavior during network testing can be visualized in a real-time manner with network information in the above 4). Moreover, in order to confirm it after network testing, this network behavior can be replayed visually.

6) Assessment of failure influence on end-to-end communication (for Step 3)

During network testing, each host continuously sends packets to other hosts by *iperf* to confirm the connectivity between any pair of hosts. This is significant to observe the capability of the network to guarantee a certain level of service quality even when failures occur.

7) Automatic log collection and analysis (for Step 4-1)

Statistical log information, such as the traffic volume and CPU utilization, is collected by Chef and Zabbix. This log information is then analyzed and the results are shown in lists and/or plots on graphs.

8) Detection of uncovered failures (for Step 3)

Chaos Monkey [26][27] provides a function to generate failures randomly at any testing point. This often helps to find system errors and faults that have not yet been found in the system. Focusing on this feature, we integrate this function into our network testing system, i.e., failures occurrence order and/or locations that are randomly chosen. Concretely, failure candidates are categorized into some groups, such as links accommodated in the same switch and routers in the same OSPF area. The system must choose a candidate within the same group, which makes this random choice much more effective.

B. *Testing Scenario*

As we introduced earlier, a *testing scenario* consists of an NtbT construction scenario and a failure scenario. It is a testing procedure that is composed of seven *scenario recipes* as shown in Table I. This testing scenario is created by the network testing operator.

Again, the failure scenario consists of one or more failure recipes. We may select recipes from DB and some examples of those recipes are; (a) traffic sending/receiving with start and end time, (b) failure occurrence/recovery, such as interface (IF) down/up, (c) latency test, (d) load test, and (e) end-to-end quality measurement. The testing scenario is stored as the NtbT construction scenario and the failure scenario. After creating the testing scenario, the execution time is scheduled at the scheduler. The execution is started automatically at the specified time and stopped when the failure scenario is completed.

TABLE I. SCENARIO RECIPES IN THE TESTING SCENARIO

Testing Scenario	No.	Scenario Recipes
NtbT construction scenario	1	Selection of NtbT topology
	2	Reconstruction of NtbT (Yes/No)
	3	Initialization of network equipment (WB-SWs, Legacy-SWs, hosts) (Yes/No)
	4	Confirmation of connectivity (Yes/No)
	5	Execution schedule (date and time, or at specific execution time)
	6	Collection of interval time of the network information and logs
Failure scenario	7	Failure recipes

C. System Implementation

Figure 3 shows the implementation of the automated network testing system. NW-CS consists of a Web server, databases that store logs, scenarios and configurations of NtbT topologies, a Chef server, and a Zabbix server on a PC. NtbT consists of an NtbT PC with vWB-SWs and virtual hosts (vhosts), physical WB-SWs, and Legacy-SWs. Chef clients run on the NtbT PC.

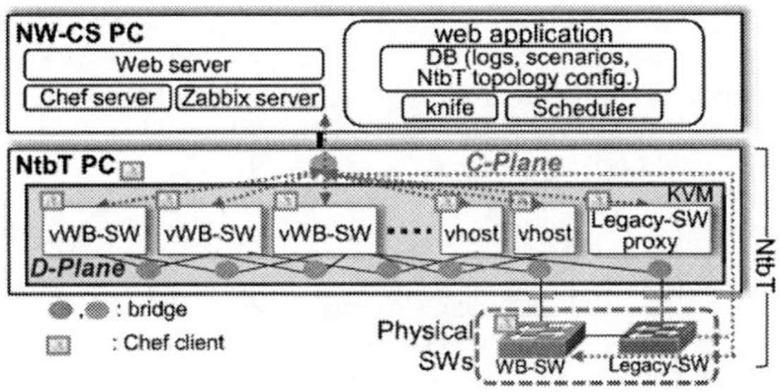

Figure 3. Implementation of automated network testing system.

When NtbT is reconstructed (if a recipe of "Reconstruction of NtbT" is "Yes"), vWB-SWs are constructed automatically in accordance with the selected NtbT. Furthermore, every adjacent SW (or host) pair is connected with a virtual link through a different bridge as logical NW cabling. The physical SW and virtual SW are also connected in the same way.

At the specified execution time, the Chef clients on each SW download the corresponding recipes from the Chef server via C-Plane. Then, the various settings are executed automatically based on the downloaded recipes. Furthermore, logs and routing tables of network equipment during the testing are collected automatically and stored in DB.

In order to separate C-Plane and D-Plane strictly where the packets in C-Plane must not leak into D-Plane and vice versa, each WB-SW arranges interfaces (IFs) and routing tables dedicated to C-Plane separated from those for D-Plane, by using two independent namespaces *mgmt* (for C-Plane) and *default* (for D-Plane) inside WB-SW [28]. Consequently, the Zabbix server collects the D-Plane information, such as routing tables of network equipment through *mgmt*.

To use uniform descriptions of the setting commands and method, it would be better that both WB-SWs and Legacy-SWs could be controlled according to the framework of Chef. Since the Chef client cannot be executed on Legacy-SW, a proxy that translates the Chef commands into the Legacy-SW commands and executes it automatically is created (called *Legacy-SW proxy*).

IV. EXPERIMENTAL EVALUATION

This section presents the evaluation results of the proposed system expressed in Section III.

A. Experimental Setup

In order to validate the effectiveness of our system implementation, we constructed NW-CS and NtbT on different PCs as shown in Fig. 3. The Chef server, Zabbix server, DB stored logs, and scenarios are implemented on NW-CS. We arranged three types of VMs as stand-alone on KVM [29] for vWB-SWs, the vhosts, and the Legacy-SW proxy composing NtbT. One WB-SW (DELL S4048-on, OS: Cumulus Linux) and one Legacy-SW (Catalyst 3750-24TS-E) also participate in NtbT via a physical interface. TABLE II summarizes the specifications of PCs for NW-CS and NtbT.

TABLE II. PARAMETERS OF THE AUTOMATED NETWORK TESTING SYSTEM

Parameter	NW-CS PC	NtbT PC
OS	Ubuntu 14.04 64bit	
Memory	64GB	
CPU	Intel® Xeon® CPU E5-2650+ v3@1.80GHz	
Chef	Server 12.4.0	Client 12.5.1
Zabbix	2.2.2(server)	2.2.2 (agent)
SW	-	Cumulus VX 2.5.6
Traffic generator	-	iperf
Routing software	-	quagga(ospf)

TABLE III. CONFIGURATION OF TESTING NETWORKS

NW No.	Network equipment (#equipment)	#Links	Failure recipes
1	vWB-SW(4), vhost(2)	7	IF down
2	vWB-SW(13), Catalyst(1), vhost(5)	25	1) IFdown 2) Silent failure
3	vWB-SW(13), DELL(1), vhost(5)	25	IF down
4	vWB-SW(12), Catalyst(1), DELL(1), vhost(5)	26	Change OSPF cost

TABLE IV. TESTING SCENARIO (NW NO. 2)

Testing Scenario	Recipe No.(*Rcp#*)	Scenario Recipes	*T* [sec]
NtbT construction scenario	1	Reconstruction of NtbT (Yes)	0
	2	Initialization of network equipment (Yes)	0
	3	Confirmation of connectivity (Yes)	0
Failure scenario	4	Start traffic send/receive	0
	5	Failure1 occurrence: wbs-core01 swp1 down	30
	6	Failure1 restoration: wbs-core01 swp1 up	30
	7	Failure2 occurrence: cat-agg20 FastEthernet1/0/2 down	30
	8	Failure2 restoration: cat-agg20 FastEthernet1/0/2 up	30
	9	End traffic send/receive	30
	10	Collection and analysis of logs	0

T: waiting time after completion of previous recipe.

To evaluate our proposed system, we created the four types of experimental networks shown in TABLE III where NtbT is constructed automatically and all hosts generated traffic by iperf between every host pair. We then conducted each scenario 10 times. Note that physical SWs are cabled by hand preliminarily.

As an example, the testing scenario of NW No. 2 is shown in TABLE IV.

B. Verification of System Functions

Firstly, we verify that our proposed system can conduct network testing automatically. In order to confirm it, we executed network testing using four types of testing networks and corresponding failure scenarios in TABLE III. We verified that our proposed system can conduct all scenarios, and every scenario was executed without error. We validated that changing the routing paths when the link failure occurs and the OSPF cost changes, the disconnect time of end-to-end connections, the transition of the traffic volume of each interface (IF) at SWs, and the transition of the routing tables by visualization. Moreover, we verified that the Legacy-SW proxy works correctly.

As an example, Fig. 4 shows our visualization of end-to-end traffic paths before/after scenario recipe *Rcp#5* of NW No. 2 in the failure scenario. We can observe the network behavior of path restoration using this visualization.

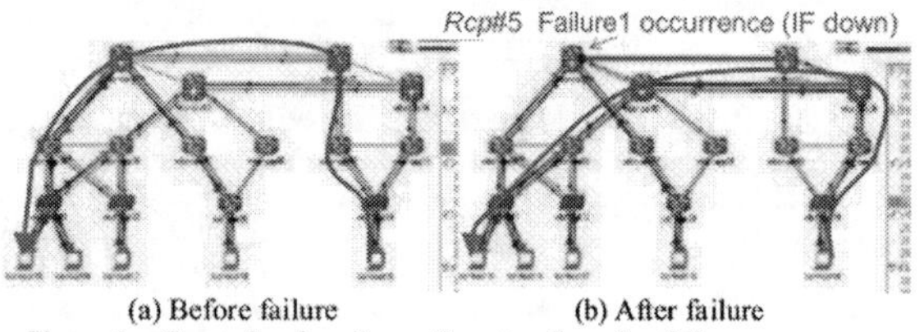

(a) Before failure (b) After failure

Figure 4. Example of routing path restoration after failure occurrence.

C. Performance Evaluation of Processsing Time

To evaluate the performance of our proposed system, we evaluated the processing time of each scenario recipe in the testing scenario during network testing. More concretely, the time to process each recipe was collected and analyzed.

The processing time of each recipe using NW No. 2 is shown in Fig. 5. The processing time differs according to the scenario recipe. The processing time has a small variance over recipes, and the maximum variance was 1.50 when the scenario recipe is the confirmation of connectivity (*Rcp#3*). The processing time of reconstruction (*Rcp#1*) was 110.0 seconds, while that of initialization (*Rcp#2*) was 138.1 seconds on average. The processing time of *Rcp#1* was less than that of *Rcp#2*. The processing time of a failure occurrence / restoration recipe is the time by which the Chef client is executed till completion of the executed failure command at the corresponding SW.

Here, we consider two cases; Case #1 that consists of *Rcp#5* and *Rcp#6*, and Case #2 that consists of *Rcp#7* and *Rcp#8*. The processing time of Case #1 was 15.19 seconds and 21.94 seconds in Case #2. These two cases are similar in the sense that they have one failure and recovery, but the time is different. Cases #1 and #2 are different since #1 is an interface down failure and #2 is a "silent" failure that is difficult to detect. As seen in these cases, the processing time differs according to the failure recipe, but it is important to know such processing time of each recipe to estimate the time to conduct tests for large-scale networks. More detailed analysis of execution time is necessary, which is part of our future work.

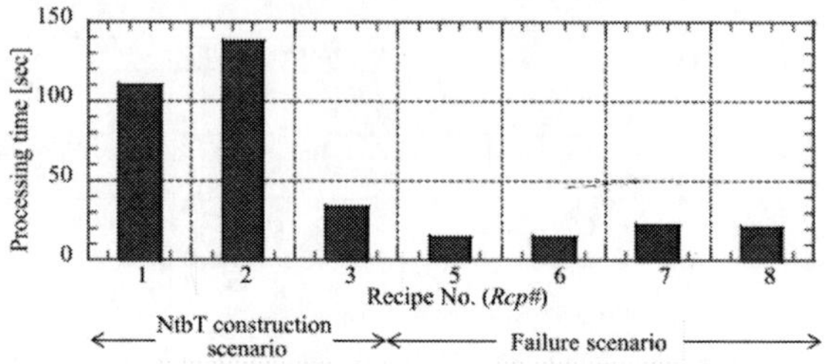

Figure 5. Processing time of each recipe (*Rcp#*).

D. Performance Evaluation of NtbT Construction Time

As our proposed system constructs NtbT including the construction and initialization of network equipment (SWs and hosts) in NtbT, it is important to perceive the processing performance of the construction NtbT for the number of SWs.

To evaluate it, we focused on the SWs because the construction time of SWs is longer than that of the hosts. In the evaluated network, vWB-SWs are connected in series on NtbT and hosts are connected to the edge of a path. Varying the number N of SWs from 5 to 60 units, we measured the processing time for constructing N vWB-SWs 10 times in each case.

Figure 6 shows the construction time on average of each recipe in the NtbT construction scenario. The processing time of each event increases in proportion to N. When N was 60, the total time for constructing NtbT was 480.4 seconds on average, and the processing time of construction increased in the following order; initialization > construction > connectivity. However, the increase rate of the processing time of *Rcp#1* was larger than that of *Rcp#2*. Therefore, we estimate that when N is over 60, the processing time of *Rcp#1* exceeds that of *Rcp#2*.

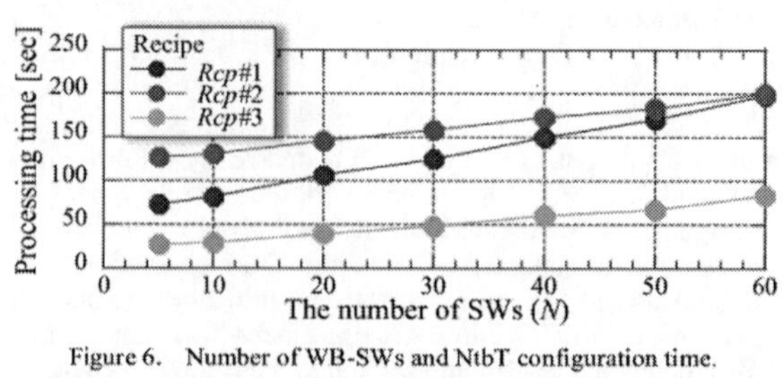

Figure 6. Number of WB-SWs and NtbT configuration time.

The reconstruction of NtbT (*Rcp#1*) creates VMs of vWB-SW only, while initialization of network equipment (*Rcp#2*) installs some software, such as OSS. Furthermore, confirmation of connectivity (*Rcp#3*) is conducted via ping between both interfaces (IFs) of a link for all links and all hosts. Therefore, the processing time depends on the number of links and hosts. In this topology, due to the fixed number of hosts (=2), the processing time increases in proportion to the number of SWs.

E. Effectiveness in Reducing Work Hours

To evaluate how our proposed system contributes to reducing the operational workload, we observed the work hours during the network testing process by comparing manual and automated operations. Using NW No. 1, we prepared the testing scenario where an interface (IF) is down and then the routing path is switched, including network cabling, initialization, and failure occurrence. In Case-A, this scenario was conducted manually, and automatically conducted by the proposed system in Case-B. We measured them 3 times in each case.

The work hours were 16.03 and 7.37 minutes in Case-A and Case-B, respectively. Namely, the work hours were reduced by 54.1%. Note that each work hour includes 30-second intervals of each recipe. From this result, we expect more efficiency in large-scale networks, and we can say that our proposed system can reduce the work hours.

V. CONCLUSION

In this paper, we assumed future-generation commercial networks where Linux-based WB-SWs and legacy-SW co-exist. So, we proposed a method of designing and implementing an automated network testing system. This system is able to observe the behavior of the network to be tested under given intended failures, collect testing results and analyze them automatically. Heterogeneity due to different SWs is completely hidden and seamless operations are provided. We implemented the automated network testing system that can automatically construct and configure the test target network containing WB-SWs and Legacy-SWs, and observed how target network performs in failure scenarios. The experimental results show the effectiveness and feasibility of the system. In particular, it is confirmed that our implementation can automate failure testing on the network with WB-SWs and Legacy-SWs and can reduce the work hours by 54.1%. In future, we intend to verify the effect of the work hours using larger networks and various scenarios.

REFERENCES

[1] J. Kim, C. Meirosu, I. Papafili, R. Steinert, S. Sharma, F. Westphal, M. Kind, A. Shukla, F. Nemeth, and A. Manzalini, "Service Provider DevOps for Large Scale Modern Network Services," IFIP/IEEE IM 2015 Workshop: 10th International Workshop on Business-driven IT Management (BDIM), pp.1391-1397, 2015.

[2] L. E. Lwakatare, T. Karvonen, T. Sauvola, P. Kuvaja, H. H. Olsson, and J. Bosch, "Towards DevOps in the Embedded Systems Domain: Why is it so Hard?," 2016 49th Hawaii International Conference on System Sciences (HICSS), pp.5437-5446, Jan. 2016.

[3] Spirent TestCenter, http://www.spirent.com/Products/TestCenter, accessed Sep. 7, 2016.

[4] IXIA, https://www.ixiacom.com/, accessed Sep. 7, 2016.

[5] OPNET Modeler, http://www.riverbed.com/products/steelcentral/opnet.html, accessed Sep. 7, 2016.

[6] Cisco Modeling Labs, http://www.cisco.com/c/en/us/products/cloud-systems-management/modeling-labs/index.html, accessed Sep. 7, 2016.

[7] GNS3, https://www.gns3.com/, accessed Sep. 7, 2016.

[8] Cumulus, https://cumulusnetworks.com/, accessed Sep. 7, 2016.

[9] Quanta, http://www.networld.co.jp/product/quanta/, accessed Sep. 7, 2016.

[10] DELL, http://www.dell.com/us/business/p/networking-s-series-10gbe/pd, accessed Sep. 7, 2016.

[11] Chef, https://www.chef.io/chef/, accessed Sep. 7, 2016.

[12] C. Ebert, G. Gallardo, J. Hernantes, and N. Serrano, "DevOps," IEEE SOFTWARE, Vol 33. No.3, pp.94-100, Apr., 2016.

[13] J. Allspaw and P. Hammond, "10+ Deploys Per Day: Dev and Ops Cooperation at Flickr," O'REILLY Velocity Web Performance and Operations Conference (Velocity 2009), Jun. 2016, http://conferences.oreilly.com/velocity/velocity2009/, accessed Sep. 7, 2016.

[14] J. Wettinger, V. Andrikopoulos, and F. Leymann, "Automated Capturing and Systematic Usage of DevOps Knowledge for Cloud Applications," IEEE International Conference on Cloud Engineering (IC2E), pp.60-65, Mar. 2015.

[15] A. Csaszar, W. John, M. Kind, C. Meirosu, G. Pongracz, D. Staessens, A. Takacs, and F. Westphal, "Unifying Cloud and Carrier Network EU FP7 Project UNIFY," IEEE/ACM 6th International Conference on Utility and Cloud Computing, pp.452-457, 2013.

[16] Puppet, https://puppet.com/, accessed Sep. 7, 2016.

[17] Ansible, https://www.ansible.com/, accessed Sep. 7, 2016.

[18] http://www.sdnjapan.org/2015/1411_torii.pdf (in Japanese), accessed Sep. 7, 2016.

[19] OPEN NETWORKING FOUNDATION (ONF), "OpenFlow," https://www.opennetworking.org/sdn-resources/openflow, accessed Sep. 7, 2016.

[20] Mininet, http://mininet.org/, accessed Sep. 7, 2016.

[21] http://www.okinawaopenlabs.org/wp/wp-content/uploads/20160205_tanabe.pdf (in Japanese), accessed Sep. 7, 2016.

[22] QualiSystems CloudShell / TestShell, http://www.qualisystems.com/products/cloudshell-add-ons/testshell-overview/, accessed Sep. 7, 2016.

[23] PicOS, http://www.pica8.com/products/picos, accessed Sep. 7, 2016.

[24] Zabbix, http://www.zabbix.com/, accessed Sep. 7, 2016.

[25] Iperf, https://iperf.fr/, accessed Sep. 7, 2016.

[26] NETFLIX, "Chaos Monkey Released Into The Wild," http://techblog.netflix.com/2012/07/chaos-monkey-released-into-wild.html, accessed Sep. 7, 2016.

[27] A. Basiri, N. Behnam, R. Rooij, L. N. Hochstein, L. Kosewski, J. Reynolds, and C. Rosenthal, "Chaos Engineering," IEEE SOFTWARE, May/Jun. 2016.

[28] Cumulus Networks, "Configuration Management Namespace," https://support.cumulusnetworks.com/hc/en-us/articles/202325278-Configuring-a-Management-Namespace, accessed Sep. 7, 2016.

[29] KVM, http://www.linux-kvm.org/page/Main_Page, accessed Sep. 7, 2016.

Creating an Intelligent, Integrated Mobility Assistance: The Elastic Trip-Chain Construction Problem

Philip Wette, Emre Cakar, Lutz Bersiner

Robert Bosch GmbH
31139 Hildesheim, Germany
Email: {firstname.lastname}@de.bosch.com

***Abstract*—The number of transport modes and mobility services has increased significantly over the last decades. To support travelers, trip planning tools are required, which can take into account not only the broad spectrum of available transport modes but also personalized user requirements and their complete daily schedule. We present the architecture of a personal mobility-assistance service taking into account daily schedules to compute multimodal journeys and we identify the *Elastic Trip-Chain Construction Problem* as an important optimization problem for modern trip planning. We describe and analyze the optimization problem and model it as a Mixed Integer Quadratically Constrained Program.**

Keywords–Elastic Trip-Chain Construction Problem; Mobility Assistance; Travel Planning Service; Trip-Chain Composition

I. INTRODUCTION

Mobility behavior has always been subject to change. Today's changes seem to be mainly governed by increasing mobility demand, exhaustion of transport capacities, and an increasing consciousness of the environmental changes caused by traffic. At present, and especially in metropolitan areas, user's willingness and ability to employ a variety of transportation means apart from private owned cars can be observed [1]. On the one hand, this tendency is strongly supported by the ubiquitous availability of real-time services for nearly all kinds of transportation. Some transportation modes, e.g., ride sharing, even depend on such real-time services. On the other hand, real-time services offer the opportunity to influence and shape mobility behavior.

To efficiently assist (and influence) users traveling with this new variety of transport modes, new personal mobility assistance tools need to be employed. In the context of this work, we investigate a mobility assistant that plans trips along multiple activities, minimizing travel efforts on a per-user basis. Those trips usually start and end at a user's home location and interlink daily activities, such as going to work, (grocery-) shopping, or leisure activities. We call a trip including multiple activities a *trip chain*. Also, in the course of one single trip chain, the use of multiple different transportation modes to move from one activity to another is allowed.

The main two contributions of this paper are a) to sketch the function of a travel planner service as part of an integrated mobility assistance, the latter to be investigated with respect to its effect on mobility within the publicly funded joint project BiE (evaluation of integrated electric mobility) [2], and b) to describe and analyze the underlying optimization problem of computing valid and effective trip chains.

The rest of this paper is structured as follows: In Section II a short overview about trip-planning problems is given. Section III introduces our mobility assistance service, along with a detailed description of the integrated travel planning sub-service. The Elastic Trip-Chain Construction Problem is formulated and analyzed in Section IV. Moreover, a mathematical formulation of the problem in form of a Mixed Integer Quadratically Constrained Program is given. Section V concludes this paper.

II. RELATED WORK

Existing commercial mobility assistance is usually confined to more or less elaborate choice of the opportunities to get from location a to location b at a given time. Recently, a few efforts have been made to develop context related (i.e., to the purpose of the trip) support for multiple activities on one journey, such as eCOMPASS [3].

Various trip planning related computation problems can be found in the literature; the closest ones to the problem at hand are the so-called *Tourist Trip Planning Problems* (for a survey, see [4]) and the *Traveling Purchaser Problem* [5]. These problems are $\mathcal{NP}$-hard, hence very hard to solve. The trip planning problem studied in this work differs from the already known problems mainly in the fact that activities (that are to be executed along the trip) do not have a single, fixed location where they should be executed, but a set of alternative locations to choose from. Timing constraints inferred by the activities are partly covered by some of the Tourist Trip Planning Problems but not to the same extent as in this work. Furthermore, in our case different transportation modes are taken into consideration, which increases the complexity of the problem considerably.

III. ARCHITECTURE MOBILITY ASSISTANCE SERVICE

A. *Mobility Assistance Service*

The architecture of the integrated mobility assistance service is shown in Fig. 1. This work focuses on a travel planning service as part of such an integrated system. Hence, Fig. 1 only depicts the essential parts from the travel planning point–of–view; the rest of the components are left out. The mobility assistant is designed as a distributed system aiming on efficient horizontal scaling. To this end, we use Vert.X [6]: an event-driven Java framework to create distributed systems. Vert.X provides an *Event-Bus* which is used as the communication medium by the system's components. The most important components for travel planing are *Organizer*, *UserPreferenceService*, *CalendarService*, *AssistanceApp*, and *TravelPlanningService*.

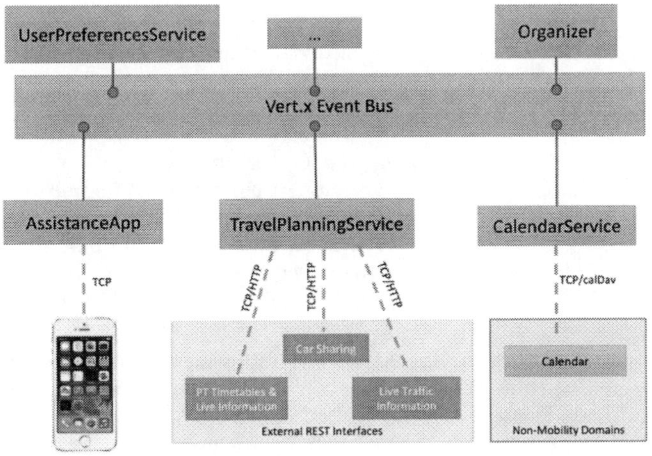

Figure 1. Architectural Overview of the Mobility Assistance Service

Both *AssistanceApp* and the *CalendarService* are the system's interfaces to external domains. The Assistance-App controls communication with the (human) users of the system. Among others, it proposes trips to the user, asks for preferences, and keeps track of the user's position. The CalendarService, on the other hand, interfaces directly with user's cloud-based digital calendars. Whenever there is a new entry in a calendar, this entry is compiled into an *activity* (the mobility assistance service's equivalent of a calendar entry) which is further analyzed and possibly annotated with additional information by the *Organizer*. The *UserPreferenceService* is the system's central component for storing and retrieving any sort of user preferences. If a user's profile is not completely filled out, it uses reasoning techniques to imply reasonable preferences. Those preferences are subsequently used by the *TravelPlanningService* to compute trip chains for all activities retrieved from external domains. The TravelPlanningService computes routes based on live traffic data. In addition, it uses REST interfaces to query for public transport information (such as time tables) and live information from car-sharing partners, for example availability of cars or the position of car-sharing stations.

B. Travel Planning Service

The travel planning service itself consists of multiple components, the most important ones for the scope of this work are *Trip-Chain Store*, *Trip-Chain Monitor*, *Trip-Chain Composer*, and *Routing Engine*.

The *trip-chain store* is the component responsible for efficient storage and retrieval of computed trip chains. It is used as a hub for other services of the integrated mobility assistance, as well as the central internal storage used by other components of the travel planning service.

The *trip-chain monitor* is used to keep trip chains up–to–date. The traffic situation undergoes constant change (e.g., due to unpredicted traffic jams). Hence, all trip chains have to be checked for feasibility under the projected future traffic situation. In the cases where they have been rendered infeasible by recent events, the trip-chain monitor triggers recomputation of the corresponding trip chains.

A *routing engine* is used to compute journeys. For any journey, all available modes of transportation are considered. Necessary real-time traffic information (public and private) is gathered via REST interfaces. These journeys are concatenated to trip chains by the *trip-chain composer*. To this end, the composer keeps a list of activities that need to be included into a trip chain and then creates journeys to connect the sites at which those activities are to be executed, making sure that no constraints, imposed by either the activities themselves or the user's preferences, are violated.

The trip-chain composer emerges as the crucial component with respect to the behavior of the travel planning service and thus of the integrated mobility assistance as a whole. As the trip-chain composer is also the component presenting the greatest challenges w.r.t. solving algorithms, it will be discussed and analyzed in more detail in the remainder of the paper.

IV. The Elastic Trip-Chain Construction Problem

The Elastic Trip-Chain Construction Problem is the core problem solved by the Trip-Chain Composer. It asks for a series of journeys interlinking one or more activities of a user such that the user arrives at the site of the activity in time (i.e., *not too late*). The activities in question have, apart from their durations, *elastic* timing constraints defining a time *interval* in which they need to start. This section further defines the underlying activity model, formally states the Elastic Trip-Chain Construction Problem, discusses its complexity and ends with a Mixed Integer Quadratically Constrained Program (MIQCP) modeling the problem.

A. Model and Problem Statement

Definition 1 *An activity a is defined to be the 4-tuple $a = (d, s_e, s_l, l_{pos})$ where d is the duration of the activity, s_e is the* earliest *possible point in time where the activity can be started, s_l is the* latest *possible point in time where the activity can be started, and l_{pos} is a non-empty set of locations where it is possible to execute the activity.*

To travel from one location where an activity is executed to another location where the next activity is executed, we define a journey.

Definition 2 *A journey j is defined as the 5-tuple $j = (src, dest, t_{dep}, t_{arr}, m)$ where src is the location to start the journey , $dest$ is the destination of the journey, t_{dep} is the point in time when the journey starts, t_{arr} is the time when the journey ends (when it arrives at $dest$), and m is the transportation mode on the journey.*

In the remainder, we use $src, dest, t_{dep}, t_{arr}$, and m as functions on journeys and d, s_e, s_l, and l_{pos} as functions on activities to describe the corresponding property (e.g., $d(a_i)$ describes the duration of activity a_i).

Definition 3 *A trip chain t is an ordered tuple of n journeys $t = (j_1, j_2, ..., j_n)$ where $dest(j_i) = src(j_{i+1})\ \forall\ 0 < i < n$. Let $A = \{a_1, a_2, ..., a_{n-1}\}$ be a set of $n-1$ activities. We say a trip chain t is* valid *for A, if t interlinks each activity $a \in A$ such that one of a's locations from l_{pos} is visited* before or on *s_e and at least d time between s_e and $s_l + d$ is spent at the location. In addition, it must be possible to make all journeys without any overlap. Hence, for all journeys $j_l \in t$*

there must not exist another journey $j_k \in t$, $j_k \neq j_l$, such that $(t_{dep}(j_l), t_{arr}(j_l))$ overlaps with $(t_{dep}(j_k), t_{arr}(j_k))$.

The Elastic Trip-Chain Construction Problem (ETCCP)
Given a set of activities $A = \{a_1, a_2, ..., a_N\}$, a location l, an earliest time s to start and latest time o to arrive (each at l), and a set of available transport modes, the elastic trip-chain construction problem asks for a valid *trip chain $t = (j_1, j_2, ..., j_{N+1})$ interconnecting all activities in A for which holds that $l = src(j_1) = dest(j_{N+1})$, $s \leq t_{dep}(j_1)$, and $t_{arr}(j_{N+1}) \leq o$.* It is worth noting that such a trip chain t does not always exist.

B. Notes on Complexity

The optimization variant of ETCCP not only asks for a *valid* trip chain that interlinks a set of activities but for the trip chain with *least* travel time or, in a general sense, *travel cost.*

The Traveling Salesperson Problem (TSP) can be reduced in polynomial time to the optimization variant of ETCCP. Reduction is done by assigning to each activity

- a time interval of unlimited size to be executed in,
- a duration of zero, and
- only one possible location to be executed at.

Due to space limitations, we omit the full construction here. However, it follows that TSP is a special case of the optimization variant of ETCCP meaning the optimization variant of our problem at hand is $\mathcal{NP}$-hard.

C. Mathematical Formulation

There is a variety of possible optimization criteria when constructing tripchains including shortest travel time, cheapest trip chain, or ecologically friendliest trip chain.

To keep the model description short, in the following we concentrate on computing trip chains with *shortest travel time* only. Note that the model can simply be adapted to meet the other optimization criteria by introducing additional model variables and using a different objective function.

1) Model variables: Our model features the following model variables as an input, describing a set of activities and their corresponding properties in detail.

In the description, with $A = \{a_1, a_2, ..., a_N\}$, we denote the set of activities to include in the trip chain. $origin$ denotes the origin (and final destination) of the trip chain. Time is modeled as a discrete series of equally spaced numbers on a time line analogous to UNIX timestamps where the spacing (i.e., the granularity) can be chosen arbitrarily.

$L \in \mathcal{N}^+$	Number of distinct possible locations from l_{pos} over all activities and the origin of the trip chain ($\mid origin \cup \bigcup_{a_i \in A} l_{pos}(a_i) \mid$)
$N \in \mathcal{N}^+$	Total number of activities on the trip chain ($\mid A \mid$)
$f^D_{k,l,t,m} \in \mathcal{N}^+$	Travel time between locations k and l with *departure* time t and using modality m. The origin of the trip chain goes by index 1 (i.e, $f^D_{1,l,t,m}$ denotes the travel time when departing at $origin$)
$f^A_{k,l,t,m} \in \mathcal{N}^+$	Travel time between locations k and l with *arrival* time t and using modality m.
$potloc_{i,k} \in \{0,1\}$	Potential locations for an activity. 1, if location k corresponds to one of $l_{pos}(a_i)$, 0 otherwise
S	The earliest possible point in time to start the trip chain
O	The latest possible point in time the trip chain needs to arrive at it's origin
M	Total number of available transport modes

2) Decision variables: The following *decision variables* tell when to execute which activity at what location and which mode to use to travel between activities.

$loc_{i,k} \in \{0,1\}$	1, if activity i is executed at location k, 0 otherwise
$t_i \in \mathcal{N}^+$	The point in time when activity i is to be started
$start_{i,k} \in \{0,1\}$	1, if execution of activity i starts at time k (in the granularity chosen), 0 otherwise
$term_{i,k} \in \{0,1\}$	1, if execution of activity i ends at time k (in the granularity chosen), 0 otherwise
$ord_{i,j} \in \{0,1\}$	The ordering of activities: 1, if activity i is the j-th activity on the trip chain, 0 otherwise.
$tt_j \in \mathcal{N}^+$	The time it takes to travel from the j-th activity to the (j+1)-th activity on the trip chain
$ttf \in \mathcal{N}^+$	The time it takes to travel from origin to the first activity
$ttl \in \mathcal{N}^+$	The time it takes to travel from the last activity back to origin
$mode_{i,m}$	1, if transport mode m is used for the i-th journey on the trip chain, 0 otherwise

3) Constraints: The decision variables have to be selected with respect to the following constraints. The notation $[a, b]$ denotes the set of natural numbers starting from a to b inclusive.

Starting activities in their „time frame" only

$$t_i >= s_e(a_i) \quad \forall i \in [1, N] \quad (1)$$

$$t_i <= s_l(a_i) \quad \forall i \in [1, N] \quad (2)$$

order of activities on the trip chain

$$\sum_{j=1}^{N} ord_{i,j} = 1 \quad \forall i \in [1, N] \quad (3)$$

$$\sum_{i=1}^{N} ord_{i,j} = 1 \quad \forall j \in [1, N] \quad (4)$$

$$\sum_{i=1}^{N} ord_{i,j} \cdot t_i < \sum_{i=1}^{N} ord_{i,j+1} \cdot t_i \quad \forall j \in [1, N-1] \quad (5)$$

no overlap of activities

$$term_i = t_i + d(a_i) \quad \forall i \in [1, N] \quad (6)$$

$$\sum_{i=1}^{N} ord_{i,j} \cdot term_i + \sum_{i=1}^{N} tt_i \cdot ord_{i,j+1} \quad \forall i \in [1, N-1] \quad (7)$$

$$< \sum_{i=1}^{N} ord_{i,j+1} \cdot t_i$$

transportation mode of journeys

$$\sum_{m=1}^{M} mode_{i,m} = 1 \qquad \forall i \in [1, N+1] \qquad (8)$$

fixing a location for each activity

$$\sum_{k=1}^{L} loc_{i,k} = 1 \qquad \forall i \in [1, N] \qquad (9)$$

$$potloc_{i,k} >= loc_{i,k} \qquad \forall i \in [1, N] \; \forall k \in [1, L] \qquad (10)$$

do not start trip chain before S

$$\sum_{t=S}^{O}\sum_{m=1}^{M}\sum_{i=1}^{N}\sum_{k=1}^{L} loc_{i,k} \cdot f^{A}_{1,k,t,m} \cdot mode_{i,m} \cdot ord_{i,1} \cdot start_{i,t} < \sum_{i=1}^{N} t_i \cdot ord_{i,1} - S \qquad (11)$$

do not arrive after O

$$\sum_{t=S}^{O}\sum_{m=1}^{M}\sum_{i=1}^{N}\sum_{k=1}^{L} loc_{i,k} \cdot f^{D}_{k,1,t,m} \cdot mode_{i+1,m} \cdot ord_{i,N} \cdot term_{i,t} < O - \sum_{t=S}^{O} term_{N,t} \cdot t \qquad (12)$$

travel times between activities

$$tt_j = \sum_{m=1}^{M}\sum_{u=1}^{N}\sum_{v=1}^{N}\sum_{k=1}^{L}\sum_{l=1}^{L}\sum_{t=S}^{O} ord_{u,j} \cdot ord_{v,j+1} \cdot loc_{u,k} \cdot loc_{v,l} \cdot f^{D}_{k,l,t,m} \cdot term_{j,t} \cdot mode_{u,m} \qquad \forall j \in [1, N-1] \qquad (13)$$

travel time from origin to first activity

$$\sum_{t=S}^{O} start_{i,t} = 1 \qquad \forall i \in [1, N] \qquad (14)$$

$$\sum_{t=S}^{O} start_{i,t} \cdot t = t_i \qquad \forall i \in [1, N] \qquad (15)$$

$$ttf = \sum_{t=S}^{O}\sum_{m=1}^{M}\sum_{i=1}^{N}\sum_{k=1}^{L} ord_{i,1} \cdot loc_{i,k} \cdot mode_{i,m} \cdot f^{A}_{1,k,t,m} \cdot start_{i,t} \qquad (16)$$

travel time from first activity back to origin

$$ttl = \sum_{t=S}^{O}\sum_{m=1}^{M}\sum_{i=1}^{N}\sum_{k=1}^{L} ord_{i,N} \cdot loc_{i,k} \cdot mode_{i+1,m} \cdot f^{D}_{k,1,t,m} \cdot term_{i,t} \qquad (17)$$

The optimization objective to minimize travel time is:

$$\min \left(\sum_{j=0}^{N} tt_j + ttf + ttl \right)$$

As this mathematical formulation contains products of decision variables in both its constraints and its objective function, it is a Mixed Integer Quadratically Constrained Program.

V. Conclusion

We described the architecture of a travel planning service as part of an integrated mobility assistance system, emphasizing that the crucial component of such a service is the trip-chain composer. This component computes the concatenation of journeys and determines when to execute which activity at what location such that travel time (or *travel cost* in general) is minimized. We call the underlying optimization problem the Elastic Trip-Chain Construction Problem and argued that it is $\mathcal{NP}$-hard. To solve the problem for small instances and to act as a benchmark for future approximation algorithms and meta heuristics, we formulated a MIQCP computing trip chains with least travel time.

Solving the MIQCP is—even for small instances—computational expensive. This not only holds for the MIQCP itself, which has a non-linear objective function but also for pre-computing the model variables. Prior to solving an instance of the problem using the MIQCP, we need to compute $f^{D}_{k,l,t,m}$ and $f^{A}_{k,l,t,m}$ which denote travel times between all locations for all departure and arrival times. As this is not practical for larger instances, future work will focus on finding fast and accurate heuristic algorithms. Further work of practical interest will address an extension of the Elastic Trip-Chain Construction Problem, which will yield multiple trip chains for a set of given activities. This will address those cases where activities are spaced so far from each other (on the time line) that one single trip chain would lead to unacceptably long waiting times between arriving at a site and starting the activity.

Acknowledgment

This work is being partially funded by the German Federal Ministry of Education and Research (BMBF) within the project „Bewertung integrierter Elekromobilität", grant identifier 16EMO0046. The authors would like to thank Mark Andrew and Peter Engel for all the fruitful discussions.

References

[1] C. Hoffmann et al. Bewertung integrierter Mobilitätsdienste mit Elektrofahrzeugen aus Nutzerperspektive. *InnoZ-Baustein*, 11, 2012.

[2] BIE - Bewertung integrierter Elektromobilität. http://www.emobil-sw.de/de/aktivitaeten/aktuelle-projekte/projektdetails/new-content-2.html, [retrieved: 09, 2016].

[3] D. Gavalas et al. A personalized multimodal tourist tour planner. In *Proceedings of the 13th International Conference on Mobile and Ubiquitous Multimedia*, pages 73–80, New York, NY, USA, 2014. ACM.

[4] Wouter Souffriau and Pieter Vansteenwegen. Tourist trip planning functionalities: State–of–the–art and future. In *In Proceedings of the 10th International Conference on Web Engineering ICWE 2010 Workshop*, pages 474–485, Heidelberg, Germany, 2010. Springer.

[5] Fayez F Boctor, Gilbert Laporte, and Jacques Renaud. Heuristics for the traveling purchaser problem. *Computers & Operations Research*, 30(4):491–504, 2003.

[6] Vert.X. http://www.vertx.io, [retrieved: 09, 2016].

Fostering Change of Individual Travel Behavior with Customized Mobility Services

Dominik Galler[a], Christoph Becker[b], Tim Hilgert[c], Martin Kagerbauer[d]

[a] *email: Dominik.Galler@esentri.com, esentri AG, Ettlingen, Germany*
[b] *email:christoph.becker@fzi.de, FZI Research Center for Information Technology, Karlsruhe, Germany*
[c] *email: tim.hilgert@kit.edu, Karlsruhe Institute of Technology, Institute for Transport Studies, Karlsruhe, Germany*
[d] *email: martin.kagerbauer@kit.edu, Karlsruhe Institute of Technology, Institute for Transport Studies, Karlsruhe, Germany*

***Abstract* — The development of new mobility services has progressed rapidly in recent years. Nowadays, users can choose from a variety of different mobility services and constantly new options become available. In this paper, we present the development of a new mobility assistance system that provides decision support for the user in order to facilitate selection of the best suiting means of transportation. Moreover, the impact of new mobility services on the user's individual travel behavior as well as the impact on the transport network in general are elaborated in this paper. The mobility assistance is a distributed system that collects and aggregates data from different providers to offer relevant, context-sensitive information for the user's current situation. Information, such as timetables of public transportation, real time data on delays, availability of car sharing vehicles or traffic congestions are aggregated, refined and then presented to the user. The mobility assistance supports the user regarding route selection, as well as scheduling of activities that are managed within the users' calendar with consideration of different starting times. Moreover, the mobility assistance implements optimization strategies to improve the user's travel needs according to his personal preferences. Activities as well as associated trips during a week can be optimally combined and rescheduled in order to achieve a lower overall travel time or low cost of mobility.**

Keywords: mobility patterns; activity generation; mobility assistance; new mobility services.

I. INTRODUCTION

Technical developments, such as the Internet of Things (IoT) offer the possibility to develop new innovative services for the user [1]. This also applies for the development of new information services in the field of mobility. New mobility services and mobility management systems are becoming increasingly important. Nowadays, users have the possibility to choose from a variety of mobility options for their daily trips [2]. Due to more flexible working arrangements and changing user preferences regarding modes of transportation, new activity patterns can be observed [3]. The variety of mobility options leads to a greater complexity in decision management. Several mobility options can be used in combination and require the users to compare complex alternatives. Hence, customer-oriented services can help users to find optimal solutions regarding trip and schedule planning in consideration of personal preferences. In this paper, we present the development of customer-oriented mobility services and their impact on the users' travel behavior.

As part of the BMBF-funded research project BiE (Evaluation of integrated Electric Mobility), several project partners are involved in the development of new mobility management services to promote the integration and acceptance of electric mobility. Therefore, electric mobility solutions have to be easily available and integrated in everyday life. In addition, they should support the user in the selection and comparison of mobility services and options. The personal mobility assistance system, which offers the user the best possible support to carry out his daily trips is currently under development. It integrates decision support, especially for complex combination of mobility options and scheduling of activities. The information provided comprises data on travel modes, possible routes and starting times of trips. Furthermore, the mobility assistance system reschedules the user's activities of one week to create trip chains that optimize the user's schedule according to individual preferences, generally to minimize travel times, travel costs or environmental pollution.

In this paper, the architecture and functionality of the mobility assistance system are presented and effects on travel behavior are analyzed. Since the mobility assistance can have an impact on the daily mobility (e.g., changing the sequence of activities due to shorter travel times or the combination of several activities into trip chains), there potentially are more effects on individual travel demand or the transport network. To investigate the reorganization of activity patterns in use of such mobility assistance systems a microscopic multi-agent traffic demand model has been extended with a module for synthetic generation of activities. The traffic demand model thus allows the quantification of the mobility assistance's impact on daily mobility.

The rest of the paper is structured as follows. Section II describes the mobility assistance. Therefore, Section II.A provides an introduction into distributed systems and microservice architectures. Then Section II.B discusses the mobility assistances architecture and subsequently, Section II.C goes into finer details with respect to the selected optimization approach. Section III describes how the mobility assistance could impact on travel behavior. Finally, the conclusion and acknowledgements close the paper.

II. MOBILITY ASSISTANCE

The mobility assistance is implemented as distributed system. The system comprises many components that act independently, but co-ordinate their actions in order to provide the required functionality. The coordination is technically based on the exchange of messages over the Internet. For the individual user of the mobility assistance, a mobile application (smartphone app) is provided as a user interface to optimize his personal travel behavior. The optimization is calculated by mobility assistance based on information received from various services (message exchange). These services include real-time information regarding different transportation alternatives, such as the availability of car-sharing vehicles, public transportation, possible delays or traffic congestions. In order to control the system's complexity, the user is only presented with information that is relevant for the current situation and scheduling of future activities. Moreover, the user will receive notifications regarding possible optimizations of his schedule according to his personal preferences. For this purpose, the system monitors the user's calendar and reacts to new events. In addition to the presentation of context related information, the system proposes alternative routes and modes of transportation. This optimization is based on individual user preferences (e.g., minimizing travel time, minimizing travel costs, selection or deselection of certain modes of transportation).

A. *Distributed Systems and Microservice Architectures*

In order to calculate optimal results for each individual user based on distributed heterogeneous data, a complex network of different subsystems is essential. In this connection, two principles of information processing are important: first, the optimization can only be provided by distributed systems and secondly, the state of an information object is subject to a certain degree of uncertainty during the optimization process. The latter is due to CAP theorem known in IT: In distributed systems, where loss of single messages (partition tolerance) can always occur due to network failures, it is not possible to ensure that a changeable data object is available (availability) and that each participant of the distributed system has a consistent (consistency) view on this respective object [4].

Therefore, a distributed system (running the mobility assistance) that relies on distributed data has to provide algorithms that can cope with this degree of uncertainty. For the design of an appropriate software architecture, the most important requirements are extracted: a) real time: the mobility assistance should calculate and present the results (schedule optimization) in (almost) real-time for each user. b) sub-optimal results are acceptable: it is more important to display an improvement than to calculate the absolute optimum. c) scalability: the system must remain functional even with an increasing number of users and data (high load).

Given these requirements, BiE project partners have selected a software architecture that is suitable for a high load and provides a good flexibility regarding future development at the same time. The latter is particularly important because the partners involved in the project focus on different aspects of the mobility assistance. The architecture should support a partner-independent implementation of services. This idea is rooted in the paradigm of service-oriented architecture (SOA). However, SOA is currently subject to an ongoing discussions regarding future development and application, where the concept of microservices attracts a lot of attention [5]. Microservices can be seen as an architectural pattern for the design of distributed software systems. Briefly: microservices are an approach to implement a system based on a large number of small services. This is similar to the primary principle of SOA. However, some more stringent requirements are generally associated with microservices. Within the concept of microservices each service should be carried out independently from other services (own process space), use its own data (database) and offer lightweight communication mechanisms (often REST) to other services. With regard to the size of a service, it is intended to bundle only functionalities within the service, which serve a single business capability. Hence, the scope of a single microservice is very limited, thereby reinforcing basic principles of service-oriented architectures. In particular, loose coupling and separation of concerns can be easily achieved this way. Additionally, microservices strengthen the following principles: intelligent services and basic communication (smart endpoints & dumb pipes), evolutionary design, strict encapsulation (shared nothing), decentralized governance, distributed data storage and automation of infrastructure (build, test and deployment processes).

Unlike traditional SOA, the microservice approach is based on simple communication mechanisms. Instead of a sophisticated Enterprise Service Bus (ESB) microservices rely on the architectural pattern pipes and filters. The intelligent processing of messages takes place within the services (smart endpoint) while the communication is implemented using simple mechanisms like REST or asynchronous messaging. Hence, microservices can be easily replaced by new implementations, thereby following the principle of evolutionary design. Strict encapsulation in turn is an important prerequisite to enable evolutionary design.

These principles allow each project partner to develop functionality independently of other partners. Within the project this enables partners to yield their specialized know-how in the best possible way and allow for algorithms and functions that can be independently developed and deployed. The microservice approach thus enables the implementation of the mobility assistance as distributed system that is capable of performing real-time traffic analysis even under heavy load (number of users). The system is based on so-called reactive microservices adopting the Vert.x framework. The individual services are implemented as verticles in Vert.x. The architecture of Vert.x contributes to a high modularity of the system and facilitates the integration of new services.

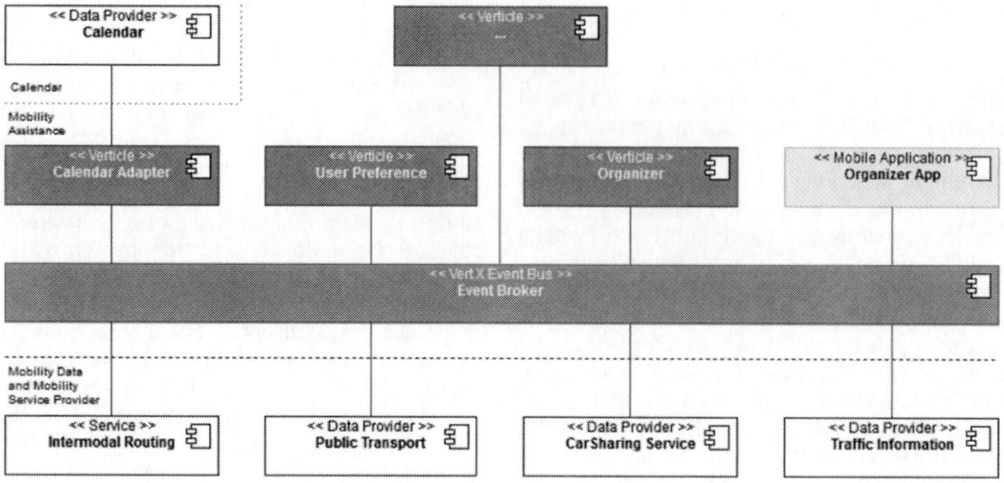

Figure 1. Mobility Assistance Architecture (Overview)

Vert.x itself is a lightweight, event based framework that supports the development of distributed systems. Different programming languages can be used to implement the services as verticle, thereby strengthening the independence of the development team. Each verticle comprises some aspects of the actual application logic of the mobility assistance system. In general, a verticle will respond to an event or create a new event. Communication between the verticles is established via an integrated and distributed bus. Communication takes place through the typical messaging patterns (publish-subscribe or point-to-point).

B. *Architecture of new Mobility Assistance*

The mobility assistance is a complex network of distributed systems and leverages a microservice-based architecture as discussed in Section II.A. In order to provide the required functionality, the mobility assistance makes use different interconnected components/subsystems that have been implemented as microservice (in this context also known as verticle). The components can be classified as follows (see Fig. 1): external data or service provider (white), Vert.x Event Bus (green), services / verticles (blue) and mobile application (yellow).

Moreover, each component illustrated in Fig. 1 can be assigned to specific domain, i.e., a) the mobility assistance domain, b) the mobility data and mobility provider domain and c) the calendar domain. Components within the mobility assistance domain implement the core functionality as well as the communication between different components and the mobile application. The remaining (non-colored) components comprise external domains that provide supporting calendar as well as mobility-related data and functions that are used by the mobility assistance.

C. *Optimization within the Organizer Verticle*

Within the organizer verticle, we developed a service called *calendar optimization service*. Its purpose is to optimize the whole week's schedule of a given user. Before the optimization process itself is presented, the different sources that induce travel demands are discussed.

Travel demands are not solely generated when a user searches actively for a route from point A to point B. More likely, the need for mobility is generated when the user is invited to an appointment and accepts the invitation in the first place. Therefore, the optimization of the user's travel demand doesn't start with the optimization of the routes between his appointments, but rather with optimizing his appointments themselves. Furthermore, there are not only appointments which generate travel demand. Thus, for the sake of simplicity, we will call all schedule elements of the user's week-schedule – regardless of whether they generate travel demand or not – activities.

Keeping this in mind, we divided the users' appointments into two different classes. The first class is the class of activities which cannot be moved in any way, e.g. appointments which involve more than one people or conference calls. The other class is called free activities and contains all other schedule elements that are more or less freely moveable within the week. There are two different subclasses within the free activities. First, there are free activities which have to take place within a certain time frame on a certain day, e.g., from 8am to 3pm on Monday. The second subclass contains free activities which have larger time frames, i.e., they last more than one day. Generally speaking, optimization is achieved when the free activities are arranged optimally around the fixed activities, which – by definition – cannot be moved. During the optimization process it must be guaranteed, that every activity can be reached within the defined time frame.

Within the time frames, activities can be attended by using various means of transport. The means of transportation may differ in departure time, which implies that they can only be used according to their departure time. Aside from this effect, traffic congestions in the morning or evening rush-hours may increase travel times as well as costs. To depict this behavior, we modelled the activities according to the asymmetric time-dependent travelling salesman problem with time windows (TDATSP-TW) as proposed by Albiach, Sanchis and Soler [6] and designed the transformation in accordance with a generalized ATSP (GATSP) presented also in this paper.

Other than Albiach et al. we had no access to CPLEX or other fast solvers for NP-hard problems. Instead of transforming the GATSP into an ATSP like Albiach et al. did, we developed an algorithm to solve the resulting GATSP while leveraging some of the GATSP's characteristics to solve the problem instances.

In order to design the algorithm, the Nearest-Neighbor-Heuristic has been adopted. If a path is found by the heuristic in the reduced GATSP within the reduction presented by Albiach et al., we initialize our algorithm with this path and try to optimize it. Since there might occur many dead ends while cutting out the clusters, the heuristic stops if it leads to a dead end to avoid a brute force solution when there is, e.g., only one feasible path within the graph. After the opening procedure, we try to optimize the initial tour in our algorithm in case an initial tour has been found. In case no initial tour has been found, we compute all feasible solutions otherwise. Therefore, we start with all possible paths from the depot to all of the reachable nodes. For any reachable node, we compute recursively all nodes, which are reachable from this node, and build the paths piece by piece. The termination criterion for the recursion is either reached if the computed path is feasible (i.e., a Hamiltonian Cycle in the GATSP-Graph) and cheaper as the cheapest path found so far, or if the path is infeasible and more expensive than the cheapest feasible path found so far. Within this process, there may occur problems without feasible solutions in the event that the combination of activities consumes more time within one day than the user can afford.

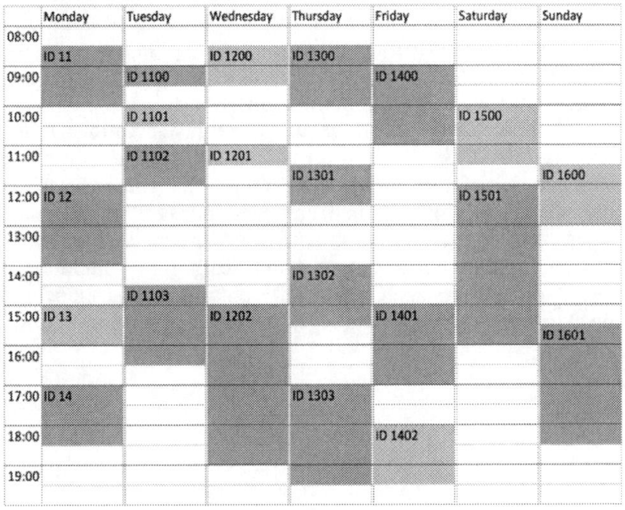

Figure 2. Initial week-schedule

To improve the runtime of the algorithm, we split the problem into various sub-problems, which can be solved on different distributed nodes. Therefore, we build the TDATSP-TW instances by computing all possible combinations of fixed and free activities for a given day. Our algorithm is then applied to each combination and returns a feasible and optimal solution – provided a solution exists – for the combination. Subsequently, the best option within all of the distributed computed solutions we've collected, is selected. The best option contains all activities, violates none of the user's preferences and has, according to the objective function, the lowest value. This solution solves the mentioned optimization problem best and thus is presented to the user.

To demonstrate the power of our solution, we provide the following case study: Since the routing service is needed to compute the edges of our GATSP and the fixed activities are always the same for each combination, we added a cache to this instance. This way, we can save many expensive requests over the network. Furthermore, network accesses, e.g., over HTTP may be slow. Thus, our algorithm was applied two times to the provided example instance. Firstly, with a cold, and then with a hot cache, to show the effect of the travel planning instance in computation time. As travel planning instance, we used Google's Distance-Matrix API [7]. The algorithm was executed on a desktop computer with an Intel i7 4770K CPU and 32GB DDR3 memory.

TABLE I: ACTIVITY SCHEDULING AFTER OPTIMIZATION

	Activity ID	Departure	Arrival	Distance (km)	Costs
Monday	11	08:10	08:20	1,74	2,914
	12	10:00	10:10	2,45	3,582
	13	14:00	14:10	2,32	3,269
	14	15:10	15:30	3,23	4,712
	0	18:30	18:50	4,53	5,944
Tuesday	1100	08:10	08:20	1,75	2,85
	1102	09:30	09:40	0	0,092
	1103	12:00	12:10	0	0,081
	0	16:30	16:40	1,17	2,111
Wednesday	1200	09:40	09:50	1,91	2,671
	1202	10:50	11:10	6,33	6,102
	1101	19:00	19:20	4,26	5,039
	0	19:30	19:40	0,08	0,159
Thursday	1300	08:00	08:20	6,28	7,444
	1301	10:00	10:20	4,55	6,146
	1201	12:30	12:40	2,72	4,033
	1302	12:50	12:50	0	0
	1303	15:30	15:40	2,34	3,653
	0	19:30	19:40	1,17	2,065
Friday	1400	08:40	09:00	6,3	6,166
	1401	11:00	11:20	8	7,394
	1402	17:00	17:20	4,78	5,927
	0	18:50	19:00	0,46	1,004
Saturday	1500	08:00	20:00	26,16	15,673
	1501	10:00	10:30	16,88	13,305
	1600	16:00	16:30	24,74	17,387
	0	18:00	18:10	1,72	2,794
Sunday	1601	08:20	08:30	1,77	2,99
	0	18:30	18:40	1,77	2,5

Fig. 2 shows the initial calendar of the week-schedule, the way any person would probably have planned it. This schedule was optimized using the calendar optimization service. We then optimized this schedule. The solution for the initial calendar was determined by using Google Maps. To compute the total solution, we chose the fastest route between the activities and the highest time value for the time variations presented by Google Maps. The described behavior could also be the one of a real person. Based on the results, we computed the total costs by applying the objective function. This lead to total costs of 164.583. Our algorithm was applied and took 355 seconds with a cold and 6 seconds with a hot cache to perform the optimization. The result was a schedule with total costs of 138.007 thereby leading to cost savings of 26.57 euro. The detailed optimization result is presented in TABLE I. Our algorithm works without penalty costs for arriving too early at the location – which is particularly permitted. However, waiting after the activity has been finished, is strictly forbidden. As a result of our evaluation, one must add penalty costs for waiting in order to avoid arriving way too early. Furthermore, it may be useful to consider waiting after the activity. This way, it's possible to wait, e.g., for an express train or plane, which could lead to a travel route, which is cheaper than all connections directly available.

III. IMPACTS ON TRAVEL BEHAVIOR

As shown above, the mobility assistance is capable – through their functionality – to influence people's travel behavior. This results in adaptions concerning activity chains, as well as influences on destination or mode choice. To quantify the impacts of the assistance on individual travel behavior but also on the transport network we use the agent-based travel demand modeling framework mobiTopp. It has been developed at the Institute for Transport Studies at Karlsruhe Institute of Technology (KIT). The framework simulates the travel demand (all trips within one week) for people – including activity, destination and mode choice – and explicitly takes into account behavioral stability and variability of peoples' travel behavior [8][9]. Within the last years it has been further developed to model also the impacts of new aspects like car sharing or electric vehicles [10][11]. For this work, we are using the mobiTopp framework to simulate the travel demand for the Greater Stuttgart Region in Germany with 2.7 million inhabitants.

To depict the impacts of the mobility assistance, the activity generation part of the model has been enhanced. Using this new module, it is possible to generate week activity schedules synthetically (which person makes what kind of activity how long and at which time). The advantage of the synthetic generation of these schedules is the modelling flexibility. Impacts of the assistance can be mapped directly into the simulation. Impacts of the assistance can also be mapped only to certain user groups and hence to investigate effects on different scenarios.

Fig. 3 shows the interaction between the mobility assistance (right side) and mobiTopp (left side) within the BiE-project. Week activity schedules are generated (see step 1) and then handed over as input to the mobility assistance. These schedules are optimized by the assistance (see step 3 in Fig. 3 or Section II in this paper) given different criteria. Following, adapted schedules feed back to mobiTopp in which they are analyzed concerning the impacts on travel behavior.

Usually the assistance suggests different optimizations of the original activity schedules. Therefore, we analyze different scenarios: First, a scenario where only the cost-minimized schedules are accepted by the agents; second a scenario where only the travel time-minimized plans are accepted and third a scenario where the agents randomly choose between the original schedules and the time- and cost-optimized schedule. Furthermore, we analyzed how the assistance impacts different user groups, e.g., commuters. The analysis of adapted schedules can evaluate changes in travel behavior: What kind of tours are adapted by the assistance? How are these tours changing? For every change in a schedule, the differences to the original schedules can be evaluated. This answers the following questions: How is the number of trips, the trip length and the travel time changing on individual level? How is the infrastructure load changing when a certain market penetration of the assistance is given? How is modal split changing within the system? Does the mobility assistance support sustainability? Does the assistance influence the infrastructure load in peak hours? How do changing trip lengths and modal splits influence the environment? After the implementation phase that is actually ongoing we will investigate these questions.

Further research will be a deeper investigation of the user's acceptance for the suggestions. Do people follow the suggestions of the assistance? Within the BiE-project we investigate only potentials of impacts on travel behavior and optimizations concerning travel times or costs. The travel demand model allows for a good scaling to simulate the usage of the assistance for different users and hence to investigate impacts for some given market penetration rates.

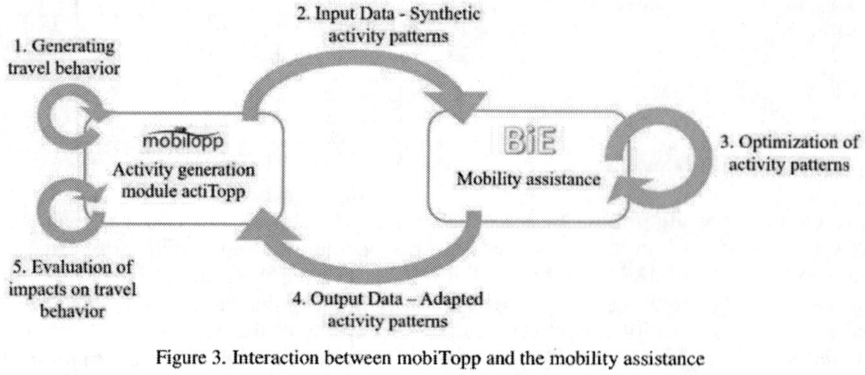

Figure 3. Interaction between mobiTopp and the mobility assistance

IV. Conclusion and Outlook

In recent years, a variety of new mobility services (e.g., multi- or inter-modal traffic management and information systems) have been created enabling users to choose from a wide range of different mobility services and options. To reduce the complexity of current mobility services the need for a customer-oriented assistance system is constantly getting more important. For this purpose, the presented mobility assistance system has been developed.

The mobility assistance gathers and aggregates information from timetables and real time information systems in public transportation, accesses mobility services, such as car sharing as well as the user's calendar and only presents selected information that is relevant in the current situation.

The mobility assistant supports the user in his daily mobility by providing routing information as well as information on alternative modes of transportation and starting times for trips. Depending on the user's individual preference, the mobility assistance may plan and reschedule activities as well as associated trips in the course of a week. To investigate the impact of mobility assistance systems on individual travel behavior, the travel demand model mobiTopp has been used. This allows for an estimation of effects at an individual level as well as network level (e.g., the shifts in the morning peak, when a certain number of people is using the mobility assistance).

As a result, it is expected that users will get better and clearer proposals and adjust their travel behavior accordingly. The proposals regarding schedule optimization will be presented on a mobile device that acts as user interface for the mobility assistance. The effectiveness of such a decision support system can only be achieved on the basis of a decentralized system, which is able to take account of a) information on general traffic situation, b) storage individual user preferences and c) calculation of optimizations regarding scheduling and trip planning. All these functionalities are currently being developed in the research project BiE.

Further research may relate to the development of assistance systems as well as to the analysis of simulated traffic behavior. In further steps for example, the acceptance of the calculated proposals from the mobility assistance system could be examined based on a user survey. In future development steps, the identification of further influencing factors (such as penalty costs for waiting times before and after activities) as well as the incorporation of these factors into the optimization routines could be addressed. Moreover, the current routines could be enhanced with adaptive algorithms (the procedure is adapted based on real-time information). Analysis results (see Section III) could be injected directly into the calculations of the organizer (see Section II.C) and thus improve the decision support offered by the mobility assistance.

Acknowledgements

The project of this publication has been funded by the German Federal Ministry of Education and Research, funding code EM1CLU039. The responsibility for the content is up to the authors.

References

[1] L. Atzori, A. Iera, and G. Morabito, "The Internet of Things: A survey," Computer Networks, vol. 54, no. 15, pp. 2787 – 2805, 2010.

[2] G. Ambrosino, J. D. Nelson, M. Boero, and I. Pettinelli, "Enabling intermodal urban transport through complementary services: From Flexible Mobility Services to the Shared Use Mobility Agency: Workshop 4. Developing inter-modal transport systems," Research in Transportation Economics, 2016.

[3] L. Adams, F. McAndrew, L. Fellows, and S. ALI, "The scope for flexible working in future," 2014. [Online]. Available: https://trid.trb.org/view.aspx?id=1316106. [Accessed: 07-Nov-2016].

[4] A. Fox and E. A. Brewer, "Harvest, yield, and scalable tolerant systems," in *Hot Topics in Operating Systems, 1999. Proceedings of the Seventh Workshop on*, pp. 174–178, 1999.

[5] C. Richardson, "Microservices: Decomposing Applications for Deployability and Scalability," *InfoQ*. [Online]. Available: http://www.infoq.com/articles/microservices-intro. [Accessed: 07-Nov-2016].

[6] J. Albiach, J. M. Sanchis, and D. Soler, "An asymmetric TSP with time windows and with time-dependent travel times and costs: An exact solution through a graph transformation," *Eur. J. Oper. Res.*, vol. 189, no. 3, pp. 789 – 802, 2008.

[7] Google, "Google Distance-Matrix-API," 2014. [Online]. Available: https://developers.google.com/maps/documentation/distance-matrix/?hl=de. [Accessed: 07-Nov-2016].

[8] M. Kagerbauer, N. Mallig, P. Vortisch, and M. Pfeiffer, "Modeling Variability and Stability of Travel Behavior in a Longitudinal View Using the Agent Based Model mobiTopp," in *Transportation Research Board 95th Annual Meeting*, 18p, 2016.

[9] N. Mallig, M. Kagerbauer, and P. Vortisch, "mobiTopp – A Modular Agent-based Travel Demand Modelling Framework," *Procedia Comput. Sci.*, vol. 19, pp. 854 – 859, 2013.

[10] N. Mallig, M. Heilig, C. Weiss, B. Chlond, and P. Vortisch, "Modelling the weekly electricity demand caused by electric cars," *Future Gener. Comput. Syst.*, vol. 64, pp. 140 – 150, 2016.

[11] M. Heilig, N. Mallig, O. Schröder, M. Kagerbauer, and P. Vortisch, "Multiple-day Agent-based Modeling Approach of Station-based and Free-floating Carsharing," in *Transportation Research Board 94th Annual Meeting*, p. 18, 2015.

Mobilty Services – Does Individual Optimization Scale Out?

Thomas Schuster
Faculty for Economy and Law
Pforzheim University of Applied Sciences
Pforzheim, Germany
e-mail: thomas.schuster@hs-pforzheim.de

Maik Herfurth
Global Information Technology
Hilti Befestigungstechnik AG
Buchs SG, Switzerland
e-mail: maik.herfurth@hilti.com

Abstract— **Mobility in industrialized nations is characterized by individual transport. Especially since the 50's of the last century, individual mobility is based on automobility. The age of automobility still influences and shapes the infrastructure development of our cities. While the model of a car-friendly city has evolved a lot, it does not seem to be capable to generate efficient means of transportation. This becomes worse in emerging metropolitan areas with large growth rates. Besides congestion, pollution is a main issue, especially in fast growing metropolitan areas. Nowadays, a lot of new mobility services are offered through the internet. Besides mobility based on cars, these services incorporate intermodal mobility, as well as third domain offers, which may reduce our individual mobility. In this article, we will provide an overview of such services and derive insights about their possible impact.**

Keywords - Mobility; intermodal mobility; sharing economy; e-services

I. INTRODUCTION

Growth of population and increased traffic because of both individual mobility as well as cargo logistics lead to congestion and pollution [1]–[3]. Metropolitan areas, especially, suffer from those effects. A large amount of these issues are caused by automobility. During the 20th century the model of a car-friendly city has been developed and evolved. Especially in industrialized countries, cars dominate infrastructure development. Areas with more than 800.000 inhabitants suffer from congestion peaks as the TomTom Traffic Index [4] indicates. The congestion level (CL) is measured as the increase in overall travel time compared to an uncongested situation. In general, the congestion level (CL) is considerably high, however, the evening peaks (EP) are typically the worst time to commute using a car (compare Tab. 1). Hence, traffic planning and management is usually focused on road planning and construction.

The public sector seeks to implement and promote alternative modes of transport. Public transport for instance is usually subsidized at community, regional or national level. In some countries, e.g., United Kingdom, public-private-partnerships are concluded to operate public transport. Sometimes regulations are made to support alternative transport modes. One famous and successful example is the London congestion charge [5]. It is observed that the charge reduces traffic, which is caused by cars by 14% and congestion, is reduced by 30% [5].

Another example of support for other modes of transport is the regulations that we put in place. In late 1950's, for instance, the ministry of transport in Germany tried to support rail based cargo by reducing maximum size of trucks and trailers. This turned out to be ineffective since manufacturers developed a new type of truck – a smaller driving cab allowed to enlarge loading. Unquestionably, there are a lot of examples where the public sector tried to or successfully influenced the choice of transportation mode of people. On the other hand, looking at individual mobility, costs associated with buying and operating a car decreased, compared to average wage and hence promoted ownership and usage of cars. In this article logistics represent an import part of traffic and we will focus on individual mobility. The remainder of this article is structured as follows: in section 2 we will present some statistics with focus on usage and change on transport modes. Furthermore, we will discuss related work on reduction of traffic congestion. Challenges which arise from these observations will be discussed in section 3. Section 4 deals with services that promise further shift in transport utilization and hence, might be able to improve the overall situation. Finally, section 5 of this article concludes with findings and an outlook on future work.

II. RELATED WORK

In this section we will analyse statistical traffic data and discuss related work. The next subsection contains statistical data about traffic development and mobility behavior of people. Especially, mono modal car utilization and increased intermodal travel behavior. The second sub sections will present typical approaches to reduce congestion levels.

A. *A statistical view on traffic*

Areas with high economic growth rates, often in developing countries, suffer most of the traffic congestion (see Tab. 1 and [1]). Typically, this is related to a significant increase in passenger car use (e.g., as recorded in Turkey). In contrast, the relative importance of the passenger car as main mode of transport in passenger traffic decreased in 13 member states of the EU. This trend is led by Italy (in the period from 2002 to 2012 passenger car share fell by 4.4 percentage points) followed by Luxembourg (2.7 points) and the United Kingdom (2.4 points) and can also be observed in three of the largest EU Member States - Germany, Spain and France. Average numbers of the ten best EU countries are shown in Fig. 1 (also see [6]).

In contrast to some decades ago, people are less attracted by a single mode of transport. While cars are still dominant we observe changes, and growth in alternative modes of transport (e.g., rail and bicycle). Both changes are often related to sharing concepts and internet based mobility services. As shown in Fig. 2, especially young people are increasingly utilizing all modes of transportation [7]. They reveal multimodal travel behavior. Multimodal travel behavior is revealed when people switch their main mode of transport for longer trips (e.g., different trips in the course of one week). Similarly, intermodal travel behavior is becoming more famous. An intermodal trip can be defined as a combination of several transportation modes during a single trip, e.g., a trip with public transport in combination with bicycle or car. Furthermore, different modes of transport seem to be adopted in respect to specific situations (context of travel and personal preferences).

TABLE 1: CONGESTION LEVEL (CL) - TOP 15 CITIES [4]

Rank	City	CL	+/-	MP	EP
1	Mexico City (MEX)	59%	4%	97%	94%
2	Bangkok (THA)	57%	0%	85%	114%
3	Łódź (PL)	54%	-2%	72%	98%
4	Istanbul (TUR)	50%	-8%	62%	94%
5	Rio de Janeiro (BRA)	47%	-4%	66%	79%
6	Moscow (RUS)	44%	-6%	71%	91%
7	Bucharest (ROU)	43%	2%	83%	87%
8	Salvador (BRA)	43%	-3%	67%	74%
9	Recife (BRA)	43%	-2%	72%	75%
10	Chengdu (CHN)	41%	5%	73%	81%
11	Palermo (ITA)	41%	-1%	62%	66%
12	Los Angeles (USA)	41%	2%	60%	81%
13	Saint Petersburg (RUS	40%	-4%	64%	88%
14	Belfast (GBR)	40%	1%	82%	86%
15	Dublin (IRL)	40%	2%	85%	81%

Looking at statistical data available for Europe, it seems that reduction of mono modal car utilization and increased intermodal travel behavior is also related to age and internet affinity. According to Eurostat [6], internet based services also experience higher growth rates in countries which are successful in promoting alternative modes of transport. This, especially, is interesting regarding forecasts of overall modal development. At this time, we know that younger people are more likely to become intermodal travelers. While there is a correlation to adoption of sharing concepts and internet usage. Nevertheless, today it is still not clear if there is also a causal connection. Thus, an open question is, if these people change their behavior once they become older or if they keep their attitude as it is – another possible causal connection might be the level of income or other personal preferences which change with age.

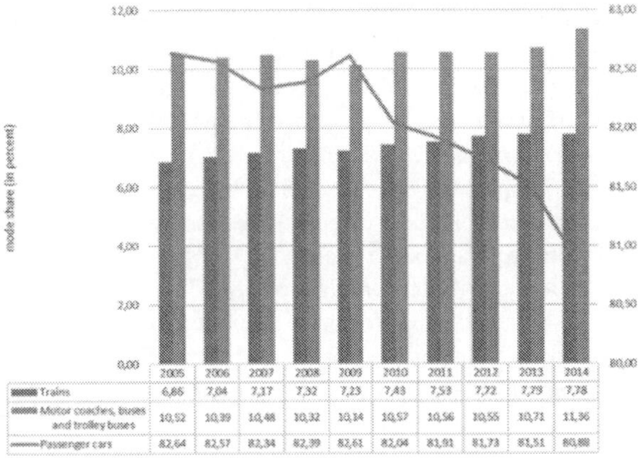

Figure 1: Modal split - Top 10 EU countries in train growth [6]

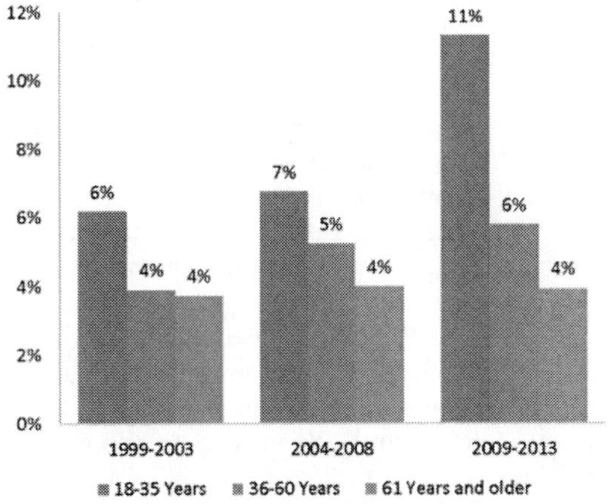

Figure 2: Share of people with multimodal transport behavior

B. Approaches taken to improve traffic flow

Different approaches have been taken to reduce traffic congestion. This incorporates basically three distinct ideas: (1) reducing congestion by upgrading infrastructure, (2) avoiding congestion based on intelligent routing and (3) reducing congestion through alternative services. The latter includes the idea of utilizing different transportation modes and the concept of services to reduce the need for individual mobility.

In this case, changes in infrastructure belong to the field of urban or regional traffic planning and management. Within the last decades a lot of research based on predictive analytics and methods of operations research has been conducted to improve traffic planning. Traffic models to support infrastructure planning characteristically recognize individual behavior (including when, where and why a user will travel). In a second step individual behavior is aggregated to an overall network behavior which can provide information for sound decisions concerning management, control, and improvement of traffic infrastructure [8], [9]. On behalf of the society, these calculations are utilized to make decisions for public investments. Hence, traffic planning is typically based on a hierarchical process [8], [10], where decisions made by the public sector seek improvements of the overall performance of the traffic network. Since many people travel by car, a lot of these efforts lead to road construction.

Since people tend to make their choice with regards to activity, route, travel mode, origin and destination of their travel and of course personal preferences, a lot of research has been conducted about route optimization [8]. This area of optimization research does not focus on individual mobility, but rather on cargo transport. For cargo and larger fleets, route optimization can save time and cost for carriers. Of course, if routes are optimal in terms of fuel consumption, the carbon dioxide emission is also reduced. Intelligent routing has been under research since almost 50 years. It includes the idea of re-routing based on the current traffic situation and pre-trip planning based on traffic prediction. The presumption for route guidance based on real-time traffic information is that traffic congestion can be reduced by intelligent routing [11]. A lot of different algorithms and types of presentation have been tested during the last decades [12]. This development was initiated by large metropolitan areas during 60's and early 70's, which began to develop and test technologies for traffic surveillance and real-time information dissemination. Nowadays the transportation development is driven by information based on Wi-Fi networks, smartphones and other GPS devices (e.g., car integrated systems) which are utilized by modern information systems and their operators – here navigation, e.g., TomTom or Google just to name a few of them [13]–[15]. It has been agreed that there is a saturation effect once information is used by a certain amount of users [16]. Therefore, routing algorithms have also been extended with parking models [17], [18] and ad-hoc mode switches [19]–[22]. Alongside several approaches have been suggested in logistics, including routing, as well as alternative transportation modes [20], [23]–[25].

Information can cause drivers to change departure times in such a way that influences congestion. Besides intelligent routing and information systems, there is another psychological aspect. Users tend to adopt suggestions once their preferences are met. This includes the design of user interface, transportation mode (in case of ad-hoc switch), cost, approximate delay, and driver comfort [12].

III. Challenges and Motivation

On one hand, in many metropolitan areas people seem to accept that they have to deal with congestion during their daily routine. Nevertheless, with high growth rates this situation even turns worse. On the other hand, looking at current growth rates of metropolitan areas and reports on traffic congestion as discussed above, it seems obvious that new solutions are needed to improve the overall mobility situation. A couple of different challenges can be derived from these issues, which apply for regions all over the globe. Amongst others, four important challenges to overcome the current problems are:

1. Service offerings to reduce mobility demand
2. Congestion level reduction
3. Options of traffic mode enlargement
4. Carbon dioxide emission reduction

If services reduce the need to travel, this would be probably the easiest solution to reduce congestion and pollution. Surrounded by current discussions on industry 4.0 and digitalization, services could transform work and life in ways which reduce travel activities because of meetings or even prevent daily commuting. Some services might just reverse current principles, so that users receive goods instead of actively obtaining them [20], [26]. Others, e.g., video conferencing or telework, promise to reduce mobility in general. The latter seems promising, but despite further development in technology, the effects in recent years where considerably low. Hence, and even in car-characterized metropolitan areas, new and alternative mobility services can be observed currently. These services are often related to sharing concepts where people either share their own goods (in this case, usually a car) with others or a commercial provider offers goods to share. This idea gains an increasing popularity in recent years.

IV. Mobility Services

Looking at the service level, it can be observed that mobility services are offered for various kinds of purposes. Within this article, we intend to have a closer look at one very promising kind, the so called *mobility services* (mobility-as-a-service or MaaS) which have been proposed and promoted as approach to achieve more sustainable transportation [27]. We strive to shed light in the current market situation, especially reachability and possible impacts are part of our exploration. MaaS are typically associated with a shift away from personally owned towards mobility solutions consumed as a service. To enact MaaS, services are currently offered by public and private transportation providers often employing a unified gateway that creates and manages trips. Opposed to subscriptions (e.g., a monthly fee), users can often pay per use, e.g., per trip based on time and distance. MaaS is offered for both people and goods. For individual mobility it often encompasses individual preferences which are considered in offers and planning of trips. Currently, mobility service offers are quite diversified and often related to sharing economy, examples are ridesharing, car sharing, carpooling, bike sharing, as well as on-demand pop-up bus services. In this article, mobility services of the following categories are further analyzed: car sharing, ridesharing, carpooling and multimodal trip planning. We will provide a definition for all of these service categories.

Carsharing is an umbrella term that covers multiple types of sharing. Carsharing (US) or car clubs (UK) is a model of car rental where people rent cars for short periods of time, often by the hour. They are attractive to customers who only occasional use a vehicle, as well as those who like to have occasional access to vehicles of a different type than they use day-to-day. The provider renting the vehicle may be a commercial business or the users may be organized as a company, public agency, cooperative, or ad hoc grouping. In consequence, car sharing includes B2B, B2C and C2C offerings including informal peer-to-peer (P2P) arrangements. Cars may be available at fixed stations (dedicated parking spots) or on a free-floating basis, which allows users to drop their vehicle at any legal spot within a defined zone. Currently, car sharing is taking hold in large urban areas. The global usage of car sharing is rapidly growing in recent years. As measured by number of vehicles, the growth rate was over 800% over a period of eight years (2006 to 2014). As measured in number of users, the growth was even 1400% in the same period [28]. More recent press releases seem to confirm this development. The largest markets currently are the Asia-Pacific region (including Australia, China, Hong Kong, Japan, Malaysia, New Zealand, Singapore, South Korea, and Taiwan), Europe (including Turkey and Russia) and North America (including Canada and the United States). Besides classic combustion engines, more and more electrically powered cars are being operated by carsharing providers.

Ridesharing, as second type of service, involves being driven rather than driving, and has existed on an informal basis for as long as there have been cars. Ridesharing has evolved into organized taxi services and more recently, into new models such as offered by companies like Uber or Lyft. *Carpooling* is the best way of reducing costs by sharing a car, which are divided among the occupants, and also reducing the number of vehicles on the road, with the corresponding reduction in pollution, consumption, accidents and parking problems [18], [29]. *Multimodal trip planning* services are smart travel assistance tools which provide pre- and on-trip travel planning. Information provided to the customer is usually planning data of public transport often enriched with real-time traffic information. The services offer information such as road network and traffic conditions. Data is typically collected from various mobility providers and often is provided with real-time precision [30].

We analyzed 51 mobility services within these categories. We included those services which have emerged in the last five years and could sustain on the mobility market. It is notable that most services somehow incorporate sharing concepts. We are classifying these mobility services into the following groups:

- *Peer-to-peer sharing services (P2P)*: private peer-to-peer arrangements to rent private owned vehicles. Typically, a mobility provider offers a marketplace.
- *Sharing service providers (B2C)*: professional mobility providers offer (rental) vehicles in station-based or free-floating models.
- *Ridesharing services (B2C)*: professional mobility providers act as a broker to provide driving services with private and business cars.
- *Carpooling services (P2P)*: Individuals are sharing a car together. Mobility providers offer a marketplace.
- *Multimodal trip planning services (B2C)*: Mobility providers are providing trip planning by offering multimodal mobility.

The analyzed mobility services are characterized by different types of services (see Tab. 1). A huge potential is given by business car rental services (32% of analyzed services). Bike and car sharing services experience huge growth rate followed by private car rental services (18%) and private car lifts (13%). Most of these mobility services can be requested instantly (55%) and are also provided as planned request (45%). 80% of the offered mobility services are single transportation mode, 20% are multi transportation mode.

Currently, the majority of multimodal services are information only services. This means they provide information but booking is not an option. Looking at geography, most of the mobility services we analyzed are provided in Germany only (25%), followed by global services and in Europe operating services (20%) and those offered in US (14%).

V. Conclusion

Recently, it is noteworthy that a lot of mobility services have been placed on the market. It is also expected that this market will be consolidated and may reach saturation. This also depends on viable or publicly subsidized (e.g., bike sharing in Germany) business models. Looking at the identified categories, various peer-to-peer sharing services with similar mobility service offerings which include acting as agency for private cars, providing a marketplace, assurance services and personal user reviews can be observed.

TABLE 2: MOBILITY SERVICES

		Mobility service	Service Type	Belongs to	Service range	Distance	Information
Peer-to-Peer car sharing services		getaround	private car sharing		US	s,m,l	200.000 users
		turo	private car sharing		US	s,m,l	
		drivy	private car sharing		Europe	s,m,l	38.000 cars
		tamyca	private car sharing		Germany	s,m,l	
		carunity	private car sharing	Opel (operated by	Germany	s,m,l	
		SnappCar	private car sharing		Europe	s,m,l	
		Ryde	private car sharing		Asia	s,m,l	
Sharing service providers	Car	Mavendrive	car sharing		US	s,m,l	
		Autolib	e-car sharing		France	s,m,l	3.000 electric cars, 6.600 charging stations
		Orix	car sharing		Japan	s,m,l	
		Park24	car sharing		Japan	s,m,l	
		eCar	car sharing	Citroen	Germany	s,m,l	250 e-cars
		EVCARD	e-car sharing		China	s,m,l	1.500 e-cars
		Car2Go	car & e-car sharing	Daimler	Global	s,m,l	14.500 cars, 1.600 e-cars, 1.900.000 users
		mobility	car sharing		Switzerland	s,m,l	
		finkster	car sharing	Deutsche Bahn	Europe	s,m,l	6.000 cars, 300.000 users
		stadtmobil	car & e-car sharing		Germany	s,m,l	4.000 cars, 52.000 users
		zipcar	car sharing	AVIS	Global	s,m,l	
		DriveNow	car & e-car sharing	BMW, SIXT	Europe	s,m,l	4.700 cars, 500.000 users
		ReachNow	car & e-car sharing	BMW	US	s,m,l	
		cambio carsharing	car & e-car sharing		Europe	s,m,l	4.600 cars, 79.600 users
	Scooter	eMio	e-scooter		Germany	s,m	
		COUP	e-scooter		Germany	s,m	
		Yugo	scooter		Spain	s,m	
		motit	scooter		Europe	s,m	
		scoo.me	scooter		Germany	s,m	
		scoot	scooter		US	s,m	
	Bike	nextbike	bicycle		Germany	s	
		Call a Bike	bicycle	Deutsche Bahn	Germany	s	
		MeinRad	bicycle		Germany	s	
		MVG Rad	bicycle		Germany	s	1.200 bikes
		bikesurf	bicycle		Global	s	
		BbikeMi	bicycle		Italy	s	
		Bycyklen	bicycle		Danemark	s	
Ridesharing services		uber	marketplace		Global	s,m,(l)	160.000 drivers
		taxi magic / curb	cab marketplace		US	s,m,(l)	50.000 taxis, 100.000 drivers, 65 cities
		mytaxi	cab marketplace	Daimler	Germany	s,m,(l)	45.000 taxis
		GroundLink	limousine marketplace		Global	s,m,(l)	45.000 cars
Carpooling services		lyft	car pool marketplace		Global	m,l	collecting Starbucks points
		bla bla car	car pool marketplace		Europe	m,l	
		karzoo	car pool marketplace		Europe	m,l	
		mitfahren	car pool marketplace		Europe	m,l	
		e-carpooling	car pool marketplace		Switzerland	m,l	
		drive2day	car & train pool marketplace		Europe	m,l	shared train rides
		via	car pool marketplace		US	m,l	
Multimodal services		Ridescout / Moovel	mobility information platform	Daimler	Global	s,m,l	
		SBB Trip Planner	mobility information platform	SBB	Switzerland	m,l	
		TripIt	mobility information platform	SAP	Global	l	110 countries
		TripCase	mobility information platform		Global	l	30 Mio trips, 40 airlines
		WorldMate	mobility information platform		Global	l	
		Qixxit	mobility information platform	Deutsche Bahn	Germany	s,m,l	meta service, partial ticket booking

Sharing service providers usually offer a single transport mode and thus, differ into bike, scooter and car sharing. While a lot of services offer the same concept, the saturation of the consumer demand is not reached yet. Additionally, and still in growth stage with rising demand, car sharing services are also provided or supported by major car manufacturers, e.g., Daimler (Car2Go) or BMW (DriveNow, ReachNow). Another car sharing service, flinkster, is even operated by Deutsche Bahn (German railroad provider). The traditional sharing business model (B2C) is difficult to scale geographically, especially to neighborhoods with lower population densities. Operators must accept fixed costs for purchase or lease of vehicles in the fleet. In contrast to that, peer-to-peer (P2P) sharing allows to rent pre-existing vehicles on a short-term basis. Most privately owned vehicles sit idle more than 90% of the day. Thus, P2P carsharing alleviates upfront costs and is more economically consistent with lower-density neighborhoods than traditional sharing. Currently carsharing services are a niche transportation option for certain demographic groups. Today, typical participants live in urban neighborhoods with medium to high household densities [31]. As a result, P2P carsharing provides greater potential for car accessibility than traditional carsharing does [32].

Unquestionable, the congestion-relief potential of sharing rises with the number of services and users. While currently bike sharing possesses even higher growth rates, carsharing has the potential to reduce the number of cars on the road significantly [31]. Carsharing business models have evolved to include both point-to-point and round-trip systems, while parking options have expanded to include both on-street and dedicated spaces in an increasing number of new developments so carsharing networks become denser and more ubiquitous. The shift in consumer preferences will further broaden the appeal of sharing.

Looking at customer level, multimodal trip planning services hold a great potential, but currently they suffer from missing booking opportunities and thus, do not unfold their full potential [22]. These services are capable to integrate all other service types. To reach this they need to be more than just information services. An interesting and promising development are multimodal mobility services supported by public transportation providers (e.g. Deutsche Bahn and SBB) in extension to their traditional business model. In summary, we identified four aspects that influence mobility services:

(1) The mobility behavior of users is changing

(2) The offer of mobility services is increasing

(3) Catalyzer effect – traditional mobility providers are joining the services market

(4) Products and services are converging

The demand for mobility services is growing since progressively, more users are using the advantage of new service types for flexible mobility instead of using individual private or public transportation modes. The amount of mobility providers is still increasing and many providers are on the market offering the same services. So far and due to market growth, this competition did not lead to a consolidation of providers yet. To participate in growth rates traditional public transportation providers and car manufacturers also enter the market for new mobility services. Instead of just selling products, cars are evolving to product service systems.

VI. Outlook

A lot of research and experimentation has been conducted to reduce traffic congestion. Nevertheless congestion is still a big issue around the globe. In consequence, numerous techniques have been applied to tackle this problem. A very promising one is coming up with combined ubiquity of internet connection and mobility e-services. As discussed these services include pre- and on-trip planning, real-time information, ticketing, mode-switch, and unquestionably re-routing. Currently services which enact intermodal mobility and just in time ticketing experience high growth rates.

While today a lot of different services are present we expect a future market consolidation. We could already observe consolidation in the long distance bus market, as well as in carsharing services. More recent service types, such as electric recharging stations or multimodal information and ticketing services, are still uprising and plenty of new providers urge to market. As next steps, we plan to collect more data on services. We intend to look into two different aspects: usage (individual behavior and preferences) and markets. Regarding market development, we plan to broaden our services analysis, especially with an extended analysis of the Asian market. This will provide insights on success factors of services, as well as on people's behavior. Furthermore, we plan to observe the development of intermodal behavior and services market development over a longer period of time. Therefore, we intend to establish an open database to store and to provide information on mobility services. Besides individual mobility, which is our main interest, we consider to broaden this to logistic services.

References

[1] A. T. H. Chin, 'Containing air pollution and traffic congestion: Transport policy and the environment in Singapore', *Atmos. Environ.*, vol. 30, no. 5, pp. 787–801, Mar. 1996.

[2] K. Zhang and S. Batterman, 'Air pollution and health risks due to vehicle traffic', *Sci. Total Environ.*, vol. 450–451, pp. 307–316, Apr. 2013.

[3] J. Beaudoin, Y. H. Farzin, and C.-Y. C. Lin Lawell, 'Public transit investment and sustainable transportation: A review of studies of transit's impact on traffic congestion and air quality', *Res. Transp. Econ.*, vol. 52, pp. 15–22, Oct. 2015.

[4] 'TomTom Traffic Index'. [Online]. Available: http://www.tomtom.com/en_gb/trafficindex/list. [Accessed: 18-Sep-2016].

[5] 'Central London Congestion Charging - Impacts Monitoring, Sixth Annual Report, July 2008.

[6] 'Passenger transport statistics - Statistics Explained'. [Online]. Available: http://ec.europa.eu/eurostat/statistics-explained/index.php/Passenger_transport_statistics. [Accessed: 27-Sep-2016].

[7] Karlsruhe Institute of Technology (KIT), Institute for Transport Studies, 'Results of the German Mobility Panel (MOP)'. Sep. 2016.

[8] A. Migdalas, 'Bilevel programming in traffic planning: Models, methods and challenge', J. Glob. Optim., vol. 7, no. 4, pp. 381–405, May 1995.

[9] P. T. Harker and T. L. Friesz, 'Bounding the solution of the continuous equilibrium network design problem', Proc. Ninth Int. Symp. Transp. Traffic Theory Delft, 1984.

[10] S. de Luca, 'Public engagement in strategic transportation planning: An analytic hierarchy process based approach', *Transp. Policy*, vol. 33, pp. 110–124, May 2014.

[11] R. Arnott, A. de Palma, and R. Lindsey, 'Does providing information to drivers reduce traffic congestion?', *Transp. Res. Part Gen.*, vol. 25, no. 5, pp. 309–318, Sep. 1991.

[12] J. L. Adler and V. J. Blue, 'Toward the design of intelligent traveler information systems', *Transp. Res. Part C Emerg. Technol.*, vol. 6, no. 3, pp. 157–172, Jun. 1998.

[13] L. De Cicco, G. Carlucci, and S. Mascolo, 'Experimental Investigation of the Google Congestion Control for Real-time Flows', in Proceedings of the 2013 ACM SIGCOMM Workshop on Future Human-centric Multimedia Networking, New York, NY, USA, pp. 21–26, 2013.

[14] G. Carlucci, L. De Cicco, S. Holmer, and S. Mascolo, 'Analysis and Design of the Google Congestion Control for Web Real-time Communication (WebRTC)', in Proceedings of the 7th International Conference on Multimedia Systems, New York, NY, USA, p. 13, 2016.

[15] R.-P. Schafer, et al., 'A Study of TomTom's Probe Vehicle Data with Three-phase Traffic Theory', Traffic Eng. Control, vol. 52, no. 5, 2011.

[16] H. S. Mahmassani and P. S.-T. Chen, 'Comparative assessment of origin-based and en-route real-time information under alternative user behavior rules', Transp. Res. Rec., no. 1306, pp. 69-81, 1991.

[17] R. Arnott and E. Inci, 'An integrated model of downtown parking and traffic congestion', *J. Urban Econ.*, vol. 60, no. 3, pp. 418–442, Nov. 2006.

[18] M. Fosgerau and A. de Palma, 'The dynamics of urban traffic congestion and the price of parking', *J. Public Econ.*, vol. 105, pp. 106–115, Sep. 2013.

[19] K. F. Abdelghany and H. S. Mahmassani, 'Dynamic trip assignment-simulation model for intermodal transportation networks', *Transp. Res. Rec. J. Transp. Res. Board*, vol. 1771, no. 1, pp. 52–60, 2001.

[20] V. Giannikas and D. McFarlane, 'Product Intelligence in Intermodal Transportation: The Dynamic Routing Problem', in Dynamics in Logistics, H.-J. Kreowski, B. Scholz-Reiter, and K.-D. Thoben, Eds. Springer Berlin Heidelberg, pp. 59–69,2013.

[21] A. Caris, C. Macharis, and G. K. Janssens, 'Decision support in intermodal transport: A new research agenda', *Comput. Ind.*, vol. 64, no. 2, pp. 105–112, Feb. 2013.

[22] E. Eryilmaz, M. Kagerbauer, T. Schuster, and O. Wolf, 'Collaborative Management of Intermodal Mobility', in Collaborative Systems for Smart Networked Environments, pp. 713–721, Oct. 2014.

[23] T. G. Crainic, N. Ricciardi, and G. Storchi, 'Models for Evaluating and Planning City Logistics Systems', *Transp. Sci.*, vol. 43, no. 4, pp. 432–454, Nov. 2009.

[24] U. Kohler, 'An innovating concept for city-logistics', in Mobility for Everyone. 4th World Congress On Intelligent Transport Systems, 21-24 October 1997, Berlin, 1997.

[25] E. Taniguchi and R. G. Thompson, *City Logistics: Mapping The Future*, 1st ed. CRC Press, 2014.

[26] A. L. Osório, L. M. Camarinha-Matos, and H. Afsarmanesh, 'Enterprise collaboration network for transport and logistics services', in Working Conference on Virtual Enterprises, pp. 267–278, 2013.

[27] J. Sochor, I. C. Karlsson, and H. Strömberg, 'Trying out mobility as a service: Experiences from a field trial and implications for understanding demand', in *Transportation Research Board 95th Annual Meeting*, 2016.

[28] 'Carsharing - Statista-Dossier', *Statista*. [Online]. Available: https://de.statista.com/statistik/studie/id/9904/dokument/carsharing-statista-dossier/. [Accessed: 26-Sep-2016].

[29] N. T. Fellows and D. E. Pitfield, 'An economic and operational evaluation of urban car-sharing', *Transp. Res. Part Transp. Environ.*, vol. 5, no. 1, pp. 1–10, Jan. 2000.

[30] N. Borole, D. Rout, N. Goel, P. Vedagiri, and T. V. Mathew, 'Multimodal Public Transit Trip Planner with Real-time Transit Data', *Procedia - Soc. Behav. Sci.*, vol. 104, pp. 775–784, Dec. 2013.

[31] E. Martin and S. Shaheen, 'The impact of carsharing on household vehicle ownership', *ACCESS Mag.*, vol. 1, no. 38, 2011.

[32] R. Hampshire and C. Gaites, 'Peer-to-peer carsharing: Market analysis and potential growth', *Transp. Res. Rec. J. Transp. Res. Board*, no. 2217, pp. 119–126, 2011.

SVM Methods in Image Segmentation

Tian Chi Zhang
College of computer science and technology
Harbin Engineering University
Harbin, China
e-mail: zhangtianchi@hrbeu.edu.cn

Jing Yang
College of computer science and technology
Harbin Engineering University
Harbin, China
e-mail: yangjing@hrbeu.edu.cn

Jian Pei Zhang
College of computer science and technology
Harbin Engineering University
Harbin, China
e-mail: zhangjianpei@hrbeu.edu.cn

Jing Zhang
College of computer science and technology
Harbin Engineering University
Harbin, China
e-mail: zhangjing@hrbeu.edu.cn

Abstract—**Support Vector Machine (SVM) is playing an increasingly important role in image segmentation methods, especially, in the medical image processing. There are many modified methods based on SVM. In this paper, SVM methods, including modified SVM methods in medical image segmentation within the last five years are reviewed. A comparison and analysis among the papers is presented, and conclusions and future research framework are suggested with the aim of helping researchers to determine their own research framework, method and content.**

Keywords- visualization technique; image segmentation; SVM

I. INTRODUCTION

Among visualization techniques, no matter in which research area, such as sea or wave image visualization, medical image visualization etc., image segmentation is the key and basic technique to achieve an exact and clear object contour of the key features in the frame. That is, image segmentation aims at dividing an image into different sub-images with different characteristics and extracts some interesting objects [1]. The most essential and important content of research on segmentation is to cluster the nodes set. It is a key technique because the quality of cluster results affects the quality of image object segmentation and recognition. The main application field of image segmentation is medical image [2]. Medical images themselves are very uncertain and inaccurate. But the accurate and certain segmentation of objects in medical image is important for object recognition [3]. In recent years, some experts made efforts to apply all kinds of clustering or classification methods in image segmentation, especially for Support Vector Machines (SVM). SVM algorithm shows excellent segmentation performance, which has been successfully extended from basic task of classification [4]. Unlike other methods, which minimize the empirical training error, SVM makes use of the structure risk minimization and can be combined with other methods to obtain a good performance in image segmentation.

In the following section, we firstly review the researches and methods of SVM in image segmentation within the last five years. Secondly, the comparison between SVM and other artificial intelligence methods is proposed. Finally, conclusions and a suggested framework for future research are presented.

II. RESEARCHES AND METHODS

This section is composed of two subsections in order to make it more comprehensible for the reader. In the first subsection, modified SVM methods in general image analysis within the last five years are reviewed. In the second part, modified SVM methods in medical image segmentation are analysed. Papers in both parts are structured in a historical and technical sequence.

A. SVM Image Segmentation

In recent years, with new theories and new methods appearing constantly, more and more modified SVM methods have achieved good effect in image segmentation [5]. We are going to review the modified SVM methods from the last five years, in a chronological sequence. Yang [6] presented an effective colour image segmentation approach based on pixel classification with least squares support vector machine (LS-SVM). Both pixel-level colour feature and texture feature were used as input of LS-SVM model (classifier), and the LS-SVM model (classifier) was trained by selecting the training samples with Arimoto entropy thresholding. Zheng [7] proposed a novel algorithm for blind watermarking by applying singular value decomposition and LS-SVM into watermark embedding and detection. Both of them proposed or utilize the method of LS-SVM. Zhang [8] studied genetic algorithm-support vector machine (GA-SVM) and used K-fold Cross Validation (K-CV) method to determine the hyper-parameters (c, g) of SVM. He studied a method of GA-SVM. Bai [9] proposed a novel visual saliency based SVM approach for automatic training data selection and object segmentation, namely, Saliency-SVM. Cheng [10] inspired by the idea of divide-and-conquer approach and discriminatively trained SVM model for object detection introduced a method of training with a mixture of weighted SVM models and Expectation Maximization (EM) algorithms. The weighted SVM with logistic function converts prediction score into pseudo-probability. Turker [11] mixed the image pixel's texture features, Maximum local energy, Maximum gradient and Maximum second moment matrix to segment colour images based on the trained LS-SVM model (classifier). Both abovementioned works modified SVM by Maximum feature in image. He et al. [12] presented an integrated approach which was the integration of SVM classification, Hough transformation and perceptual grouping for the automatic extraction of rectangular-shape and circular-shape buildings from high-resolution optical space borne images. That is, integrated method can be successfully used in modified SVM.

To summarise, there are studies about the modified methods of singular value decomposition and least squares support vector machine, GA-SVM, training mixture of weighted SVM models and EM algorithm, Saliency-SVM, LS-SVM, Maximum local energy adding Maximum gradient and Maximum second moment matrix of LS-SVM, Hough transformation and perceptual grouping for the automatic extraction feature with SVM. All the methods above can be grouped into two types; one of the groups is formed by SVM methods mixed with other artificial methods, such as GA-SVM. The other group modifies parameters or function in SVM, such as LS-SVM method, which modifies function in SVM. These modified SVM methods aim at obtaining effective image segmentation, searching for parameters to determine hyper-parameters (c, g) of SVM in order to achieve automatic training data selection and automatic feature extraction. In a word, researchers seek automatic and effective image segmentation. However, for medical image segmentation, the most important thing is not effectiveness or automatic segmentation, but accuracy [13]-[20]. Methods for medical image segmentation that aim at offering accurate results are described in the following paragraphs.

B. *Medical Image Segmentation*

For medical image segmentation, Wu [21] introduced an automated method, which was called prior feature Support Vector Machine-Markov Random Field (pSVMRF) to segment three-dimensional mouse brain Magnetic Resonance Microscopy (MRM) images. In her study, pSVMRF reduced training and testing time for SVM while boosting segmentation performance. Segmentation accuracy for new strains is 80% for hippocampus and caudate putamen, indicating that pSVMRF is a promising and exact approach for phenotyping mouse models of human brain disorders. Alajlan [22] used an ensemble of linear support vector machine classifiers (SVMs) for classifying a subject as either patient or normal control. Image voxels were first ranked based on the voxel wise t-statistics between the voxel intensity values and class labels. Then voxel subsets were selected based on the rank value using a forward feature selection scheme. Finally, an SVM classifier was trained on each subset of image voxels. The class label of a test subject was calculated by combining individual decisions of the SVM classifiers using a voting mechanism. Varol [23] presented a class of nonlinear kernel SVMs admits approximate classifiers with runtime and memory complexity that was independent of the number of support vectors. The class of kernels, which they referred to as additive kernels, included being widely used kernels for histogram-based image comparison, such as intersection and chi-squared kernels. Additive kernel SVMs can offer significant improvements in accuracy over linear SVMs on a wide variety of tasks while having the same runtime, making them practical for largescale recognition or real-time detection tasks. Shao [24] proposed method essentially generates new synthetic support vectors (SVs) from the obtained by training a standard SVM with the available label samples. Then, original and transformed SVs were used for training the virtual SVM. They incorporated invariances to rotations and reflections of image patches for improving contextual classification. Then, added an invariance to object scale in patch-based classification. They also focused on the challenging problem of including illumination invariances to deal with shadows in the images. Very good results were obtained when few label samples were available for classification. The obtained classifiers revealed enhanced sparsity and robustness. Interestingly, the methodology can be applied to any maximum-margin method, thus constituting a new research opportunity. Maji [25] has presented an improved SVM method, which combined the SVM with the canny algorithm, the morphological algorithm and the fixed circle method to obtain a better segmentation result. In addition, the initial image was pre-processed by using the image contrast enhancement and median filtering. L [26] developed an improved support vector machine (SVM) framework to segment hepatic tumour from CT data. By this method, the one-class SVM (OSVM) and two classes SVM (TSVM) were connected seamlessly by a boosting tool, to tackle the tumour segmentation via both offline and online learning. An initial tumour region was first presented by an OSVM classifier. Then the boosting tool was employed to automatically generate the negative (non-tumour) samples, according to certain criteria.

As a summary, these are the most common modified SVM methods: prior feature Support Vector Machine-Markov Random Field (pSVMRF), SVM adding canny algorithm, morphological algorithm and the fixed circle method, additive kernels in SVM, new SVs in SVM, aggregate the obtained set of spectro-spatial maps used in SVM and boosting tool adding SVM. We divide the methods above into two groups: the first group is an improved method by adding medical image features, such as method of pSVMRF; the second group is a modified method and then applied to medical image segmentation, such as additive kernels in SVM. All the modified SVM methods aim at offering the results of accurate, fast clinical and automatic segmentation.

III. COMPARISON AND ANALYSIS

In this section, we firstly make a comparison between SVM and other typical artificial intelligence methods in image segmentation, such as, GA, K-means clustering and neural networks (NN), finally, the analysis of modified SVM methods is presented.

There are many image segmentation methods, which are based on difference theories and principles. This work will review the methods of Genetic algorithm (GA), K-means and NN to compare with SVM. GA [27] is a metaheuristic algorithm inspired by the process of natural selection that belongs to the larger class of evolutionary algorithms (EA). The principles of genetic algorithms are that they use the operators such as mutation, crossover and selection to achieve optimization. It is commonly used to generate high-quality solutions to optimization and search problems. Actually it combines with other methods to segment images. K-means [28] is a kind of cluster method; it segments images by the theory of grouping or dividing pixels in an image into a set. The principle of this method is that it partitions n pixels into k clusters in which each pixels belongs to the cluster with the nearest mean. K-means is a cluster method, not good at classification. Neural network [29] is the theory of self-studying and fault-to-learnt, it utilizes the training and learning method to segment images. Its principle is that it has the capacity of parallel computing, distributed saving and nonlinear function approximating. Before applying NN to segmentation, it requests large samples to be learned, so it has the limitation of the need of training techniques.

Compared with the above mentioned methods of optimization, clustering and learning, SVM [30] is a classification method. It classifies pixels into one-class, two or many classes. The aim of image segmentation is to classify an image into one, two or more classes. So from the point of theory and principle, the advantages of SVM are that it is more suitable to segment images. The disadvantage of SVM is that it is not sensitive to noise that leads to the inexact segmentation. The advantages or disadvantages of them are analyzed in Table I.

TABLE I. COMPARISON AMONG SEGMENTATION METHODS

	SVM	GA	K-means	NN
Advantages	Fit to classify and segment	Can optimizate	Suit to group	Can Train and learn
Disadvantages	Not exact	Not accurate	Not accurate	Learn ahead
Result	Good	Limited	Limited	Limited

The typical modified SVM methods in this paper are: GA-SVM and LS-SVM in general image segmentation; pSVMRF and additive kernels in medical image segmentation. GA-SVM represents the type of two method combination; it is composed of GA mixed with SVM method. The method of two method combination improves the principle and theory of SVM. Its disadvantage is that it is not sensitive to noise leading to that it cannot segment images accurately. LS-SVM represents the method that improves SVM by modifying its parameters or function. It does not change the principle and theory of SVM. It can improve the accuracy of segmentation. However, the disadvantage of this method is that it still cannot achieve exact segmentation.

In medical image segmentation, there are modified methods of pSVMRF and additive kernels SVM. On one hand, pSVMRF method represents the type of adding medical image features to modified SVM methods. It does not change the principle and theory of SVM. As the focus of this method is medical image features, such as medical image noise, it can achieve better performance in segmentation. On the other hand, additive kernels represent the type that it firstly improves the method of SVM, and then applies it to medical image segmentation. This means that the additive kernels not only can be utilized in medical image, but also in other research areas. The result of comparing and analysing the explained techniques is that the method of adding some features of medical images to modify SVM is superior to other method. Thus, the future research frame of modified SVM in medical image segmentation is suggested to combine medical feature with SVM method.

The advantages or disadvantages of modified SVM are analyzed in Table II.

TABLE II. COMPARISON AMONG MODIFIED SVM

	GA-SVM	LS-SVM	Additive kernels SVM	pSVMRF
Advantages	modified by other method	Modified SVM theory	Modified SVM principle	modified by medical feature
Disadvantages	Not exact	Not exact	Not exact	Exact
Result	Good	Good	Good	Better

GA-SVM is modified SVM method based on combination with GA method. This type of SVM method is modified by other methods. LS-SVM is SVM method modified by changing the theory of SVM. SVM of additive kernels is a method obtained by changing the principle of SVM. pSVMRF is a method modified by adding medical feature. All four types of methods above represent four different modified SVM. As for medical image segmentation, pSVMRF modified SVM has better performance than the other three methods.

IV. CONCLUSION

In this paper, many modified SVM methods within the last five years have been reviewed, especially modified SVM in medical image segmentation. A comparison and analysis among modified SVM methods both in general image and medical image are presented. Future research frameworks are suggested.

In future research of medical image segmentation, there are two research tendencies and frameworks: on one hand researchers improve methods and then apply them to medical image segmentation; on the other hand, they modify the

SVM method by adding the medical image features and then apply it to medical image segmentation. Both of the research frameworks above are feasible. As future research, we are planning to add medical image features to modified SVM combination with artificial intelligence algorithm to improve SVM method for medical image segmentation.

ACKNOWLEDGMENT

This research is supported by: (1) 2017-2020 The National Natural Science Fund of China (Project No. 51679058). (2) 2013-2016 China Higher Specialized Research Fund (PhD supervisor category) (Project No. 20132304110018).

REFERENCES

[1] B. H. Menze, A. Jakab, S. Bauer, J. Kalpathy-Cramer and K. Farahani, "The Multimodal Brain Tumor Image Segmentation Benchmark (BRATS)," IEEE Transactions on Medical Imaging, 99(10):1.vol.34, pp. 1993–2024, 2014

[2] S. Saha, A. K. Alok, and A. Ekbal, "Brain image segmentation using semi-supervised clustering," Expert Systems with Applications, vol. 52, pp. 50–63, 2016.

[3] Wang. Y. , T. Z. Huang, and H. Wang, "Region-based active contours with cosine fitting energy for image segmentation," Journal of the Optical Society of America A Optics Image Science & Vision, vol. 32, pp. 2237–46, 2015.

[4] Ravikumar, S. "Image segmentation and classification of white blood cells with the extreme learning machine and the fast relevance vector machine," Artificial Cells, pp. 985–989, 2015.

[5] Rajalakshmi, Natarajan, and V. L. Prabha, "MRI brain image classification—a hybrid approach," International Journal of Imaging Systems & Technology, vol. 25, pp. 226–244, 2015.

[6] H. Y. Yang, X. Y. Wang, Q. Y. Wang and X. J. Zhang, "LS-SVM based image segmentation using color and texture information," Journal of Visual Communication & Image Representation, vol. 23, pp. 1095–1112, 2012.

[7] P. P. Zhang, J. Feng, Z. Li and M. Q. Zhou, "A novel SVD and LS-SVM combination algorithm for blind watermarking," Neurocomputing, vol. 142, pp. 520–528, 2014.

[8] Z. Zhang, J. Yang, Y. Wang, D. Dou and W. Xia, "Ash content prediction of coarse coal by image analysis and GA-SVM," Powder Technology, vol. 268, pp. 429–435, 2014.

[9] X. Bai and W. Wang, "Saliency-SVM: An automatic approach for image segmentation," Neurocomputing, vol. 136, pp. 243–255, 2014.

[10] D. Cheng, J. Wang, X. Wei and Y. Gong, "Training mixture of weighted SVM for object detection using EM algorithm," Neurocomputing, vol. 149.PB, pp. 473–482, 2015.

[11] Turker, Mustafa, and D. Koc-San, "Building extraction from high-resolution optical spaceborne images using the integration of support vector machine (SVM) classification," Hough transformation and perceptual grouping. International Journal of Applied Earth Observation & Geoinformation, vol. 34, pp. 58–69, 2015.

[12] M. He, T. Wu, A. Silva, D. Y. Zhao and W. Qian, "Augmenting cost-SVM with gaussian mixture models for imbalanced classification", vol. 4, air.v4.n2.p93, 2015.

[13] Sidibé, Désiré, I. Sadek, and F. Mériaudeau, "Discrimination of retinal images containing bright lesions using sparse coded features and SVM," Computers in Biology & Medicine, vol. 62, pp. 175–184, 2015.

[14] S. R. Prasad, K. S. Jhaveri, S. Saini, P. F. Hahn and E. F. Halpern, "CT tumor measurement for therapeutic response assessment: comparison of unidimensional," bidimensional, and volumetric techniques initial observations. Radiology, vol. 225, pp. 416–9, 2002.

[15] X. Zhang, J. Tian, D. Xiang, X. Li and K. Deng, "Interactive liver tumor segmentation from ct scans using support vector classification with watershed," Conference : International Conference of the IEEE Engineering in Medicine & Biology Society IEEE Engineering in Medicine & Biology Society ConferenceConf Proc IEEE Eng Med Biol Soc, pp. 6005–8, 2011.

[16] M. A. Khan, and M. N. A. Syed, "Image processing techniques for automatic detection of tumor in human brain using SVM," International Journal of Advanced Research in Computer and Communication Engineering, vol. 4, pp. 541–544, 2015.

[17] M. Freiman, O, Cooper, D. Lischinski and L. Joskowicz, "Liver tumors segmentation from CTA images using voxels classification and affinity constraint propagation." International Journal of Computer Assisted Radiology & Surgery, vol. 6, pp. 247–255, 2011.

[18] A. Sharma, Gulista, "Performance Comparison of Kmeans & Canny Edge Detection Algorithm On MRI Images," International Journal of Mobile Network Communications & Telematics (IJMNCT) Vol.l, pp. 1–12, September 2011.

[19] J. Zhou, W. Xiong, Q. Tian, Y. Qi and J. Liu, "Semi-automatic Segmentation of 3D Liver Tumors from CT Scans Using Voxel Classification and Propagational Learning. 2008."

[20] S. R. Prasad, K. S. Jhaveri, S. Saini, P. F. Hahn and E. F. Halpem, " CT tumor measurement for therapeutic response assessment: comparison of unidimensional," bidimensional, and volumetric techniques initial observations. Radiology, vol. 225, pp. 416–9, 2002.

[21] T. Wu, "A prior feature SVM-MRF based method for mouse brain segmentation",Neuroimage, vol. 59, pp. 2298-306, 2012.

[22] N. Alajlan, Y. Bazi, F. Melgani and R. R. Yager, "Fusion of supervised and unsupervised learning for improved classification of hyperspectral images," Information Sciences, vol.217, pp. 39–55, 2012.

[23] E. Varol, B. Gaonkar, G. Erus and R. Schulrz, "Feature ranking based nested support vector machine ensemble for medical image classification," Proceedings, pp. 146–149, 2012.

[24] G. Shao, T. Wang, W. Hong and Z. Chen, "An improved SVM method for cDNA microàrray image segmentation. International Conference on Computer Science & Education IEEE," pp. 391–395, 2013.

[25] S. Maji, A. C. Berg, and J. Malik, "Efficient Classification for Additive Kernel SVMs," IEEE Transactions on Pattern Analysis & Machine Intelligence, vol. 35, pp. 66–77, 2013.

[26] L. Lei-Lei, H. X. Wang, J. Y. Huang, P. Ling and J. Sheng-Guo, "Segmentation of hepatic tumor from abdominal CT data using an improved support vector machine framework," Conference: International Conference of the IEEE Engineering in Medicine & Biology Society IEEE Engineering in Medicine & Biology Society Conference Conf Proc IEEE Eng Med Biol Soc, pp.3347–3350, 2013.

[27] Akbari, Ziarati, "A multilevel evolutionary algorithm for optimizing numerical functions" IJIEC,vol. 2, pp. 419–430, 2011.

[28] Y. Zhou, H. B. SHI, "Adaptive K-means clustering for Color Image Segmentation," Advances in Information Sciences & Service Sciences. Vol. 3, pp.216–223, 2011.

[29] L. J. Zhang, X. C. Deng, " The Research of Image Segmentation based on Improved NeuralNetwork algorithm,"Sixth International Conference on Semantics, Knowledge and Grids, pp. 395–397, 2010.

[30] G. F. Shao,T. Wang, W. P. Hong, Z. G. Chen, " An Improved SVM Method for cDNA Mieroarray Image Segmentation," The 8th International Conference on Computer Science & Education, pp. 391–395, 2013.

The Need of a Framework for the Digital Transformation of Industry Ecosystems

Handling Intercompany Collaborative Workflows

Marco Peter and Stella Gatziu Grivas
Institute for Information Systems
FHNW School of Business
Olten, Switzerland
e-mail: marco.peter@fhnw.ch and stella.gatziugrivas@fhnw.ch

Abstract—**This research paper, describes the specifics of an industry ecosystem and its definition, as well as the challenges occurring while transforming the ecosystem. The goal is to demonstrate the need for further research towards creating a systematic approach to solve these challenges. A framework of an industry ecosystem and its transformation towards digitalization would solve this.**

Keywords-industry ecosystem; digitalization; collaboration; framework.

I. Introduction

The term ecosystem is usually considered in the literature as interconnecting and interacting stakeholders who together form a system [2][4]. Industry ecosystems are today in the digitalization era in a transformational digital wave, which has been put in motion by the technologies enabling digitalization like mobile, big data or cloud. As defined in [2], digital transformation is "the seamless, end-to-end connectivity of all areas of the economy, and as the way in which the various players adapt to the new conditions that prevail in the digital economy."

The strive for automated processes and new ways to collaborate is omnipresent with the best example of internet of everything, where communication of things is omnidirectional and autonomous [7]. New technologies like cloud allow for example the central data and document storage and enable new ways of collaboration supporting the execution of intercompany collaborative workflows, i.e., of workflows, which span over several organizations. The main benefit out of a digitalized industry ecosystem is the improvement in collaborative processes between the different actors of the ecosystem.

Main challenges for ecosystems today are the transformation of the industry ecosystem towards a digitalized industry ecosystem and the integration and maintenance of the ecosystem actors. In [2], we propose three levels of transformation at the enterprise IT level (e.g., with new roles or governance models) at process level and the ecosystem level (e.g., with new business models).

The literature still has a gap for systematically describing the industry ecosystem and its transformation towards digitalization and the need for a framework to do so. The goal of this research paper is to demonstrate the need for a systematic framework to master the challenges during the transformation of the industry ecosystem.

The paper is organized as follows: in Section II, the authors' definition for an industry ecosystem is stated and the challenges of ecosystems are elaborated. Section III discusses two representative frameworks and a model, which describe relevant parts of a business ecosystem. In Section IV, the literature gap is pointed out. The last section, Section V, evinces the conclusion of this research paper.

II. Industry Ecosystem

This section includes a definition for industry ecosystem created by the authors and the challenges which industry ecosystem usually face, both based on literature findings.

A. *Definition*

The literature does not have analyzed the term industry ecosystem thoroughly; still there are some definitions to it. Industry ecosystems are complex systems as they consist of a large number of actors, which interconnect in a complicated way [1]. The term ecosystem can be defined as interconnecting and interacting stakeholders who together form a system [2]. It is a value adding system to which all relevant actors are connected with. An industry ecosystem consists of companies and their partners [3]. Such ecosystems come along with network-effects: the bigger the network gets through adoption of new users, the more valuable the ecosystem becomes.

From these definitions, in combination with the definitions of business ecosystem, which are highly related, the following main elements, which define an industry ecosystem, have been derived:

The goal for an industry ecosystem is...

- to support/allow/enable the exchange of information between actors by means of an uniform platform through overcoming the company boundaries
- to support/allow/enable the collaboration between actors through the management of collaborative intercompany workflows

An industry ecosystem is...

- a highly complex integrated system to exchange information
- a platform to increase industry innovation
- a system where competition as well as collaboration is nurtured
- a network of actors, which have a link to the industry
- optimally led by the industry association

The actors within the industry ecosystem are...

- highly integrated to the point where they become an integral part of the ecosystem
- highly diverse from any size
- collaborative industry stakeholders
- partners, suppliers, distributors, customers, competitors, investors, government agencies, research facilities, industry associations

B. *Challenges*

Industry ecosystems have to face challenges, which need to be overcome, in order to provide a sustainable ecosystem to its involved actors. Fig. 1 illustrates our understanding of all relevant dimensions along with the challenges of how building and managing ecosystems can be classified.

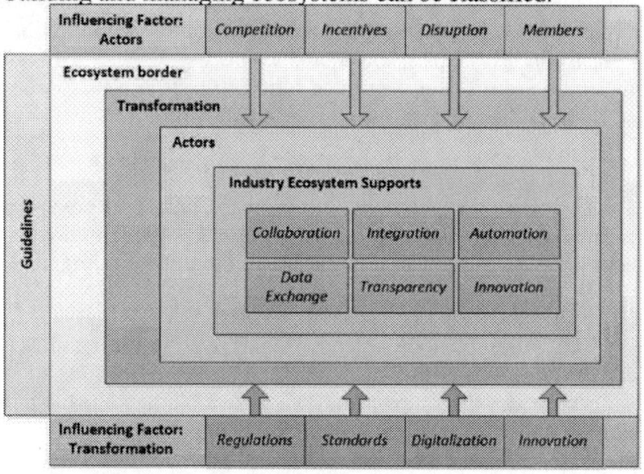

Figure 1. Challenges in Industry Ecosystems.

In the following sub-sections the challenges are explained in more detail.

1) Challenges Regarding Transformation of Ecosystems

There are four main factors which are challenging regarding transformation of ecosystems.

a) Regulations

Legal regulations differ from country to country, which makes it very challenging for an industry ecosystem to have actors involved from different countries [7]. Legal regulations as well as policies of the individual actors are challenging to handle for the industry ecosystem [10]. Therefore, it is important that the industry ecosystem covers the industry regulations and policies. For industry ecosystems it becomes difficult to handle the regulations, since different industries blur into each other [12][9].

b) Standards

Technology standardizations especially for data transfer are considered an important conditional factor for a successful ecosystem [10]. The electronic data interchange needs standardization across all actors [7]. An industry ecosystem is challenged by defining standards for naming or for industry specific items, such as standards for container sizes in the logistics industry [7].

c) Digitalization

The megatrends and enabling technologies cloud, mobile, big data, and social are the pillars for a digitalized industry [17]. The four technologies are not only deployed by the business leaders to gain efficiency or to cut costs. Instead, companies use those technologies to create new business models and to craft new revenue streams [17]. The future customers are going to be fully digitalized and thus, industries and its actors need to be digitalized in order to not get disrupted.

d) Innovation

It is challenging for an industry ecosystem to define its direction of innovation, since it has several different actors involved. The innovation directions need to be kept close to the regulations, otherwise the outcome might bring trouble to the involved actors [9]. It is difficult to define innovative directions by taking the incentives for the involved industry actors into account [4]. Therefore, it is important to define a strategic landscape of which the innovation is an essential part. Businesses need innovative business models, which nowadays need industry members to be innovative and sustainable [11].

2) Challenges Regarding Actors

There are four main factors which are challenging regarding actors.

a) Competition

When industry ecosystems emerge, the power balance in the industry might change [4]. Thus, it is an important task for the industry association to maintain a certain level of competition between the actors, since competition nurtures innovation after all, but at the same time keeping the relation between the actors in good will [4].

b) Incentives

The association of the industry ecosystem has to find incentives for the actors to join the ecosystem as well as integrate their businesses into the ecosystem.

c) Disruption

New players, mostly entrepreneurs, will disrupt the ecosystem of the different industries of today; if the industries do not transform their ecosystem into a digitalized world through for example cloud computing [5]. The best way to avoid disruption of businesses is to predict the future [5]. This can be achieved by exchanging information in the industry as well as to collaborate for more efficient and economical results.

d) Members

It is necessary to define a leader over the industry ecosystem, who defines the components of the industry ecosystem. A company or a small group of companies need to be defined to act as the leader [4]. It might be more useful to create an industry association, to which not only one or a small group is part of, but a greater number of actors can be part of it. In addition, it is important to have an overview of all involved actors in the industry ecosystem. To do so, first the actors, which need to be considered for the industry ecosystem, need to be identified [9].

3) Challenges Regarding Industry Ecosystem Support Activities

There are four main factors which are challenging regarding industry ecosystem support activities.

a) Collaboration and Automation

A transformation requires the intercompany workflows, especially the collaborative workflows, to be automated by support of cloud services [2]. Furthermore, automation of intercompany workflows needs a platform on which not only the exchange of information can be done but as well the process conducted. Only an industry ecosystem could bring all the actors together and provide the required platform to perform automated workflows and collaboration workflows.

b) Integration

An industry ecosystem has a huge number of actors involved. To integrate them is a big effort [7]. The challenge is to integrate such heterogeneous actors, which have to compete as well as to collaborate with each other within the industry ecosystem [4].

c) Data exchange

Information needs to be timely exchanged between actors. Thus, an efficient data exchange needs to be established within the ecosystem and provided to its actors. Data exchange is furthermore needed as a base for digitalized collaboration activities within the industry.

d) Transparency

Not only the processes of the industry stakeholders are heterogeneous, the actors themselves are very heterogeneous as well as some of their goals [7]. So it is important for the ecosystem to keep it transparent for all the parties. The actors within the ecosystem are unlike one from another, which leads to a very diverse ecosystem [9].

e) Innovation

Innovation through technology is essential for not only businesses but the whole industry, in order to stay competitive within the market. Current processes need to be revolutionized by innovation and technology to automate processes and to stay competitive [7]. A difficult challenge for industry ecosystems is to handle an ongoing industry innovation [4].

III. INDUSTRY ECOSYSTEM FRAMEWORKS

Our literature review about frameworks for describing industry ecosystems revealed two frameworks, the 6C and the performance framework as well as one model, the business ecosystem architecture model, which describe relevant parts of business ecosystems.

A. 6C Framework

The framework 6C is for describing an Internet of Things (IoT) -based business ecosystem [13]. According to the 6C framework, the following six dimensions are considered a must for a business ecosystem:

TABLE I. COMPONENTS OF THE 6C FRAMEWORK [13]

Dimension	Objective
Context	To specify the environmental features of the ecosystem.
Cooperation	To specify the mechanisms, which the actors use for interaction to accomplish the common strategies.
Construct	To specify the basic structure and auxiliary infrastructure of the business ecosystem.
Configuration	To specify the stakeholder relationships and their configuration patterns in the business ecosystem.
Capability	To specify the key success features of the business ecosystem.
Change	To specify the shift of system configuration pattern from one lifecycle to the other.

Table I lists the objective and the description for each of the six dimensions.

B. Performance Framework

The performance framework is to help organizations during the selection process of finding the best matching ecosystem [14]. For this goal, the framework has the following three key steps:

1. Assessing the existing ecosystems and current capabilities
2. Assessing the ecosystem options
3. Continually improve the ecosystem through key management practices

Relevant to mention in detail is the key step three. The reason for this step is the fact that most organizations are not effectively using the management practices to maximize their ecosystem performance [14].

TABLE II. KEY MANAGEMENT PRACTICES OF ORGANIZATIONS [14]

Management practice	Explanation
Loose Coupling	To be flexible and scalable.
Access Management	Expand the ecosystem by number of actors according to the objective and scope of the ecosystem.
Behavior Management	Increase the potential for productive interactions among actors through behavioral norms and enforced rules.
Incentives	Foster capability building and cumulative learning through the use of intrinsic- and extrinsic-based incentives.
Action Points	Incorporating several action points leads to opportunities for efficient friction, which forces and sharpens choices. This can be achieved through embedded integration or decision milestones where shared outcomes are achieved.
Interaction Archive	Store rich content information regarding actors' interactions to enable a long-term view of the ecosystem's opportunities.

There is generally a chance to increase value within existing ecosystems just by refining management practices, which are shown in Table II.

C. Business Ecosystem Architecture Model

The business ecosystem architecture model defines that there are three levels of actors involved in a business ecosystem [15]. On the first level, the local level, there are five actors: the core unit, which is the company for which the business ecosystem is designed, the clients, the distribution channels, the suppliers, and the standardization bodies. Actors of the first level are mainly the actors, which are usually part of the supply chain of a business and thus, these actors cooperate closely between each other. The competitors, governmental agencies, and stakeholders are part of the second level, the intermediate level. On the third level, the global level, the actor's international partners and international competitors are placed [15].

The actors of the intermediate level, the competitors, the governmental agencies, and the stakeholders as well as the standardization bodies of the local level are the environmental elements, which play a main role in the development of the core units' entire model [16]. They are important for establishing legal background, for developing competitiveness and diversity, and for attracting new investments [16]. The actors within a business ecosystem collaborate with each other to achieve common goals.

IV. Gap in the Literature

Although there have been some approaches for the description of industry ecosystems, there is no systematic way. A systematic approach entails an illustrative system for industry players usually in form of a framework. A common case is the need of intercompany collaborative workflows. For such a case it is important to have all relevant factors, like all involved actors, within the framework. Otherwise, it becomes very complicated to understand the behavior and the constellation of the ecosystem. Under such conditions, an introduction of an intercompany collaborative workflow might be too complex. Furthermore, a systematic approach provides transparency for the industry and its actors and thus, it is essential and beneficial for the transformation and the evolvement of the ecosystems.

Challenges regarding industry ecosystems and their transformation towards digitalization are well defined. But the literature gives almost no input on how to approach these challenges in order to master them. The industry could make sure with the help of a framework that the awareness of the challenges is given and therefore, no challenge is overlooked. Furthermore, a framework could provide an approach on how to solve the challenges to have a successful and sustainable industry ecosystem.

V. Conclusion

This research paper, analyzed the current definitions on industry ecosystem. Due to the fact that there is no all including definition for it, the following definition has been created. An industry ecosystem is a complex system of diverse integrated actors, which all interact, exchange information and/or collaborate through collaborative intercompany workflows to common goals, to have an overview of all involved actors within an industry. An industry ecosystem is led by an association of several industry actors, which together define standards and boundaries of the industry ecosystem and push the industry innovation forward.

Researchers have mentioned several challenges for ecosystems transforming into digitalization. This paper, collects these challenges and created a framework for illustrating the challenges of industry ecosystems. Intercompany collaborative workflows are a main benefit and therefore a main driver for industries to handle the challenges of such transformations.

Two frameworks and a model for describing industry ecosystems are explained within this paper. These frameworks are required for gaining insights to build a framework for tackling the challenges described in this paper and thus to help industries in their transformation processes.

The identified gap in the literature leads to the current state of the research team. The current work evolves around the design and development of such a framework. In order to do so, the relevant dimensions of the framework with focus on integration, collaboration, and actor management need to be identified and brought together in a systematic way. Such a methodical framework would close the literature gap and would bring new knowledge into this research topic.

References

[1] A. Tsvetkova and M. Gustafsson, "Business models for industrial ecosystems: A modular approach," Journal of Cleaner Production, 29-30, pp. 246–254, 2012.

[2] B. Bloching et al. (2015), The Digital Transformation of Industry,http://www.rolandberger.com/media/pdf/Roland_Berger_digital_transformation_of_industry_20150315.pdf [retrieved: 07, 2016]

[3] S. Gatziu Grivas, C. Giovanoli, and S. Grand, "Cloud on the way to transform whole enterprises : Reasons and the several levels of transformation," Olten, Solothurn, Internal Report, 2015.

[4] A. Gawer and M. A. Cusumano, "Industry Platforms and Ecosystem Innovation," Journal of Product Innovation Management, 31(3), pp. 417–433, 2013.

[5] Deloitte Digital and Heads! (2015), Überlebensstrategie "Digital Leadership." Deloitte, https://www2.deloitte.com /content/dam/Deloitte/de/Documents/technology/20150414_%C3%9Cberlebensstrategie Digital Leadership_final.pdf [retrieved: 07, 2016]

[6] M. Gomez, S. Grand, and S. Gatziu Grivas, "Digitalisation in Logistics and the Role of Cloud Computing," VNL Zeitschrift, Logistics, 2015.

[7] M. Heikkilä and L. Kuivaniemi, "Business Ecosystem under Construction," EBRF Conference (Research Forum to Understand Business in Knowledge Society), 2011.

[8] B. Chew, D. Derosby, E. Kelly, and B. Miracky, "Regulating ecosystems," Deloitte Business Trends, pp. 43–55, 2015.

[9] J. Guo and H. Bouwman, "An analytical framework for an m-payment ecosystem: A merchants' perspective," Telecommunications Policy, 40(2-3), pp. 147–167, 2015.

[10] J. Bruun-Jensen and J. Hagel, "Minimum viable transformation," Deloitte Business Trends Series, pp. 91–103, 2015.

[11] E. Kelly, "Introduction: Business ecosystems come of age," Deloitte Business Trends Series, pp. 3–16, 2015.

[12] K. Rong, J. Wu, Y. Shi, and L. Guo, "Nurturing business ecosystems for growth in a foreign market: Incubating, identifying and integrating stakeholders," Journal of International Management, 21(4), pp. 293–308, 2015.

[13] J. Hagel, J. S. Brown, and D. Kulasooriya, "Performance Ecosystems," Deloitte University Pres, 2011.

[14] E. Galateanu and S Avasilcai, "Business Ecosystem Architecture," Annals of the Oradea University, Fascicle of Management and Technological Engineering, 22, pp. 79 – 84, 2013.

[15] E. Galateanu and S. Avasilcai, "Business Ecosystem "Reliability"," Procedia - Social and Behavioral Sciences, 124, pp. 312–321, 2014.

[16] Harvard Business Review, "The Digital Transformation of Business," Harvard Business Review, 2015.

Integrated Modeling Approach iServMod for Modeling, Analysis and Execution of collaborative Service Processes in Service Chains

Maik Herfurth
Global Information Technology
Hilti Befestigungstechnik AG
Buchs SG, Switzerland
email: maik.herfurth@hilti.com

Thomas Schuster
Faculty for Economy and Law
Pforzheim University of Applied Sciences
Pforzheim, Germany
email: thomas.schuster@hs-pforzheim.de

Abstract – **Increasing market competition between service providers leads to further differentiation, currently often driven by offering so-called hybrid services. Hybrid services are typically implemented between several service providers as service chain. Hence, within service chains the effectiveness of collaborative, cross-company service processes constitute a major competitive factor. While basic service processes are typically company internal, service chains include cross-company administration, especially for service e-procurement. Hence, the collaborative service chains also require domain specific information about procurement and have to support information systems engineering. In turn, information systems have to support service e-procurement and operations in an integrated fashion. To improve the transition from planning to implementation of collaborative service processes with incorporated e-procurement, we suggest an integrated and formalized modeling approach. Our modeling approach will be practically demonstrated by case studies taken from the domain of industrial service procurement.**

Keywords – Service processes; service e-procurement; hybrid services; integrated modeling approach; modeling language; business process analysis

I. INTRODUCTION

Current surveys highlight that services increasingly create value offerings to customers and thus constitute an integral element of many products [1], this includes industrial services as one example of hybrid services. Industrial services make a significant share of companies total spending and ensure required operational levels and availability of systems and facilities. As a consequence, industrial service e-procurement is gaining importance and an integrated perspective of goods and services is required [2][3]. An example of service chains in this domain are industrial maintenance services. They are typically delivered through third-party service providers to grant availability and reliability of industrial facilities and infrastructures. For the procurement of these industrial services, several service providers and service consumers have to interact in industrial service chains [4].

In multilateral service chains where capital goods producers, goods and service requesters, as well as specialized service providers interact to produce, operate and administrate hybrid services. These cross company value added chains with flows of goods, cash and information are called *service chains* [5]. Hence, the ability to integrate and share products and services offerings of external business partners turns out to be a major competitive factor. In consequence, service suppliers take focus on supporting customer's processes or even offering to provide larger parts of value creation processes. Service suppliers and service requesters are collaborating in industrial service chains. In these service chains, the production of services is in focus.

Since service requesters request different service types from different service suppliers, new ways of flexible collaborations are emerging. In this case service e-procurement constitutes an important segment of e-business activities. It compasses extensive use of *Information and Communication Technology* (*ICT*) to improve productivity and business processes. Electronic processes support business interactions reducing interfaces, process and throughput times and support improved harmonization of meta data, activities, procedures and integration of resources. E-business standards can help to support a shared process understanding and increase process transparency amongst business partners by harmonization and structuring of exchanged business data. In this way, e-business standards facilitate enhanced interoperability.

Electronic service processes of service chains are in focus throughout planning (modeling level) and operation (execution level). Nevertheless, there is still a lack for a precise modeling, analysis and benchmarking of these service processes. The paper is focusing on the development of an integrated analysis and modeling service processes in service chains. We suggest a formalized modeling method for collaborative business processes in service chains for further improvement. Our focus within that is the service e-procurement. The overall research approach is based and evaluated on case studies of a research and standardization project [6]. The remainder of this article is structured as follows: In section 2 the challenges of service e-procurement are outlined and the approach of iServMod is motivated. In section 3, the modeling approach of iServMod is presented while in section 4, the modeling of service objects, in section 5, the modeling of eSN and in section 6, the modeling of hSN are described in detail. After the application of iServMod (section 7), conclusion and outlook are drawn in section 8.

II. Challenges and Motivation

Service chain collaborations achieve economies of scale, economies of scope and lower transaction costs. These collaborations are confronted with several challenges: The missing harmonization, integration and standardization of cross-company service processes. Therefore, the creation of new collaborations suffers from low quality of business interactions caused by integration and transaction costs, manual exception handling, offline communication (media breaks) and long procurement lead times; also resulting in less transparency and low quality of processes and data. The aforementioned shortcomings result from missing standards in document exchange and lack of information harmonization. Also, in the past service processes for administrative order processing in service chains did not draw much attention. However, especially these processes require many resources and incorporate long process and throughput times.

Inefficiencies result from internal and especially cross-company handling und coordination of transactions and non-harmonized and non-integrated electronic service processes. Service processes must support procedural rules and service logic of required interactions and communication between service suppliers and requesters [2]. Industrial service e-procurement is still source of high cost because underlying business processes are error prone. Errors and failures occur foremost through the absence of coherent e-business standards and reference frameworks offering meta models of processes, data objects and interaction patterns taking into account the service logic.

A. Research Objectives

Within this paper, we follow paradigms defined in design science. Thus, knowledge can be gained by creation and evaluation of artifacts in the form of models, methods and systems. In contrast to empirical research, the goal is not necessarily to evaluate the validity of research results with respect to their truth, but to the usefulness of the built artifacts as a tool to solve certain problems [7].

In this spirit, we will impose requirements driven by analysis of service and service e-procurement literature, interviews with domain experts as wells as hypotheses. The requirements analysis will disclose the decisions for the design concept of our planning approach. In contrast to an approach driven by theory, the basis for the design not necessarily has to be formulated as hypothesizes. Hence, the planning method will be constructed, implemented and tested in a real environment.

The paper proposes a model-based approach for the following reasons: information and knowledge has to be captured, before it can be part of sound analysis and utilization. Informal, semi-formal as well as formal models offer an abstract possibility to represent information and knowledge. Furthermore, graphical representations such as class diagrams, data-flow diagrams, state-transition diagrams or Petri nets ease understanding between stakeholders both for the expert and the non-expert. Overall this facilitates the communication between persons of different domains. In addition, formal languages allow to describe a certain phenomenon uniquely and precisely, but with a high level of abstraction of reality. They can be easily evaluated and verified or be used to automate certain tasks. The goal of this article is the definition of a modeling method which improves the quality of service chain definition by a domain-specific modeling approach, linked collaborative, cross-company service processes, hierarchical modeling structures, and precise modeling of processes and data.

B. Planning and modeling requirements

Due to these challenges, the modeling of service processes seeks for an adequate and precise integrated modeling approach as well as a precise system design for information systems. So far no adequate modeling approach based on a modeling language focusing the domain specific context of service e-procurement is existing. The modeling approach for system design should be based on a formal modeling language to enable the following advantages [8]:

- *adequate concept* for representation for domain specific description of data flow and control flow
- *formal semantics* of workflow processes due to a formalized syntax
- *uniqueness of syntax* and graphical descriptions for an easy understanding
- *expressiveness* for a precise system modeling
- *mathematical foundation* for evaluation and sound proof of system design
- *analysis of information systems* for properties like deadlocks, performance or the correctness of information systems (regarding requirements)
- *interoperability and vendor independence* of the modeling language, to support different modeling and analysis tools
- consideration of *static and dynamic elements* in business processes to describe the control flow and data flow.

III. State of the Art

Scientific literature reveals several approaches for service procurement with different focus and different granularity. *FlexNet Architect* [20] offers reusable modules for the scenario-based modeling of hybrid value creation. For planning and modeling of hybrid value creation networks, the cooperation definition, actors, areas and information flows can be modeled. The *HyproDesign* [21] modeling language was developed for modeling customer specific configurations and calculations of hybrid bundles of services and is based on a meta model to describe variants and configurations. Single modules are described as semantic models via *Entity Relationship diagrams* [22]. Winkelmann and Luczak [23] propose a Petri net based approach for the cooperative supply of industrial services by using *colored Petri nets* (*CPN*) [24].

Becker and Neumann [25] define central components like processes and activities, technical objects, contacts and service offers based on data models for the order transaction of technical services. Che et al. [26] are using *XML nets* [11] for modeling, execution and monitoring of cross-company business processes. Mevius and Pibernik [27] propose XML nets for the support of business processes for the *Supply Chain Process Management* (*SCPM*). Every approach considers certain aspects of the description of services and service processes. But none of these approaches represents a comprehensive model for the description of service objects and service processes for industrial services based on a formalized approach. For modeling collaborative service processes and service objects in service transactions of service e-procurement, no such domain-specific approach considering the characteristics of service processes for service e-procurement is existing yet.

IV. Integrated Modeling Approach for Service Modeling *iServMod*

To meet the challenges and requirements described before, an integrated modeling approach based on a formal modeling language considering the domain specific context of service procurement will lead to the following advantages:

- *increased transparency in service chains*: service processes lack transparency due to individual internal service processes of service providers and service requesters.
- *precise modeling of collaborative service processes and data flow*: the precise modeling of service processes and service objects serves as a basis for high quality documentation and analysis. Internal service processes can be modeled separately and put together in service process models with an adequate modeling approach support.
- *analysis of service processes*: application of analysis methods for the quantitative and qualitative evaluation of service process models serve as a basis for benchmarking.
- *integration of domain specific context*: integration of service e-procurement context for its integration into information systems.
- *support of modeling and execution layers*: the modeling and the execution of service processes rounds up the comprehensive analysis of service process models.

Such a modeling approach results into the improvement of the efficiency (performance) and productivity of the service processes due to the reduction of process costs, reduction of process times, reduction of process throughput time, the improvement of process quantity, improvement of process transparency and increase of process flexibility. The integrated modeling approach *integrated service modeling* (*iServMod*) is based on Petri nets [9]. A Petri net is a formal mathematical modeling language for the description of distributed systems. A Petri net is a directed bipartite graph, in which the nodes represent transitions and places. The directed arcs describe which places are pre- and/or post-conditions for which transitions. With Petri nets, major network structures like sequence, iteration, alternative, concurrency, synchronization and contact can be modeled and dynamic properties like liveness, reachability, boundness and soundness can be analyzed [28]. High level Petri nets fulfill these requirements and support an integrated modeling of service processes and service objects.

A. *Modeling Concepts*

Based on *modeling concepts*, service processes and corresponding service objects can gradually be modeled in a top-down approach in detail or on a higher abstraction level. Service processes can stepwise be transformed into different formalization stages and their hierarchical scaling and modularization. For the modeling of different formalized service processes, the *screen model* [10] serves as a modeling concept for Petri nets. The modeling concept support four different formalized Petri nets modeling language types, starting from informal modeling languages (Petri nets) up to programming modeling language types for an automated execution (XML nets [11]). The modeling concept describes the successive transformation of these modeling language types of Petri nets. The hierarchical and modular modeling of service processes is supported by the *layer model* [12]. On a higher abstract modeling level, process phases are choreographed. On a detailed modeling level, complex electronic processes based on web services are orchestrated.

B. *Petri Net based Modeling of Service Processes*

Petri nets are extended by syntactical extensions. Therefore, the semantic of Petri nets and its characteristics aren't changed. The extensions serve as a basis for a detailed and precise modeling of service processes (design time) in order to integrate service processes on the execution level (run time). In the first step, the modeling of *service objects* as static components of data schemas is presented. Service nets as dynamic components of business processes are developed: *single Service nets* (*eSN*) based on place/transition nets are defined. *High level service nets* (*hSN*) based on XML nets in a second step are developed. With these Petri nets types, the screen model is supported.

V. Modeling of Service Objects

Service objects describe static object-oriented components in service processes. Service object are identified data objects which describe central service master data and transaction data. These data are service requesters and service provider data, materials, service and business documents. Service objects are input and output objects of service processes. Service objects are economically relevant data objects which are executed in electronic service processes as workflows. Service objects are relevant data objects like a service specification, a service order, a service invoice or another service-relevant data object for service transactions of service e-procurement.

For the graphical modeling representation, service objects are modeled with the XML schema model (XSM) [11] as modeling constructs in XML nets. XSM serves as a formal object description method to describe complex object structures in conjunction with organizational processes. As an example, the service object *industrial service description* is shown (Fig. 1).

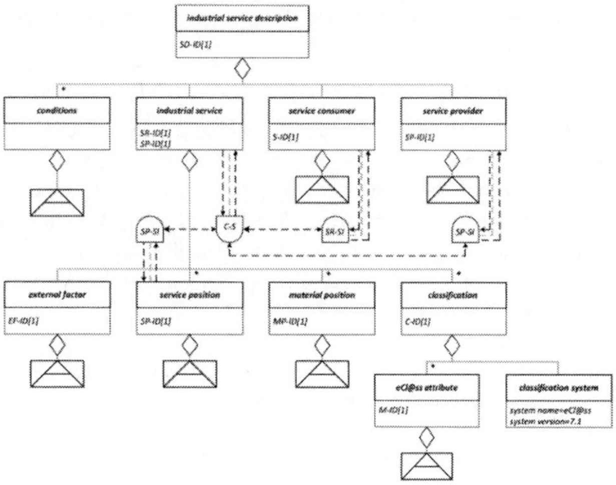

Figure 1. Service object *industrial service description*

XML schema diagrams are used to describe service objects. Data structures in XML nets are determined by Petri nets places. Places combine structured service objects with a common schema (typification of places). The modeling constructs of XML schema models are element types represented by UML classes and dependencies represented by association types.

VI. SINGLE SERVICE NETS ESN

For the modeling of *eSN*, we utilize places/transition nets (P/T nets) to support initial modeling phases. Places and tokens of these nets represent the current status of a service chain. Domain specific process interface place types and process transition types are defined to standardize modeling. Internal (private) service processes are modeling by *pools*. The interface place types *service object places* (*SO*), *service interface places* (*SS*) and *service document places* (*SD*) are defined. *SO* places are containers for general service objects.

SS places are internal and cross-company interfaces for the data flow. Static interface places between service processes and dynamic interface places for capsulated interface processes are defined. *SD* places serve as containers for service document types. For transition concepts, *service process phases* (*SP*) are defined to reflect the specific process phases in service procurement. *Service process modules* (*SM*) represent service processes of a collaboration participant (service provider or service requester). *SP* and *SM* represent both a black box for further detailed modeled service processes. A service process phase consists out of service process modules. Service process phases and modules represent and apply hierarchical modeling concepts to support the layer model. As an example, the singe collaborative service process between a service provider and a service requester is shown in Fig. 2.

VII. HIGH LEVEL SERVICE NETS

The use of P/T net concepts accompanies a couple disadvantages: the semantic correctness cannot be checked, domain specific modeling constructs are not supported, communication and information concepts are not designed, the structured hierarchical modeling is not supported and tokens cannot be specified individually. Thus we introduce modeling extensions of *eSN* with transfer to higher level service nets on the basis of XML nets with individual tokens.

High level Service nets (*hSN*) are based on XML. Thus operational sequences and the document flow are based on XML and all tokens of are represented by complex structured XML objects. All activities correspond to operations on XML documents. *hSN* are characterized by domain specific extensions, and individual tokens. Furthermore, within *hSN* the phases of service chains are standardized. Thus, *electronic service processes* and their data flow can be precisely modeled, analyzed, simulated, executed and maintained.

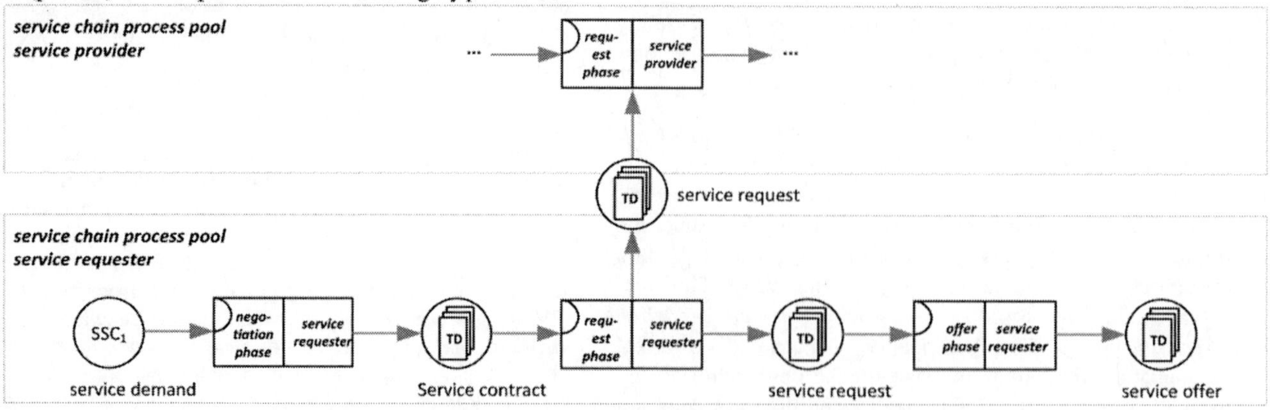

Figure 2. Single collaborative service process with pools of service provider and service requester

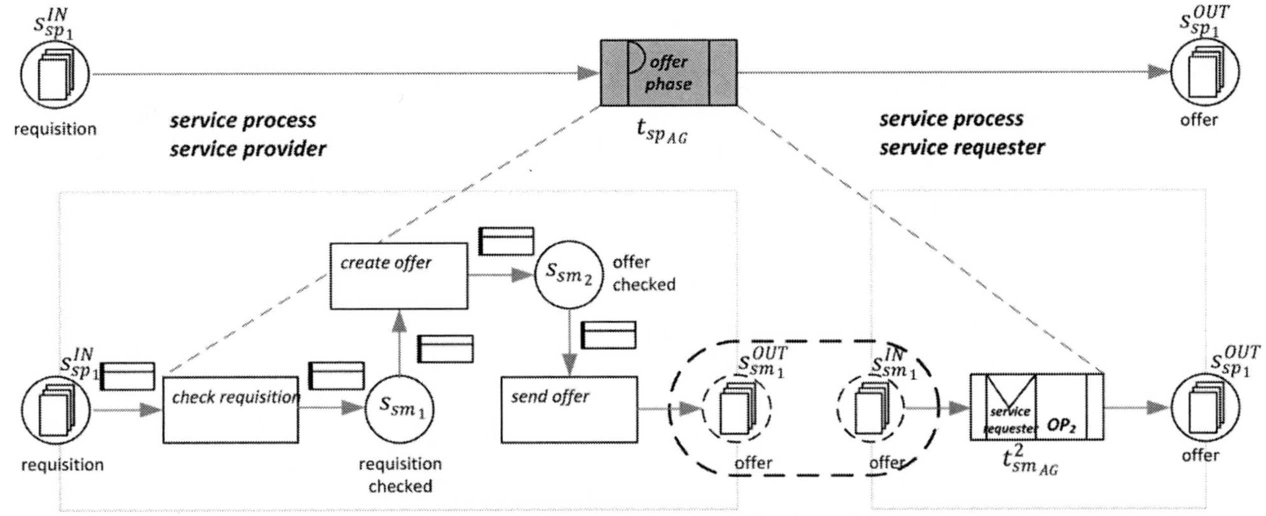

Figure 3. Modularization of a service process phase by service process modules

For the process interface place types, places are typified based on the domain specific context. *Service process phases (SP)* are represented by coarsened transitions with capsulated service processes based on service process modules. Service process modules are also coarsened transitions and contain capsulated service processes of one process participant (internal service process). Service process modules contain a service process which fulfills the requirements of a Workflow net [13].

A service process module is defined by an internal structure and communicates with other modules based on process interface places. *Service process modules (SM)* describe unidirectional and bidirectional interaction and communication patterns. Service process phases and service process modules contains typified input and output places *SO*, *SS* and *SD*. Service process phases are defined with specific typified places in dependence on process patterns. Service process phases and service process modules are syntactically compatible.

The service process phase offer ($t_{sp_{AG}}$) is modularized by two service process modules (Fig. 3). The service process consists of the service process $hSN'_{\ sm_1}$ of the service process module $t_{sm_{AG}}^{1}$ and $hSN'_{\ sm_2}$ of the service process module $t_{sm_{AG}}^{2}$. $hSN'_{\ sm_1}$ of the service provider is modeled as an XML net. The representation of XML filter schemes FS_i, transition inscriptions TI_i and place type definition ST_i are not modeled. The service process of the service requester is represented by the service process module $t_{sm_{AG}}^{2}$. The place $s_{sp_1}^{IN_1}$ and the place $s_{sp_1}^{OUT_1}$ are the in- and output of hSN. The input place $s_{sm_1}^{IN_1}$ ($s_{sp_1}^{IN_1}$) and the output place $s_{sm_1}^{OUT_1}$ as the input place $s_{sm_2}^{IN_1}$ and the output place $s_{sm_1}^{OUT_1}$ ($s_{sp_2}^{OUT_1}$) are module interface places of the service process modules. Thus a high level Service net hSN is defined as follows:

A Service net is defined as a tuple $hSN = (S, SSO, SSI, SSD, T, TSP, TSM, F, \Phi, I_S, I_T, I_F, I_{SSO}, I_{SSI}, I_{SSD}, M_0)$, where

1. $XN = (S, T, F, \Phi, I_S, I_T, I_F, M_0)$ is an XML net.
2. $\Phi = (\mathrm{E}, \mathrm{FKT}, \mathrm{PRE})$ is a structure consisting of a non-empty and finite individual set E of Φ, a set of formula and term functions FKT defined on E, and a set of predicates PRE defined on E.
3. The set of places is structured in the sets process object places SPO and service object specific places SPS. The set of SPS is further structured in the sets of service object places SSO, service interface places SSI and service document places SSD.
4. The set of transitions is structured in the sets of process activities TPA and service process activities TPS. The set of TPS contains of service process phases TSP and service process modules TSM. The set of TPS is defined as a real set of transitions T: $TPS \subseteq T$.
5. I_{SSO} is the function that assigns a valid XML schema as a place typification to each place $s_{so} \in SSO$.
6. I_{SSI} is the function that assigns a valid XML schema as a place typification to each place $s_{si_s} \in SSI$.
7. I_{SSI} is the function that assigns a valid XML schema of a service documents type j as a place typification to each place $s_{sd_j} \in SSD$.
8. I_T is the function that assigns a predicate logical expression as inscription to each transition on a given structure Φ and the set of variables which are contained on all adjacent arcs.
9. I_F is the function that assigns a valid XSLT expression to each arc which is conform to the adjacent XML scheme.

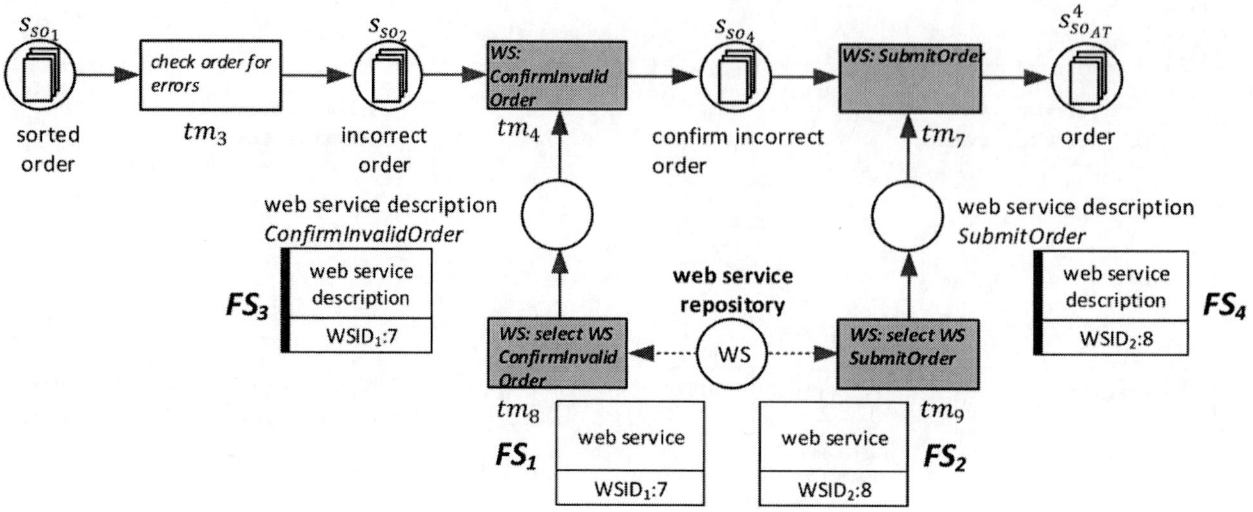

Figure 4. Web Service net with web service selection

A. *Modeling of distributed Service Processes based on SOA*

Service processes can be modeled as dynamic interface processes and be executed by web services in *service oriented architectures* (*SOA*). *iServMod* supports the modeling and analysis of distributed service processes based on web services by *Web Service nets* (*WSN*) [14]. A web service is considered as an implementation of a local service process (interface process). A distributed service process can be realized by the composition of web services. Input and output messages represent the data flow in Web Service nets. Web Service nets also support the composition concepts like the orchestration and choreography. The example service process *validation of incorrect orders* is models as an abstract Web Service net with web service selection (Fig. 4).

B. *Transformation and Execution of Web Service Nets*

Based on the precise modeling of all aspects of service processes with Web Service nets, *Web Service Business Process Execution Language* (*WS-BPEL*) elements can be derived to use standardized web service technologies like interface description (*WSDL*), protocols (*SOAP*) or service discovery (*UDDI*). Web service process models [15] can be modeled and the transformation of Web Service nets into executable WS-BPEL code is based on control flow and data flow structures. Specific structures and elements can be identified and transformed into equivalent WS-BPEL structures. A detailed transformation of Web Service net structures into WS-BPEL code with a transformation algorithm is defined in [16].

VIII. APPLICATION OF ISERVMOD IN USE CASES

The integrated modeling approach *integrated Service Modeling (iServMod)* serves as an adequate method for a precise modeling and analysis of service processes. The advantages of *iServMod* increase the value of business process simulation and business process benchmarking. The simulation of service processes based on key performance indicators reveals gaps and weaknesses. The execution of a process benchmarking identifies differences of relevant factors like throughput times, resource assignments or cost items. The causes of performance gaps can be analyzed. For the modeling and simulation of service process models, the software tool *Horus* [18] was enhanced by the new modeling extensions of Service nets and used for a software based simulation. As business process simulation method, a discrete event driven business process oriented simulation was used [19]. The strengths of the independent simulative analysis are the possibility of a "*playground*" by simulating different process alternatives. Evaluation of simulation results can shed light on correlations of system parameters at build time and can be used to develop action strategies [1]. Unlike analytical procedures, the simulation can be used for the analysis of large systems. Based on benchmarks, performance gaps can be quantified. Redundant service processes and non-value creating activities as well as automation potentials for service processes can be identified and the error data is reduced. Also the cost-effectiveness of service processes can be ensured.

The integrated modeling approach *iServMod* has been successfully applied in a research projects in the domain of service procurement [2]. The service process models of 18 use cases between six service suppliers and four service requesters were analyzed, modeled, simulated and benchmarked [1][6][17]. Service process models were modeled with high level Service nets. The modeling of Service nets was based on a reference process model [2] to structure and align the individual service processes. *iServMod* supported the precise modeling of service processes and service objects in a syntactical correct and semantic formal way. The data flow could be modeled based on XML. Service processes could be model in a hierarchical modeling approach based on different abstraction levels to support modeling user groups with different modeling experiences. Service processes could be modeled top down from high level process description to detailed service processes as workflows using web services and representing and supporting a further implementation in information systems. Service process phases and service process modules allow for reusability of pre-defined concepts by assuring the syntactical and semantic compatibility in service process models. The evaluated uses cases were compared pairwise for benchmarking by applying the presented procedure model.

IX. Conclusion and Outlook

We presented the integrated modeling approach *iServMod* based on formalized modeling techniques. *iServMod* supports integrated modeling of service processes and service objects. Additionally, *iServMod* offers an adequate modeling approach for the precise analysis and implementation of service processes. *iServMod* is focusing on collaborative service processes which are modeled independently by different companies and their domain experts (modelers). It furthermore supports the domain specific requirements of service e-procurement in service chains.

The presented modeling concepts enact different formalization levels, starting from a semi-formal description of service process models up to highly formalized and executable service process models. This includes a hierarchical order of service processes typically modeled ion a top down approach utilizing service process phases. The modeling approach is concluded by integrated description of web service calls to implement sound information systems at execution level. The syntactic domain specific extensions both of service object specific process interface place types and process transition types enable a precise hierarchical modeling of process participants, modular service processes, e-procurement service phases, pre-defined process patterns, interfaces and service data objects.

While *eSN* serve as an initial modeling approach and further analysis based on Petri nets, *hSN* enable an integrated modeling of service processes and service objects for the design of information systems. The integrated modeling and design approach was evaluated with real-life case studies [2]. The service process models have been modeled and analyzed and the developed extension of the software tool *Horus* supports the overall modeling of collaborative service chains.

As next steps, we foresee the evaluation of *iServMod* by a survey of domain specific users to determine. We also strive to further evaluate the performance, quality and efficiency of this approach together with several leading companies in the domain of industrial services. Furthermore, the adoption and application of *iServMod* in different domains and hence different types of service chains are planned.

References

[1] M. Herfurth, T. Schuster, and P. Weiß, "Simulation-based Service Process Benchmarking in Product-Service Ecosystems", Proceedings of Collaborative Systems for Reindustrialization: 14th IFIP WG 5.5 Working Conference on Virtual Enterprises, PRO-VE 2013, Dresden, Germany, pp. 40-47, (2013)

[2] P. Weiß, M. Herfurth, and J. Schumacher, "Leverage Productivity Potentials in Service-oriented Procurement Transactions: E-Standards in Service Procurement", Proceedings of RESER 2011, (2011)

[3] A. Eggert, C. Thiesbrummel, and C. Deutscher, "Heading for new shores: Do service and hybrid innovations outperform product innovations in industrial companies?", Industrial Marketing Management, vol. 45, pp. 173-183, (2015)

[4] J. Johanson and L. G. Mattsson, "Internationalisation in Industrial Systems — A Network Approach", in Knowledge, Networks and Power, pp. 111-132, (2015)

[5] T. Baltacioglu, E. Ada, M. Kaplan, O. Yurt, and C. Kaplan, "A New Framework for Service Supply Chains", Services Industry Journal, vol. 27, No. 2, pp. 105-124(2007)

[6] M. Herfurth, T. Schuster, and P. Weiß, "E-Business for Services: Simulation-based Analysis of E-Business Solution Concepts for Service Procurement Scenarios". eChallenges e-2012 Conference Proceedings, Paul Cunningham and Miriam Cunningham (Eds), IIMC International Information Management Corporation Ltd 2012, ISBN 978-1-905824-35-9, ISBN: 978-1-905824-35-9, (2012)

[7] A. R. Hevner, S. T. March, J. Park, and S. Ram, "Design Science in Information Systems Research", MIS Quarterly, 28(1), pp. 75-105, (2004)

[8] W. M. P. van der Aalst, "The Application of Petri Nets to Workflow Management". The Journal of Circuits, Systems and Computers, 8(1), pp. 21-66, (1998)

[9] W. Brauer, W. Reisig, and G. Rozenberg, "Petri Nets. Part I and Part II", Lecture Notes in Computer Science 254 and 255, Springer Verlag, (1987)

[10] J. Desel and A. Oberweis, "Petri-Netze in der Angewandten Informatik: Einführung, Grundlagen und Perspektiven". in: Wirtschaftsinformatik, vol. 38(4), Vieweg Teubner, pp. 359-367, (1996)

[11] K. Lenz and A. Oberweis, "Interorganizational Business Process Management with XML Nets", in: Petri Net Technology for Communication Based Systems, LNCS 2472, pp. 243-263, (2003)

[12] M. Herfurth, T. Karle, and F. Schönthaler, "Reference Model for service oriented Business Software based on Web Service Nets", Third AIS SIGSAND European Symposium on Analysis, Design, Use and Societal Impact of Information Systems SIGSAND-EUROPE, pp. 55-69, (2008)

[13] W. M. P. van der Aalst., "Modeling and Analyzing Interorganizational Workflows". In: Lavagno, L.; Reisig, W. (eds): Proceedings of the International Conference on Application of Concurrency to System Design (CSD'98), IEEE Computer Society Press, pp. 1-15, (1998)

[14] A. Koschmider and M. Mevius, "A Petri Net based Approach for Process Model Driven Deduction of BPEL Code", OTM Confederated International Conferences, Agia Napa, Cyprus, Springer Verlag, pp. 495-505, (2005)

[15] A. Martens, "Analyzing Web Service based Business Processes", in: Proceedings International Conference on Fundamental Approaches to Software Engineering (FASE), volume 3442 of LNCS, Edinburgh, Scotland, pp. 19-33, (2005)

[16] M. Herfurth, T. Karle, and R. Trunko, "Model Driven Implementation of Business Processes Based on Web Service Nets", Proceedings of the 2008 SIWN Congress/ 2nd

International Conference on Adaptive Business Systems (ABS 2008), Glasgow, pp. 32-38, (2008)

[17] M. Herfurth, T. Schuster, and P. Weiß, "Decision Support Based on Simulation Analysis of Service Procurement Scenarios". eChallenges e-2013 Conference Proceedings, Paul Cunningham and Miriam Cunningham (Eds), IIMC International Information Management Corporation Ltd 2013, ISBN 978-1-905824-40-3, ISBN: 978-1-905824-40-3, (2013)

[18] Y. Li and A. Oberweis, "A Petri Net-Based Software Process Model for Developing Process-Oriented Information Systems", Proceedings of the 18th International Conference on Information Systems Development (ISD2009), Nanchang, China, pp. 27-39, (2009)

[19] J. Banks, J. S. Carson, B. L. Nelson, and D. M. Nicol, "Discrete-Event System Simulation", Pearson Education, (2005)

[20] J. Becker, D. Beverungen, R. Knackstedt, M. Matzner, O. Müller, and J. Pöppelbuß, "Flexible Informationssystem-Archtitekturen für hybride Wertschöpfungsnetzwerke (FlexNet)", Arbeitsbericht des Instituts für Wirtschaftsinformatik No. 130, Westfälische Wilhelms-Universität Münster, (2011)

[21] J. Becker, D. Beverungen, R. Knackstedt, and O. Müller, "Konzeption einer Modellierungssprache zur softwarewerkzeugunterstützten Modellierung, Konfiguration und Bewertung hybrider Leistungsbündel", in: O. Thomas, and M. Nüttgens, (eds.), "Dienstleistungsmodellierung", Physica-Verlag, pp. 53-70, (2009)

[22] P. P.-S. Chen, "The entity-relationship model - towards a unified view of data", ACM Transactions on Database Systems 1 (1976) 1, pp. 9-36, (1976)

[23] K. Winkelmann, "Prospektive Bewertung der kooperativen Erbringung industri-eller Dienstleistungen im Maschinenbau durch Simulation mit Petri-Netzen", Dissertation RWTH Aachen, (2007)

[24] K. Jensen, "Coloured Petri Nets: A high-level Language for System Design and Analysis", LNCS vol. 483, Springer Verlag, (1990)

[25] J. Becker, and S. Neumann, "Referenzmodelle für Workflow-Applikationen in technischen Dienstleistungen", in: H.-J. Bullinger, and A.-W. Scheer, "Service Engineering", Springer Verlag, pp. 623-647, (2006)

[26] H. Che, M. Mevius, Y. Ju, W. Stucky, and R. Trunko, "A Method for Interorganizational Business Process Management", Proceedings of the IEEE International Conference on Automation and Logistics, China, (2007)

[27] M. Mevius, R. Pibernik, "Process Management in Supply Chains - A New Petri-Net Based Approach", Proceeding of the 37th Hawaii International Conference on System Sciences (HICCS'04), IEEE Computer Society, (2004)

[28] W.MP. van der Aalst, W.M.P. and K. van Hee, "Workflow Management: Models, Methods, and Systems", MIT Press, (2004)

International Academy, Research, and Industry Association (IARIA)
412 Derby Way
Wilmington, DE 19810

ISBN 978-1-5108-3374-6

CURRAN ASSOCIATES INC.
proceedings.com